MICHIGAN BUSINESS STUDIES
Volume I Number 3
*New Series*

# bank lending policies

## domestic and international

### second edition

douglas a. hayes

Division of Research
Graduate School of Business Administration
The University of Michigan

ISBN 0-87712-180-X

A Publication of the
Division of Research
Graduate School of Business Administration
The University of Michigan
Ann Arbor, Michigan



SECOND PRINTING

# CONTENTS

## TABLES

## FIGURES

## PREFACE

This book is primarily concerned with the lending policies of, and their operational implementation in, large commercial banks. Although banks have greatly expanded the scope of their financial services over the years, lending programs of various types continue to represent their major functional role in the financial markets.

The unquestioned acceptance of the view that the size and structure of the investment portfolio must accommodate to the needs and configuration of the loan portfolio and not vice versa is prime evidence of the high priority attached to the lending operation. Loan policies and their implementation, therefore, represent the focal point of managerial activities in commercial banks. Indeed in most cases, loans constitute at least two-thirds of earning assets, and an equivalent proportion of management personnel are assigned to this function.

Over the past decade or so there have been major changes in the banking process that have had a major feedback to lending policies. Perhaps the most important has been a structural change in the composition of the liability mix. In large banks demand deposits long dominated the liability structure; until perhaps the mid-sixties management strategies were largely oriented toward demand deposit customers and the solicitation of savings and time deposits was regarded as a peripheral activity at best. It was probably largely due to competitive pressures that banks introduced new types of savings and time deposit instruments, aggressively marketed these innovations, and in addition developed other sources of purchased funds. As a result, interest-bearing instruments now dominate their liability structure.

The consequence has been that "yield spread" banking has become increasingly important in the banking process; the yield spread approach, it is interesting to note, has long dominated the European banking scene because demand deposits have always been a relatively minor source of funds abroad. Spread banking essentially means that the average and marginal yield spreads between the cost of funds on the one hand and asset acquisitions on the other are of crucial significance in structuring managerial policies. In the new context of banking, for example, pricing policies on loans have become considerably more complex to reflect a mix of yield-spread variables. This edition, therefore, includes a separate and extensive chapter on pricing policies for the first time.

In addition, we found considerable evidence that the effects of the 1974–75 recession had a significant impact on asset management policies of large commercial banks. During these years loan losses escalated to levels exceeded only during the Great Depression. Although the basic solvency of the system remained strong, we witnessed the highly visible failures of a few large banks and a major decline in the earnings of others, consequent in considerable part to greatly increased loan losses. Given these circumstances, it was not surprising that there seemed to be a general consensus that policy revisions should be instituted to improve the quality of and control over the loan portfolio. There was no evidence that banks had become highly restrictive and negative in their policy orientation, but there seemed to be a pervasive attitude that moderate constraints should be imposed to reduce the exposure of the loan portfolio to serious credit losses.[1]

My approach to structuring the book was basically the same as in the first edition. Senior loan officers of selected large banks were personally interviewed in depth and in addition were requested to complete a series of detailed questionnaires covering

1. A statement of the chief executive officer of a major bank reinforces this point: "The very sharp recession which began two years ago upset our comfortable assumptions about the business cycle. . . . It became apparent that bank loan portfolios were much more vulnerable than had been generally realized. The business cycle is still very much alive; the banking industry has losses to prove it. The lesson is now incorporated into our frame of reference, and we ought to be better prepared the next time the economy falters." (E. C. Patterson, Chairman of the Board, Morgan Guaranty Trust Co., "Credit Quality: Lessons of Recent Experience," *Journal of Commercial Bank Lending* 59 [Oct. 1976]: 15.)

all aspects of their lending activities.[2] The respondent banks were most cooperative in articulating not only their existing policy guidelines but also the reasoning behind policy formulations and their views on the possible future trends in the lending programs of large banks.

Because the emphasis is on the evaluation of credit policies in relation to the major goals of the bank, it is hoped that the book may be of considerable interest to practicing loan officers and also to management charged with the responsibility for policy formulation. At one point in the text it is suggested that a major policy requirement might be a periodic review of all policy guidelines, followed by such changes as seem appropriate in the light of dynamic developments in the economy and financial markets. Static policies should be avoided in a rapidly changing world, and, therefore, I considered it highly important to indicate alternative views of both existing lending policies and their possible future trends.

In addition, it is hoped that the book might be useful as a reference work for college courses in financial institutions, money and banking, and bank management. Most textbooks in these areas, because of the wide scope of their material, cover the important subject of commercial bank lending policies in a cursory fashion. My objective is to offer students the opportunity to obtain greater insight into the issues involved in formulating credit policies than textbooks on banking and financial institutions typically afford.

Finally, because of their recurring needs for loan officer personnel, large banks regularly employ a number of loan officer trainees. Much of the material in this book, it is hoped, might be useful to such trainees in their education programs.

Personal interviews at all the respondent banks, together with the written answers to the detailed questionnaires, provided the basic research data for the book. The following bankers, in particular, were of great assistance in providing information and data for the project: Messrs. Joseph G. Conway, Philip G. Moon, and Gerald B. O'Neill of the National Bank of Detroit; Messrs. Donald R. Mandich, Frederick C. Hertel, Albert W. Holcomb,

2. The content of the questionnaires is reproduced in the Appendix.

Gerald E. Brielmaier, and James R. Waterson of Detroit Bank and Trust Company; Mr. Dean E. Richardson of the Manufacturers National Bank of Detroit; Messrs. Lowell L. Peacock, Thomas R. Stewart, Frank D. Alandt, and John R. Engler of Security Bank and Trust Company, Southgate, Michigan; Messrs. Charles M. Bliss, Beryl W. Sprinkel, and B. Kenneth West of Harris Trust and Savings Bank, Chicago; Messrs. David W. Fox and Thomas F. Duffy of Northern Trust Company, Chicago; Messrs. James K. Suhr, Leo H. Gorman, and Harrison F. Tempest of the First National Bank of Chicago; Messrs. Ralph W. Abelt, Gerald Keeley, and Roger H. Sherman of Continental Illinois National Bank and Trust Company, Chicago; and Messrs. Rodney Galpin, and G. M. Gill of the Bank of England, London.

Without the full cooperation of these senior bank officers and others in their banks, this book would not have been possible. I am greatly indebted to them for their assistance, but it also should be added that they are not responsible for any errors or omissions in the material or any opinions presented unless so indicated in the text. Mrs. Henrietta H. Slote edited the entire manuscript and Mrs. Sandra Laurie and Mrs. Susan Owen typed most of it; I am very grateful for their considerable assistance. Finally, the University of Michigan's Graduate School of Business Administration, Division of Research, under the direction of Professor Alfred L. Edwards, provided financial support and research assistance for the study, and I particularly would like to express my thanks to Dean Floyd A. Bond for his full support and cooperation on this project.

*Ann Arbor, Michigan* Douglas A. Hayes
*December, 1976*

# 1

# LENDING POLICIES: OBJECTIVES AND ECONOMIC CONTEXT

# I

## INSTITUTIONAL STRUCTURE AND CORPORATE GOALS

### Corporate Goals: Private Sector

Subject to legal and ethical constraints, the major goal of corporations in the private sector is generally conceded to be to maximize long-term returns to their shareholders. Conceptually these returns can take the form of either cash dividends or long-term appreciation in the market value of common stock. Under any reasonable assumptions, however, both forms of returns are likely to be functions of existing earning power, its growth potential, and the degree of market confidence in the earning power and growth potential.

To implement the goals of maximizing the amount, growth, and consistency of earnings, the corporation engages in a set of financing and operating decisions wherein the costs of finance are related to the net returns expected from the operation of the assets acquired with the proceeds of the financial decisions. To formalize the functional relationships, financial theory has developed rather sophisticated capital-budgeting models designed to show the effects of alternative finance and asset decisions on internal rates of return and consequent present values of the assets and equity.

These models of course incorporate the well-known principles of financial leverage, wherein debt finance is used to the extent that expected returns from the assets acquired with the proceeds from debt issues exceed the cost of the debt. But while higher debt in relationship to stock equity may increase returns to the latter, risk constraints presumably limit the process. Risk constraints have two dimensions: (1) variance in returns to the equity are magnified as the debt/equity ratio increases, and (2) the probability of default under adverse economic circumstances necessarily increases as debt service requirements become higher in relation to total operating cash flows. Therefore, decisions to use senior finance in the typical corporation logically involve assessments of the trade-off between possible higher returns to the equity on the one hand and the increase in both dimensions of risk on the other.

## Institutional structure of commercial banks

Although the above summary of general corporate goals and their implementation applies in a broad sense to commercial banks as part of the private corporate sector, banks have several unique characteristics which affect the earning potential attached to the common equity. These features are as follows:

1. A large proportion of their liabilities represent either transaction money ($M_1$ or demand deposits) or near moneys that constitute a large segment of the liquidity reserves of the public ($M_2$ or time and savings deposits).
2. In a developed industrial economy, the needs and preferences for both money and near moneys are very large. In addition, normative monetary policy seeks to encourage their stability and growth at about the rate (at least) of economic output. As a result the universe of commercial banks has enjoyed a fairly constant growth of relatively favorable proportions in its deposit liability structure.
3. Because the soundness of the money supply depends on the soundness of commercial banks, public policy in the United States historically has been to subject banks to extensive and detailed regulatory supervision by governmental units under special legislative statutes.[1]

1. In Michigan the objective of the regulatory statute is stated as follows: "It is the policy of this state that the business of all banking organizations shall be supervised and regulated in such manner as to insure the safe and sound conduct of such business . . . and thus to maintain public confidence in such business and protect the public interest and the interests of depositors, creditors, and shareholders." Act No. 319, Mich. Public Acts of 1969, ch. 1, § 2.

4. In all jurisdictions, the asset universe eligible to banks is strictly limited. Outside of fixed-asset requirements (subject, by the way, to legal limitations), assets may consist only of debt obligations—such as loans, bonds, and similar instruments—plus, of course, cash and the equivalent.

5. Historically the growth in deposit liabilities has proceeded at a rate more rapid than the ability of the banks to attract equity capital. Moreover, given the constraints imposed on the asset universe, adequate returns on equity can be achieved only with a high leverage of deposits to capital. As a consequence, debt leverage (mainly in the form of deposits but also including other borrowings) typically amounts to between ten and fifteen times capital.

6. Finally, public policy in the United States has accepted the view that it is desirable to limit concentrations of economic and financial power in the private sector. As a consequence, while a few states allow statewide banking facilities, most limit banks to a very restricted geographic area. Some states, in fact, allow banks to have only a single domestic office, although foreign branches are allowed at the discretion of the Federal Reserve. The result is that, while most large banks usually seek business on a national and international basis, the market scope of the majority is geographically limited to a relatively small area and their viability and growth are intimately associated with the economic strength of the community in which they are located.

## Bank Objectives

### Policy guidelines for financial performance

Given the institutional framework outlined above, banks must necessarily establish policy guidelines in two major areas. First, there must be policies designed to acquire the optimal amount and mix of deposits and other sources of funds. Second, policies must be established to convert these funds into eligible assets. However, as will be shown below, these policy areas are not completely independent of each other. Moreover, most statutes also allow banks to engage in "the business of banking and any business related or incidental thereto."[2] Under the "related and incidental" authorization, large banks in particular have expanded their product lines to include trust services, corporate financial planning, bond trading, and other services, but for the most part these activities remain peripheral to attracting funds on the one hand and converting funds on the other.

On the positive side, the policy objectives are to acquire the maximum amount of deposits and other funds at the lowest cost possible and to convert these sources of funds into eligible assets with the highest return potential from a long-term standpoint. The constraints on these policies are (1) regulatory requirements, (2) the need to maintain (or have assured sources of) liquidity to meet depositor demands, and (3) the need to constrain the risk of losses on assets within reasonable limits—which necessarily become more restrictive as deposit and borrowing leverage on equity capital increases.

In order to visualize the set of dynamic asset and income relationships that typify large banks. Table 1–1 summarizes the major income and asset ratios of member banks with over $500 million of assets in the Seventh Federal Reserve District for the 1971–75 period inclusive.[3] The following observations on these data suggest the nature of the functional relationships:

1. Gross operating income as a percentage of assets was between 5.7 percent and 8.2 percent, which reflects the weighted average of gross returns on assets that consisted of about 13 to 16 percent cash, 7 to 9 percent governments and agencies, 9 to 12 percent tax-exempt municipals, and 57 to 64 percent loans. As cash is a nonearning asset, it might be estimated that the gross yield on the mix of earning assets was about 15 percent higher than that on total assets. As the loan portfolio is by far the dominant asset, average loan

2. *Ibid.*, ch. 4, § 151.
3. The period 1971–72 was generally marked by expansive monetary policy, 1974 was a period of restriction, and in 1975 monetary policy was again eased to a moderate extent. Therefore, the data for these years should indicate the dynamics of the income and asset relationships under various conditions in the financial markets.

TABLE 1–1

INCOME AND ASSET RATIOS OF MEMBER BANKS OVER $500,000,000

Seventh Federal Reserve District

| | 1971 | 1972 | 1973 | 1974 | 1975 |
|---|---|---|---|---|---|
| Percentage of Total Assets | | | | | |
| Total operating income | 5.76 | 5.77 | 7.05 | 8.22 | 7.17 |
| Less costs of funds | | | | | |
| Interest on deposits | 2.11 | 2.10 | 2.76 | 3.41 | 2.48 |
| Interest on borrowings* | 0.41 | 0.43 | 0.94 | 2.68 | 1.88 |
| Net interest spread | 3.24 | 3.24 | 3.35 | 2.13 | 2.81 |
| Less other expenses | 2.56 | 2.50 | 2.64 | 1.42 | 1.99 |
| Net income† | .68 | .74 | .71 | .71 | .82 |
| Assets/Capital and Reserves | 13.00 | 13.00 | 13.20 | 13.60 | 13.20 |
| Percent Return on Capital† | 9.20 | 10.60 | 10.30 | 10.30 | 11.70 |
| | *Percentage of Total Assets* | | | | |
| Asset Distribution | | | | | |
| Cash | 16.2 | 15.2 | 13.6 | 13.2 | 13.5 |
| U.S. Treasury and agencies | 9.1 | 8.9 | 7.4 | 7.0 | 7.0 |
| Municipal securities | 11.6 | 11.5 | 10.3 | 9.6 | 9.0 |
| Loans | 57.6 | 59.1 | 63.4 | 64.0 | 61.5 |
| Other | 4.5 | 5.3 | 5.3 | 6.4 | 9.0 |

Source: Federal Reserve Bank of Chicago, *Operating Ratios of Seventh District Member Banks.*

* Includes costs of Federal Funds purchased in 1974–75; not reported separately in 1971–73.

† After taxes and before securities gains and losses.

yields necessarily dominate the determination of gross operating income.

2. The ratio of gross operating income to total assets varied as interest rates fluctuated, but to a considerably lesser degree. The reason is that a significant proportion of the total earning asset portfolio at any given time is not "interest sensitive" in a short-term sense. Bonds with maturities beyond a year and loans made at fixed rates are examples of nonsensitive assets.

3. The interest costs of deposits and borrowed funds absorb a very large proportion of gross income. Until 1974 interest on Federal Funds purchased was not broken out, and, as

most large banks have used these funds extensively for many years, it is presumed that total interest costs were significantly understated for 1971–73 in Table 1–1.

4. After all other operating expenses are deducted (wages, salaries, and fringe benefits represented more than half of the "other" expense category), net income as a percentage of assets amounted to about .70 to .82.

5. Leverage finance in the form of deposits and borrowings, however, has regularly amounted to more than 13 times equity capital, and when the leverage ratios are multiplied by the net return on assets (.70–.82), the consequent returns on equity have been a respectable 9 to 12 percent.

6. If it is assumed that both net income as a percentage of assets and the leverage ratio will remain relatively constant, then the growth rate in earnings necessarily becomes a function of the growth rate in equity capital. If the sources of additional equity capital continue to be largely retained earnings (as has been true for years), then the growth dynamics of a bank can be expressed by the following simple model:

$$Rg = Re\ (1 - PO)$$

where

$Rg$ = growth rate in equity capital;

$Re$ = rate of return on equity$\left(\frac{\text{assets}}{\text{capital}} \times \text{return on assets}\right)$; and

$PO$ = payout ratio of earnings.

On the basis of the empirical data shown in Table 1–1 the nature of the specific long-range planning objectives that a bank might establish are shown in Table 1–2.[4] The specific percentage targets are given for illustrative purposes only. In any given instance the specific guidelines presumably would be based on projections and managerial judgements that seemed appropriate in view of the bank's operating environment. The guidelines

4. The functional relationships in a commercial bank were the basis for the long-range planning objectives indicated in Table 1–2. If planning is conducted at the holding company level, then modifications based on the relative importance and characteristics of nonbank subsidiaries would, of course, be necessary.

TABLE 1–2

LONG-RANGE PLANNING OBJECTIVES
(Illustrative Guidelines Data)

| *Major* | FIVE-YEAR OBJECTIVE |
|---|---|
| Deposit growth (average annual) | 6–8 % |
| Return on assets (average) | .7–.8 % |
| Assets to total capital, including reserves (average) | 14 |
| Assets to equity capital (average) | 16 |
| Return on equity (average) | 13 % |
| Dividend payout (average) | 40 % |
| Growth in equity capital (average annual) | 7– 8 % |
| Earnings per share increase (average annual) | 7– 8 % |
| *Secondary* | |
| Purchased money* as a percentage of total deposits | 15–25 % |
| Growth in noninterest expenses (average annual) | 6– 8 % |
| Loans to assets | 55–65 % |

* Includes CDs over $100,000 and short-term borrowings.

given in Table 1–2 are internally consistent in the sense that the realization of each would be consistent with realizing the others. Moreover, they appear realistic in that they generally conform to the empirical data on large banks in the Seventh Federal Reserve District.

Policy guidelines of this sort may provide considerable assistance to management in their long-range planning and major policy decisions. In addition, as operational targets they provide a basis for monitoring results and possibly suggesting areas in which performance might be improved. Finally, a Board of Directors might find these guidelines helpful in evaluating and approving major policy decisions. For example, if the rate of deposit growth exceeds this target for several years yet equity capital increases only at or possibly below the indicated rate, then from these guidelines the alternative decision options would appear clear. The options would be (1) reduce the dividend payout ratio by not increasing dividends in proportion to the percentage increase in earnings; (2) cut back on deposit and asset growth; (3) obtain additional capital, possibly a subordinated debenture issue might be appropriate.

## Social responsibilities

As noted above, most state banking statutes place strict geographical constraints on the location of bank facilities.[5] For this reason, the economic and social trends of the local community are logically of more concern to banks than to most corporations in the private sector, whose facilities and markets may extend over wide geographic areas. Moreover, nonfinancial corporations may move their facilities from communities plagued by severe social and economic problems. This option is generally not open to banks, as their charters specifically indicate their operating areas. Therefore, a strong case can be made that, in their own self-interest, banks should be motivated to become involved with programs designed to prevent deterioration in the social structure of their communities.

Large banks in particular have a considerable stake in metropolitan markets and would seem particularly exposed to deterioration in the condition of their cities. It is, therefore, salutary to find the president of one such bank making the following statement about the need for enlightened social policies:

> Perhaps we should be applying the old phrase of enlightened self-interest to loans of the type we are discussing here—those with social or civic overtones. I do this because I wonder what good profits will mean at all in the long run if the whole rest of our society, particularly the big cities, is torn apart by strife. This just might be the case if institutions such as the commercial banks don't step in.[6]

The clear recognition that policies instituted to alleviate environmental and social decay are not dictated by a peripheral concern for public welfare considerations outside the mainstream of corporate goals would seem salutary. If corporate managements

5. The National Banking Act governing the federal chartering of banks provides that the state statutes shall govern branching authority of national banks in each state. However, holding companies are allowed to own statewide subsidiary banks in most states. Interstate banking by the holding company device requires specific legislative approval in each state on a reciprocity basis. As of 1976, such legislation had been proposed in several states, but passage in most seemed doubtful because of strong political lobbies against interstate banking operations.

6. H. F. Still (President, Central-Penn National Bank, Philadelphia), "Asset, Liability, and Capital Management," *Journal of Commercial Bank Lending* 53 (Jan. 1971): 24.

generally accept the view that such policies are not only compatible with but perhaps essential to their goals of long-term profit maximization, then such policies probably will be more carefully conceived and forcefully implemented. The concept that long-term profit goals make it necessary to solve problems ordinarily considered beyond the concern of individual private companies may seem to be a self-serving approach, but it might well provide the incentive to more dedicated action on these problems than has been evidenced in the past.

In addition, favorable political relations are highly important to banks. As a result, clear evidence that their operational policies are concerned with the major problems of the nation and their communities would seem desirable, if not imperative, in order to convince political bodies that their activities are positively in the public interest and not insensitive to it. For example, vigorous programs to render financial and management aid to businesses operated by minority groups in the inner city would seem particularly relevant for major urban banks; special priority for financing pollution control systems in their communities also could be supported for these reasons.

Finally, because banks offer a wide spectrum of financial services to the general public, the consumer movement has increasingly directed attention to banking policies as they relate to consumer interests. For example, in 1973 a Nader Group published a highly publicized and presumedly objective investigation of the policies of First National City Bank of New York. The study covered a wide range of topics, and its conclusions can only be characterized as highly biased and prejudicial, perhaps to be expected since a main objective of Nader studies often seems to be sensational revelations to obtain maximum media exposure. To illustrate the nature of activist complaints against banks, the following are some of the charges made in the report:

1. The bank consciously makes loans to many low income people who cannot service them and then actively seeks legal remedies in the courts when defaults occur.
2. The bank ignores the "credit-starved" residential mortgage market while holding large quantities of individual savings accounts.

3. Financing of large corporate customers dominates the lending operation which, according to the report, is to be expected because corporate executives dominate the board of directors. In fact, the report charges that the bank makes major loans at lower-than-competitive rates to large companies in financial difficulty.

4. No serious attempt is made to counsel and finance minority enterprises, although the bank pays lip service to this objective. Moreover, the regulatory agencies "have failed to monitor banks to ensure that community needs are met."[7]

In a reply Citibank observed that these charges were based on limited evidence which often had been interpreted improperly and it cited numerous failures of the investigators to use data which conflicted with their apparently preconceived hypotheses. The Citibank response, being less sensational, received minimal attention in the media, but it indicated the degree to which social concerns have become an integral part of the activities of the corporation. The following statement is indicative of the scope of the effort:

> An Economic Development Center with a full-time professional staff has been set up to handle situations requiring specialized know-how or a centralized financial capability. This unit evaluates loan applications and works closely with clients on financial planning matters. As compared to previous arrangements which tended to be more passive, the Economic Development Center actively works to generate referrals for our combined loan and investment program from the branch system and from other sources, most particularly community-based local development corporations.[8]

Given their high visibility, their considerable political vulnerability, and their significant dependence on regional, if not local, economic growth for their progress, large banks may increasingly institute such programs as an integral part of their corporate affairs.

7. D. Leinsforg and D. Etra, *Citibank*, Ralph Nader's Study Group Report on First National City Bank (New York: Grossman Publishers, 1973), pp. xxvi–xxx.

8. First National City Bank, *Citibank, Nader and the Facts* (New York: First National City Bank, 1974), pp. 32–33.

# II

## MANAGEMENT GOALS: IMPLEMENTATION POLICIES

### Deposit Determinants in the Banking System

From a macro point of view, economists perceive a bank as part of the institutional system wherein asset and liablity management decisions determine the level and growth of the major monetary aggregates—demand deposits on average have composed more than 70 percent of transaction money ($M_1$) and savings and time deposits constitute a large proportion of the near money ($M_2$ and $M_3$). The process requires the Federal Reserve Board to make legal reserves available to the system; then each bank in the system lends or invests the excess legal reserves up to the maximum allowed by the fractional reserve requirement. Borrowers are assumed to spend the proceeds, and the recipients deposit the funds in other banks. These banks in turn may increase their earning assets to the extent permitted by their legal reserve ratio requirements. The simplified model of these systematic relationships can be expressed as:

$$\text{Total Legal Reserves} \times \frac{1}{\text{Average Reserve Ratio}} = \text{Deposits of Banks.}$$

As legal reserve ratios against savings and time deposits are much lower than against demand deposits, the weighted average reserve ratio depends to a large extent on the percentage composition of the deposit mix. In addition, reserve requirements are scaled upward against demand deposits as their amount increases in a bank, so that shifts in such deposits from large to small banks will decrease the average systemic reserve ratio, and shifts in the opposite drection will have the reverse effect. Although the composition and distribution of deposits complicates the results obtained from the model, the essential point is that a systemic model of banking dynamics views deposits as the dependent variable, with loans and investments and legal reserves provided by the Federal Reserve the major independent variables.

## Sources of Funds

### Deposits

From the point of view of the individual bank, the receipt of deposits precedes loan and investment decisions on the asset side. Only as a bank obtains additional cash reserves through new deposits or from other sources can it acquire earning assets. Then if deposits decline, earning assets must be liquidated or other funds obtained as replacement. Therefore, it is conceptually accurate to view the first financial function of a bank as establishing policies and implementing programs to obtain deposits and other sources of funds.

Table 2–1 shows the trends in the various sources of funds for all insured banks over the past twenty-five years. As of 1951 demand deposits heavily dominated the liability structure, almost 80 percent of total deposits and 69 percent of total footings including capital accounts were represented by such deposits. In 1961, a decade later, the dominance of demand deposits had declined only moderately; at that time they constituted 65 percent of total deposits and 58 percent of total footings. As a consequence, liability policies were relatively simplistic for most banks: maximize services to the demand deposit market, generally affluent individuals, and corporations.

While attracting demand deposits remains an important banking function, the composition of the deposit structure has changed radically in the past fifteen years or so. By the end of 1975 time and savings deposits in all insured banks were about 60 percent of total deposits, which represented a change in the deposit mix unprecedented in the history of the banking system, and unless regulatory policies are drastically changed in the future, it is generally agreed that the trend will continue, although possibly at a slower pace.

Table 2–1

LIABILITY STRUCTURE OF INSURED BANKS
(Selected Years; in Billions of Dollars at December 31)

| Year | Deposits* | | Borrowings | Capital | Ratios | | |
|---|---|---|---|---|---|---|---|
| | Demand | Time | | | Demand/Time | Cap./Deposits | Cap./Liab.'s† |
| 1951 | 110.4 | 37.7 | .03 | 11.9 | 2.93 | .08 | .08 |
| 1961 | 147.0 | 82.1 | .46 | 22.1 | 1.79 | .10 | .10 |
| 1963 | 147.4 | 110.7 | 1.5 | 24.2 | 1.33 | .09 | .09 |
| 1965 | 165.2 | 146.1 | 4.3 | 29.8 | 1.13 | .10 | .09 |
| 1967 | 188.2 | 183.1 | 5.5 | 33.9 | 1.03 | .09 | .09 |
| 1969 | 212.3 | 194.2 | 18.0 | 39.5 | 1.09 | .10 | .09 |
| 1971 | 229.2 | 271.8 | 25.6 | 46.7 | .84 | .09 | .09 |
| 1973 | 271.4 | 363.3 | 57.5 | 57.6 | .75 | .09 | .08 |
| 1975 | 279.5 | 433.4 | 56.8 | 68.5 | .64 | .10 | .09 |

* Excludes interbank deposits.

† Includes total deposits and borrowings.

A number of reasons have been cited for the remarkable change in the deposit mix. Frst, demand deposits have been allowed to grow only in accord with the $M_1$ growth targets set by Federal Reserve monetary policy—generally about 4 to 8 percent per annum. Second, corporations have increasingly adopted sophisticated money-management techniques designed to reduce holdings of demand deposits and to substitute liquid earnings assets for such deposits. As a result, it became clear to the managements of large banks, which relied heavily on corporate business, that their growth probably would be seriously inhibited unless they found means to retain the liquid assets of the larger corporations. The major change in policy which first was instituted by large money center banks and then spread rapidly through the banking system as a competitive response, was to adopt an aggressive rather than a passive posture in connection with the acquisition of time deposits. A complete new line of deposit instruments, certificates of deposit, was designed and vigorously sold to both small and large customers. In the money market centers, the certificates in denominations of $100,000 or more were sold as negotiable open market instruments in competition with Treasury bills and commercial paper. Maturities were structured to tap both short- and intermediate-term funds. Thus they have varied from thirty days, the minimum allowed by law, up to several years.

However, it is important to note that the explosive growth in these new types of deposit instruments required regulatory cooperation. Under an amendment to the Federal Reserve Act, the Board of Governors of the Federal Reserve System ("the Fed") was empowered to set maximum rates payable on time and savings accounts by member banks.[1] Under the provisions of Regulation Q issued to implement this authority, the maximum rates had been held below 4 percent, except for time deposits with a maturity of a year or more, which of course had a very limited appeal. But as Table 2–2 shows, since about 1963 Regulation Q has been liberalized repeatedly.

1. This authority was granted to the Federal Reserve in 1935 on the grounds that excessive competition for deposits through high rates would lead banks into acquiring high-risk assets with sufficient yields to offer a positive yield spread and that such assets might impair the soundness of banks. The failure of some banks during the Great Depression was allegedly due to this propensity.

TABLE 2–2

MAXIMUM RATES PAYABLE ON SAVINGS AND TIME DEPOSITS
(Regulation Q of the Federal Reserve, Selected Dates)

| | Percentage Paid | | | | |
|---|---|---|---|---|---|
| Deposit Category | 1963 | 1964 | 1968 | 1970 | 1976 |
| Savings deposits | 4 | 4 | 4 | 4½ | 5 |
| Other time: | | | | | |
| Less than $100,000 | | | | | |
| 30–89 days | 1 | 4 | 4 | 4½ | 5 |
| 90 days–1 year | 2½ to 3½ | 4½ | 5 | 5 | 5½ |
| 1–2 years | 4 | 4½ | 5 | 5½ | 6 |
| 2½ to 4 years | 4 | 4½ | 5 | 5¾ | 6¼ |
| 4–6 years | 4 | 4½ | 5 | 5¾ | 7¼ |
| 6 years or more | 4 | 4½ | 5 | 5¾ | 7½ |
| Over $100,000 | | | | | |
| 35-59 days | Not Separately | | 5½ | 6¼ | * |
| 60–89 days | Classified | | 5¾ | 6½ | * |
| 90–179 days | Until | | 6 | 6¾ | † |
| 180 days to 1 year | 1968 | | 6¼ | 7 | † |
| 1 year or more | | | 6¼ | 7½ | † |

Source: Federal Reserve bulletins.

* Restriction eliminated on June 24, 1970.

† Restriction eliminated on May 16, 1973.

The first notable change occurred in late 1964 when the Fed permitted a significant increase in the rates payable on time deposits with maturities of less than one year. Demand for this range of maturities is usually a large proportion of the total, because seasonal fluctuations in corporate and government cash flows are normally adjusted in this area. If one makes the reasonable assumption that most negotiable CDs mature within one year, Table 2–3 shows that time deposits in this maturity range have come to represent about half of the total. In addition, the removal of rate ceilings on large denomination CDs in 1970 and 1973 made it possible for banks to be fully competitive in all maturity ranges. Consequently, large time deposits (over $100,000) have more than quadrupled since 1970. At the same time, the Fed finally recognized the logic of a term structure of interest rates (so far as Regulation Q is concerned), and permitted rates to scale

TABLE 2–3

TYPES OF TIME AND SAVINGS DEPOSITS FOR INSURED COMMERCIAL BANKS*
(In $ Billions)

| TYPE | JULY 31 | | | JAN. 31 |
|---|---|---|---|---|
| | 1970 | 1974 | 1975 | 1976 |
| Savings deposits (passbook) | 92.2 | 144.2 | 152.0 | 165.5 |
| Time deposits in denominations of less than $100,000 with maturities of: | | | | |
| Less than 1 year | 40.6 | 36.1 | 37.4 | 38.4 |
| 1–2½ years | 15.1 | 41.0 | 35.9 | 36.0 |
| Over 2½ years | 13.2 | 36.7 | 55.4 | 57.2 |
| Total | 68.9 | 123.8 | 128.7 | 131.6 |
| Time deposits in denominations of $100,000 or more: | | | | |
| Negotiable CDs | 13.0 | 68.2 | 62.8 | 58.8 |
| Non-negotiable CDs | 7.4 | 27.6 | 26.2 | 26.2 |
| Total | 20.4 | 95.8 | 89.0 | 85.0 |
| Total time deposits | 89.3 | 219.6 | 217.7 | 216.6 |

Source: Federal Reserve bulletins.

* For individuals, partnerships, and corporations.

upward significantly as maturities lengthened. As a consequence, retail certificates of deposit (less than $100,000) with maturities of more than one year have enjoyed considerable growth, and maturities of less than one year have remained relatively constant.

## Borrowings

Although the design and aggressive marketing of new time deposit instruments was the major innovation in fund attraction policies during the past fifteen years or so, more aggressive policies in the use of borrowings have emerged since about 1967, particularly in many large banks. Table 2–1 shows that from relatively trivial levels as recently as 1967 such borrowings expanded tenfold by 1975 for all insured banks. To indicate the alternative sources, Table 2–4 shows the composition of borrowings for the large, weekly reporting banks for 1970–76 inclusive. Although published data on borrowings do not give maturities, Fed Funds and Repos. (securities sold under agreements to repurchase), the major sources, are almost entirely limited to maturities of a week or so and most Fed Funds borrowings are one-day transactions.

It is apparent that there has been an evolutionary change in the views of many large banks as to the appropriate use of short-term borrowing. Prior to the mid-sixties the general view was that such borrowings should be used only to accommodate short-term liquidity needs consequent to random fluctuations in deposits and loans. If liquidity needs persisted after several days, liquidation of short-term money market assets, such as Treasury bills, was considered appropriate. But with the development of the concept that the wholesale certificate-of-deposit portfolio could be actively managed both to provide funds for growth and to offset seasonal and cyclical fluctuations in other deposits and loans, it was probably inevitable that some banks would conclude that borrowed funds might serve the same purpose.

TABLE 2–4
WEEKLY REPORTING BANKS' SOURCES OF BORROWED FUNDS
(In $ Billions)

| JUNE 30TH* | FED. FUNDS, ETC.† | FEDERAL RESERVE | OTHER | TOTAL |
|---|---|---|---|---|
| 1970 | 17.7 | .7 | 2.0 | 20.4 |
| 1971 | 19.5 | .4 | 1.0 | 20.9 |
| 1972 | 28.9 | .4 | 1.6 | 30.9 |
| 1973 | 37.1 | 1.1 | 3.9 | 42.1 |
| 1974 | 51.3 | 2.3 | 6.4 | 60.0 |
| 1975 | 49.7 | .2 | 3.5 | 53.4 |
| 1976 | 51.3 | .2 | 3.8 | 55.3 |

Source: Federal Reserve bulletins.

* Week ended nearest to that date.

† Includes securities sold under agreements to repurchase (Repos.).

In fact, large negotiable CDs sold in the money market are essentially borrowed funds rather than customer deposits. Because Federal Reserve regulations require a minimum thirty-day maturity on all CDs, and because significant amounts of corporate funds seek placement for periods of less than thirty days, the innovative borrowing techniques to acquire short-term funds on a regular basis are a logical extension of an active liability-management policy. Thus, although short-term borrowings of large banks still fluctuate with seasonal and cyclical needs for liquidity, the secular trend has been clearly upward.

Table 2–5 shows the asset and liability relationships for the large weekly reporting banks that developed during the first five years of the seventies consequent to the implementation of active liability management policies. From these data the following percentage increases can be derived:

| *Liability Category* | *Percentage Increase, 1970–76* |
|---|---|
| Demand deposits | 27.0 |
| Negotiable CDs | 401.4 |
| Other time | 77.1 |
| Short-term borrowings | 172.4 |
| Capital accounts | 65.7 |

As a consequence of the explosive growth in negotiable CDs, these became 18 percent of total deposits in 1976 as compared to only 6 percent in 1970. And the ratio of total money market liabilities (negotiable CDs and short borrowings) to money market assets increased from 2.65 to 3.30. Although the loan-to-deposit ratio showed no significant trend during these years, if negotiable CDs are excluded from deposits, the loan-to-deposit ratio increased from 76 percent in 1970 to over 100 percent in 1974 before declining to 84 percent in 1976.[2] In short, there has been a clear trend for short-term debt to increase relative to short-term liquid assets and for a significantly larger proportion of the loan portfolio to be funded with "purchased" funds rather than "natural" deposits.[3] Moreover, largely because "purchased" funds increased at a much

2. The decline in loan demand during the recession of 1975 resulted in a significant decline in borrowings and negotiable CDs, indicating the cyclical usage of these fund sources. It was uncertain as of 1976 whether this was a cyclical interruption in the trend or would be permanent in view of the public concern with the risk exposure of banks that emerged at that time.

3. "Natural" deposits are usually defined as those obtained from regular customers of the bank on an ongoing basis, whereas "purchased" funds are those obtained impersonally in the market strictly on a competitive rate basis. Some negotiable CDs may be sold to regular customers but their nature suggests that the great majority are sold on an impersonal basis in the open market.

TABLE 2–5

ASSET AND LIABILITY STRUCTURE OF WEEKLY REPORTING MEMBER BANKS

(At June 30 of Each Year, in Billions of Dollars)

| | 1970 | 1971 | 1972 | 1973 | 1974 | 1975 | 1976 |
|---|---|---|---|---|---|---|---|
| *Assets* | | | | | | | |
| Fed. Funds sold, etc. | 7.4 | 7.8 | 11.1 | 12.0 | 16.2 | 18.8 | 19.3 |
| U.S. Treasury, less than one year | 5.6 | 7.9 | 8.4 | 8.0 | 5.2 | 12.1 | 18.9 |
| Total money market assets | 13.0 | 15.9 | 19.5 | 20.0 | 21.4 | 30.9 | 38.2 |
| U.S. Treasury, over one year | 16.4 | 18.7 | 17.6 | 13.8 | 15.8 | 19.9 | 23.2 |
| Other securities | 38.3 | 49.7 | 54.1 | 55.5 | 63.1 | 60.2 | 59.2 |
| Total investments | 67.7 | 84.1 | 91.2 | 89.3 | 100.3 | 111.0 | 120.6 |
| Loans | | | | | | | |
| Commercial* | 118.4 | 124.6 | 135.9 | 172.4 | 199.4 | 190.8 | 180.7 |
| Real estate | 33.5 | 35.6 | 41.9 | 50.0 | 58.2 | 59.2 | 61.4 |
| Consumer instalment | 20.6 | 22.6 | 25.6 | 30.3 | 33.9 | 33.9 | 36.7 |
| Total loans | 172.5 | 182.8 | 203.4 | 252.7 | 291.5 | 283.9 | 278.8 |
| *Liabilities* | | | | | | | |
| Demand deposits | 139.1 | 153.0 | 146.2 | 150.0 | 158.5 | 169.1 | 176.7 |
| Time and savings deposits | | | | | | | |
| Negotiable CDs | 14.1 | 28.5 | 35.9 | 59.5 | 80.2 | 81.4 | 70.7 |
| Other large CDs† | n.a. | n.a. | n.a. | n.a. | n.a. | 33.8 | 28.3 |
| Other time | 87.5 | 103.4 | 113.8 | 120.5 | 130.4 | 108.0 | 126.7 |
| Total deposits | 240.7 | 284.9 | 295.9 | 330.0 | 369.1 | 392.3 | 402.4 |
| Short-term borrowings‡ | 20.3 | 20.4 | 30.9 | 42.0 | 63.3 | 53.4 | 55.3 |
| Capital accounts | 23.9 | 25.8 | 28.2 | 30.5 | 33.0 | 35.5 | 39.6 |
| Ratios: | | | | | | | |
| Negotiable CDs and short borrowings to money markets assets | 2.65 | 3.11 | 3.43 | 5.08 | 6.71 | 4.36 | 3.30 |
| Negotiable CDs to total deposits | .06 | .10 | .12 | .18 | .22 | .21 | .18 |
| Loans to total deposits | .72 | .64 | .69 | .77 | .79 | .72 | .69 |
| Loans to deposits less negotiable CDs | .76 | .71 | .78 | .93 | 1.01 | .95 | .84 |
| Risk assets to capital accts.§ | 8.82 | 9.01 | 9.13 | 10.10 | 10.75 | 9.69 | 8.54 |

Source: Federal Reserve bulletins.

* Total Loans less real estate and consumer instalment.

† Included in "other" time deposits until 1975; n.a.—not available.

‡ Sum of Federal Funds purchased, etc.; borrowings from Federal Reserve banks and others.

§ Risk assets defined as sum of Other Securities and Total Loans.

more rapid rate than the capital accounts, the leverage ratio of risk assets to capital accounts has increased steadily.

Some bankers and regulatory authorities view this sharp upward trend in the use of purchased money with concern. In their opinion heavy reliance on such funds might seriously increase liquidity problems under some circumstances rather than representing a source of liquidity relief. The opinion is based on the fact that these funds are "hot" money in the sense that large quantities must be rolled over constantly in the impersonal open money market. If access to this market becomes restricted for any reason, then the bank necessarily experiences severe liquidity problems in meeting maturing CDs and borrowings.[4] The inability of several large banks (Commonwealth of Detroit and Franklin National of New York are examples) to roll over open market borrowings seriously compounded their financial difficulties. Therefore, some banks have imposed strict policy limits on the use of borrowing and large CDs and even prohibited the use of certain types, such as negotiable CDs sold through money brokers.

## Allocation of Funds

The second major financial function of a bank is asset management. While conceptually this function would appear to be independent from the first major function, obtaining funds, there are several interfaces between them. First, a major means of soliciting deposits is to offer customers the opportunity to obtain bank credit when and if the need arises. Therefore, it has been traditional and entirely logical to give high priority to loans requested by depositing customers. Second, pressures from fund usage departments (loans) have a feedback effect on fund attraction policies. If the pressures from borrowing customers are

4. Although indicated as a personal opinion, the views of an officer of a Federal Reserve Bank are indicative of the negative position on liability management: "At least three potential dangers associated with the practice of Liability Management are recorded in banking history. These include borrowing short to lend ong, excessive interest rate competition, and reverse fund flows resulting from confidence crises or other reasons." (L. G. Gable, "Liability Management: An Indictment," *Journal of Commercial Bank Lending,* Aug. 1974, p. 4.)

strong, an aggressive search for funds becomes imperative. On the other hand, if the demand for loans declines, aggressive bidding for borrowed funds, including negotiable CDs, can be relaxed to some extent, although opportunities for money market "spread" operations may continue to keep most large banks active in these markets.

Third, active management programs with respect to "purchased" funds have had significant effects on asset management policies. If fluctuations are expected in the level of "natural" deposits, then traditonal banking concepts held that allocations to liquid earning assets should be sufficient to cover the anticipated variations. However, if the availability of "purchased" funds obtained on the initiative of the bank seems reliable, one can argue that liquidity needs against deposits of the traditional types can be met largely through additional fund purchases rather than through the disposal or runoff of assets. Some banks have therefore concluded that there is little need to orient asset management policies to the probable behavior of customer deposits. As noted earlier, the data in Table 2–5 suggest that large banks with access to funds in both the national and international markets have adopted this approach. On the other hand, most moderate-sized banks have generally been reluctant to adopt a liability management approach to liquidity needs, on the grounds that their access to the national open markets for funds might be marginal since they do not enjoy a national reputation.

A fourth interface between the major financial functions occurs when large banks often "purchase" money for arbitrage and market-making purposes wherein the asset and liability items are identical. A significant proportion of operations in the Fed Funds market apparently is along these lines. Smaller banks routinely sell (or possibly sometimes buy) these funds to (from) their large city correspondent. Those funds which are not required for their own needs are resold to other banks throughout the country. Thus it is common to find on published balance sheets of large banks both a considerable amount of Fed Funds purchased as a liability and Fed Funds sold as an asset. Because the amounts involved are large, even very small rate differentials make the operation quite profitable.[5] In addition, foreign branches, particularly in London, to remain active in the Eurodollar market buy Eurodollar deposits continually and redeposit significant portions in other banks. Thus foreign deposit liabilities are, to a significant extent, matched by deposits in foreign banks as an asset.

Finally, while the new devices for attracting funds have been effective, they also have been very costly. As was shown in Chapter 1, the unprecendented growth of time and savings deposits, coupled with substantial increases in the interest rates offered on such deposits, has produced an explosive increase in interest paid on time deposits as a percentage of gross operating income as well as greater sensitivity of these costs to changing levels of interest rates. The significantly greater sensitivity and cost of funds undoubtedly has had a feedback effect on asset allocation policies by encouraging a shift in the asset mix to higher-yielding items. In particular, up until 1975 when regulatory concern with risk asset exposures became evident, asset management policies emphasized the acquisition of loans and "other securities" (municipals for the most part), and the disposition of government securities.

Table 2–6 shows that the portion of assets devoted to cash and government securities declined from 38 percent in 1961 to 28 percent in 1975 for all insured banks, while loans and municipals increased substantially both in absolute amounts and in percentages. While the recurrent tight money conditions that marked the decade of 1965–75 probably induced some involuntary liquidation of government securities to meet loan demand, the significant voluntary increase in municipals as a percentage of earning assets clearly suggest more aggressive asset allocation policies.[6] In addition, the percentage of assets devoted to loans of all types has shown a sharp upward trend. Because it seems probable that the extensive use of interest-sensitive money is a permanent aspect of the banking

5. A lively description of the history and current activities of large banks buying and selling Federal Funds on a daily basis is contained in Martin Mayer, *The Bankers* (New York: Ballantine Books, 1974), pp. 215–32.

6. In many large banks, alternative tax shelters in the form of direct leasing programs and foreign tax credits on international earnings reduced the need for tax exempt municipal income. Heavy loan losses in 1975–76 had the same effect. As a consequence some large banks have actually reduced their municipal portfolios in recent years.

TABLE 2–6
ASSET STRUCTURE AT ALL INSURED BANKS
(In Billions of Dollars)

| Date (as of Dec. 31) | Cash Items | Fed. Funds Sold | Securities: Govt. & Agencies | Securities: Other | Loans: Com'l. & Agricultural | Loans: Financial* Inst's. | Loans: Real Estate | Loans: Consumer Loans | Other Assets | Total Assets | Capt'l. Acct's. | Ratios: Cash & Govts. / Total Assets | Ratios: Other Securities / Total Assets | Ratios: Loans / Total Assets | Ratios: Capt'l. Acct's. / Risk Assets† |
|---|---|---|---|---|---|---|---|---|---|---|---|---|---|---|---|
| 1951 | 44.2 | n.a. | 60.5 | 13.0 | 29.1 | 2.5 | 14.5 | 7.7 | 5.7 | 177.2 | 11.9 | .59 | .07 | .30 | 16.4 |
| 1961 | 56.1 | n.a. | 66.0 | 23.5 | 51.2 | 14.5 | 30.2 | 27.7 | 52.2 | 321.4 | 22.1 | .38 | .07 | .38 | 11.1 |
| 1963 | 50.3 | n.a. | 62.7 | 34.6 | 60.2 | 20.8 | 38.9 | 34.4 | 60.5 | 362.4 | 25.3 | .31 | .10 | .43 | 10.1 |
| 1965 | 60.3 | 2.1 | 59.1 | 44.4 | 79.1 | 23.5 | 49.0 | 45.3 | 11.3 | 374.1 | 29.8 | .32 | .12 | .53 | 11.8 |
| 1967 | 77.3 | 3.9 | 62.1 | 60.9 | 97.1 | 24.0 | 58.2 | 51.4 | 14.0 | 448.9 | 33.9 | .31 | .14 | .51 | 9.8 |
| 1969 | 89.1 | 9.7 | 54.4 | 70.9 | 118.0 | 27.0 | 70.0 | 63.0 | 25.5 | 527.6 | 39.4 | .27 | .13 | .53 | 10.5 |
| 1971 | 98.3 | 19.6 | 64.7 | 104.0 | 130.1 | 32.0 | 81.4 | 74.3 | 31.4 | 635.8 | 46.7 | .26 | .16 | .50 | 10.3 |
| 1973 | 116.3 | 35.3 | 86.9 | 100.7 | 174.8 | 51.4 | 118.0 | 99.6 | 11.4 | 827.1 | 57.6 | .25 | .12 | .54 | 9.8 |
| 1975 | 128.3 | 37.3 | 116.6 | 109.6 | 194.4 | 49.8 | 134.6 | 106.0 | 13.1 | 889.7 | 68.5 | .28 | .12 | .54 | 11.3 |

* Defined as loans to domestic and foreign banks, other financial institutions, brokers, and other loans to purchase/carry securities.
† Defined as all assets except cash items, Federal Funds sold, and government securities.

industry, it follows that banks will be concerned with obtaining both reasonable yield spreads and interest senstivity on asset commitments. Loan pricing policies in particular have become much more sophisticated in recent years in order to achieve these objectives.

The need to hold risk exposure within reasonable limits in relation to capital and reserves ultimately limits policies to acquire a more aggressive asset mix. Maintaining depositors' and regulatory authorities' confidence in the integrity of the bank as a going concern is a necessary constraint on asset management policies. Appraising real trends in risk exposure is difficult, however, because important matters, such as possible changes in the quality of the asset portfolio, cannot be discerned from the aggregate data. The ratio of capital to risk assets is conventionally used as a rough index of risk exposure, since this ratio shows the maximum percentage losses on such assets that could occur before creditor claims would be affected.

The data in Table 2–6 show that the ratio of capital accounts to risk assets declined significantly between 1951 and 1963, and since then the ratio has fluctuated moderately around a mean of about 10 percent. At this level, it is actually moderately below the stated Federal Reserve normative guide for capital-to-risk assets of 12 percent.[7] In addition, the highly adverse loan loss experience of many banks during the recession of 1975—unique since the Great Depression—resulted in public concern with the integrity of the banking system. Although the communications media, as is their custom, undoubtedly exaggerated the problems, both bank managements and regulatory authorities indicated that retention of public confidence suggested the desirability of prudent management of risk exposure from both an asset and a liability point of view. It is conjectural whether the concerns of

7. The comments of a member of the Board of Governors of the Federal Reserve System are indicative of the regulatory view: "There has been a dramatic drop in the capital ratios of many banks in recent years, accompanied by a sharp rise in return on equity capital. . . . Thus we should pause and vigorously resist a further decline in bank capital ratios while we reflect carefully on the complex issues involved and make certain that banks remain in a sound capital position." (John E. Sheehan, "Bank Capital Adequacy—Time to Pause and Reflect," *Journal of Commercial Bank Lending*, Jan. 1974, pp. 2–3.)

1975–76 will persist in asset management policies, but Table 2–6 shows that during 1975 commercial banks on balance shifted a large portion of their net asset acquisitions to government securities. This reversal in the trend may have occurred partly because of a decline in loan demand and a lower need for tax-exempt income from municipals, but it also suggests the emergence of a more conservative posture with respect to asset management policies.

The tarnished image of the banking industry consequent to the problems of a few banks in the 1974–76 period also has made it more difficult for banks (or their holding companies) to improve their capital positions through the sale of new equity or subordinated debenture debt issues. Because internal capital generation through retained earnings is likely to result in only a 6-to-8-percent equity growth, the ability of the banking system to fund an increase in loan demand considered normative to support economic growth as come into question. A major executive of a large bank has been quoted as follows:

> I personally don't believe that the nation has the financial base for a sustained economic expansion. Because of inadequate capital, the banking system's share of total financing will shrink in this recovery from those in past recoveries.[8]

Therefore, although the evidence is far from conclusive that the asset trends of the past two decades will materially reverse in the future, at least a moderate shift to less aggressive asset-allocation policies seemed probable as of 1976.

## Special Aspects of the Lending Function

As indicated previously, one of the major interfaces between the fund attraction and fund allocaton functions is the use of the latter as a marketing device for the former. According to a corporate financial officer:

> There are various and sundry services that a corporate customer requires of its bank, varying in complexity and magnitude with the

8. E. H. Yeo, III, Vice Chairman, Pittsburgh National Bank, as quoted in the *Wall Street Journal,* June 13, 1975, p. 13.

> size and diversity of the customer's business. But none is more important, regardless of whether the customer is large or small, than the ability of banks to make loans. Without this ability, business as we know it today could not exist.[9]

Therefore, a bank which is positive and ingenious in its commercial lending policies can use this fact as a major selling device to retain existing and obtain new depositors. On the other hand, a bank which is timid and negative in its lending practices may well find that some depositors will move their accounts to more aggressive banks. Competition for customers has been and is likely to remain intense in the banking industry.

The relation between deposit relationships and commercial loan commitments will be analyzed in more detail subsequently. The point to be made here is that a wide difference exists between the approach to customer loans and the acquisition of most securities. The latter operation is conducted on a completely impersonal basis; purely objective criteria, such as relative interest rates, credit qualities, maturities, and marketability, form the context of decisions. The only exception is the acquisition of security issues of local municipal units which carry their operating funds and short-term liquidity reserves as deposits in the banks. Purchases of local municipals are essentially analogous to extending commercial loans. Indeed some banks logically assign commercial loan officers to handle local municipal accounts, including their borrowing needs. In fact for functional analysis purposes, there may well be a breakout of local municipals from the total investment account and the prospective amounts that may have to be acquired in the next several months may be shown as part of the analysis of loan demand.

To generalize, decisions regarding customer credit commitments tend to be influenced by many singular, subtle, and subjectve factors, such as the history and prospective future of the borrower's relationship with the bank. In other words, most business customers have unique features and problems which can be evaluated and resolved only on the basis of personal contacts between the

9. T. A. Gudiness, "Lending Rituals and Sacred Cows," *Journal of Commercial Bank Lending* 52 (May 1970): 31. Mr. Gudiness, at the time of writing, was a financial officer in a leading manufacturing corporation.

two parties.[10] As a consequence, the number of officers required for the commercial loan operation is much greater than the number needed to manage the security portfolio, even though the dollar totals of the security portfolio are usually a significant percentage of total assets.

With some justification it has been held that the major difference between commercial banks and other financial intermedaries is that banks are prepared to custom tailor the financing arrangements they offer good customers. Financing packages are designed specifically for particular needs, and, moreover, the packages are continuously subject to modification as customer requirements change through time. Therefore, loan officers start with the premise that borrowing relationships may have to be structured in unusual ways. As a result, while lending decisions are usually conducted within a broad framework of policy, there is a clear tendency to avoid establishing a highly specific set of detailed policy constraints. In fact, the managements of large banks seem to have a pervasive attitude that in the management of the loan portfolio specific policy guidelines should apply to only a few major areas.[11]

It is tempting to conclude that a complete absence of definitive policies characterizes commercial lending operations, and in some respects this conclusion does not appear to be far from the truth. However, it is probably more accurate to conclude that commercial lending operations are conducted within an accepted set of policies but that these policies are reasonably elastic, in the sense

10. Reference here is particularly to the commercial loan operation. For the most part, consumer and mortgage borrowers are less likely to have important deposit relations with their banks; hence these operations tend to be more homogeneous and require less individual attention on the part of the management.

11. One large bank disclosed that at one point a "Loan Operations Manual" had been considered desirable by top management and great time and effort had gone into its preparation. It attempted to set forth in some detail the lending policies and techniques that the bank thought appropriate for various types of customers. When it was almost completed the senior vice-president in charge of all lending activities decided to keep it under lock and key in his confidential file, because he had concluded that such a manual would inhibit the flexibility and imagination of loan officers in working out desirable credit accommodations for borrowers. In other words, a positive policy decision was taken to avoid establishing definite benchmarks to guide lending decisions. The manual remains under lock and key, and neither loan trainees nor officers have access to it.

that they are often open to ad hoc trade-offs and individual exceptions. In short, while a set of loan policies guides the decision-making process, most banks also consider it essential to be flexible in implementing policy in order to survive in a highly competitive environment.

Because lending policies are quite flexible, loan officers are usually given wide latitude to structure appropriate financing packages for customers. Moreover, many loan requests involve the commitment of many millions of dollars for one or more years. Commercial loan officers must therefore have considerable intelligence, education, and experience in order to evaluate large and complex loan requests and then to structure decisions that will be in the best interest of both the bank and the customers. As a result, the greatest proportion of senior officers in large banks are assigned to the commercial lending function, although the mechanical handling of deposits and other transactions requires a much larger total number of employees. Consequently, large banks' greatest demand for college graduates is for potential loan officers, and these officers as a group generally enjoy the highest status within the institution.

# III

## EVOLUTION OF LOAN POLICIES 1950–76

The determination and implementation of loan policies of large commercial banks have several dynamic dimensions. First, as noted in the preceding chapter, implementation of policy is flexible at any given time to meet competitive pressures or unusual needs and circumstances of particular customers. Second, policies have been subject to considerable variance in response to cyclical fluctuations in the money markets. In fact, Chapter 12 will devote considerable attention to the specific modifications in policy that are likely to take place in response to changes in Federal Reserve monetary policies. Third, loan policies are also dynamic in a long-term, evolutionary sense. Sudden radical changes in the policy framework are the exception, but over a considerable time span the cumulative impact of evolutionary developments may be considerable. This chapter will examine the trends in the economy and financial markets since World War II in order to show how these trends have produced changes in commercial bank lending policies.

Because change has always marked the economy of the United States, loan policies are expected to continue to follow a dynamic pattern in the future. Although existing social and economic trends can be evaluated relative to their probable impact on credit policies, it clearly is not possible to predict all the major developments that may occur in the years ahead. Therefore, while the broad framework of existing loan policies may remain more or less intact in the future, continued innovations and modifications in many aspects of the lending function can be expected. In fact, policy statements might well include a directive that existing lending policies should be periodically and critically reviewed.

## The Growth Decade: 1950–59

When World War II ended in 1945, the asset structure of commercial banks reflected their wartime role of financing the significant portion of the government's budgetary deficits that could not be met with savings flows. Member bank holdings of Treasury obligations had increased from $15.8 billion in 1940 to $78.3 billion in 1945, whereas loans had increased only modestly from $15.3 billion to $22.8 billion. During the following five years, marked generally by an inflationary boom in business activity, loans doubled and government securities were liquidated in substantial amounts, but even so holdings of government obligations still exceeded the loan account at the end of 1950.

Despite the significant increase in loans, interest rates did not advance appreciably from their low wartime levels because of the official policy to support government bond prices at par.[1] In fact, Table 3–1 shows that only very modest yields were available on governments, municipals, and prime commercial loans through most of the decade of the fifties despite the fact that the pattern of the economy was both inflationary and growing during most of these years; the exceptions to this pattern were short and mild recessions in 1953–54 and again in 1957–58.

In summary the environmental context of bank policies at the beginning of the fifties exhibited these features: (1) portfolios were still dominated by government obligations on which yields were relatively low; (2) alternatives in the form of municipals and prime commercial loans also offered modest yields; (3) there was an active consumer demand for durable goods (and housing) and for credit to finance these purchases; and (4) most corporations of substantial size enjoyed strong liquidity positions, because their cash flows had substantially exceeded cash requirements during and immediately after World War II.

These conditions clearly favored innovative asset management

1. This policy undoubtedly contributed to the postwar inflation and became highly controversial, but the Treasury view that unpegging the market would lead to an inability to conduct refunding operations on reasonable terms prevailed until the "accord" of 1951, wherein the Federal Reserve reasserted its right to conduct open market operations on the basis of monetary policy considerations rather than on the basis of supporting government bond prices at a prescribed level.

TABLE 3–1
SELECTED INTEREST RATES IN PERCENTAGES: 1950–59
(Average for Year)

| YEAR | GOVERNMENTS | | GOOD GRADE MUNICIPALS | | PRIME RATE |
|---|---|---|---|---|---|
| | 3-MONTH | 5-YEAR | 5-YEAR | 10-YEAR | |
| 1950 | 1.18 | 1.54 | 1.15 | 1.50 | 2.25 |
| 1951 | 1.49 | 2.03 | 1.40 | 1.60 | 2.75 |
| 1952 | 1.70 | 2.26 | 1.40 | 1.70 | 3.00 |
| 1953 | 1.90 | 2.57 | 1.85 | 2.25 | 3.25 |
| 1954 | 0.92 | 1.89 | 1.30 | 1.75 | 3.00 |
| 1955 | 1.70 | 2.58 | 1.80 | 2.15 | 3.25 |
| 1956 | 2.64 | 3.13 | 2.40 | 2.15 | 3.75 |
| 1957 | 3.17 | 3.63 | 2.95 | 3.25 | 4.50 |
| 1958 | 1.81 | 2.98 | 2.50 | 2.80 | 3.50 |
| 1959 | 3.26 | 4.26 | 2.95 | 3.35 | 4.50 |

Source: Based on data in Salomon Brothers & Hutzler, *An Analytical Record of Yields and Yield Spreads* (New York: n.d.).

policies, and it was during these years that many banks became active in loan areas outside the traditional short-term commercial loans. Consumer and mortgage loan departments were established by many large metropolitan banks that formerly had remained aloof from such activities. The levels of interest rates prevailing in these markets can only be estimated, because they are for the most part determined locally, but by and large mortgage rates were from 4.5 percent to 6 percent, and consumer loans offered gross yields (before costs) of 9 percent to 12 percent. In any case, as the prime commercial loan rate averaged about 3 percent until 1956, there were very favorable rate spreads between commercial loan yields and those prevailing in the mortgage and consumer loan markets, and this situation provided a substantial incentive for banks to become active in the latter. In addition, an increasing proportion of business loans were made to small and growing firms, and fairly continuous borrowing arrangements were generally tolerated; rates, of course, were well above the prime rate to reflect the increased risk and longer maturities of such loans.

In short, new loan markets were aggressively promoted, and lending officers were generally encouraged to provide liberal credit arrangements for their business customers. A leading book on bank management commented on the scene of the early fifties as follows:

> Banks hunt for borrowers and offer good service and attractive rates. The picture of the successful bank lending officer has changed greatly. He is a salesman at heart, albeit a salesman with a sense of financial prudence but more disposed to view the applicants' case favorably than not.[2]

Because liquidity positions were generally excessive and earnings could be improved by shifting assets from the bond portfolio to the loan accounts, competition for borrowing customers was intense. As a result, credit terms were liberalized across the board and many traditional policies, such as rigorous requirements for supporting balances, were either eliminated or ignored. In fact, a senior officer of onc largc bank stated that procedures were instituted which made it more difficult for a loan officer to reject than to grant a loan request.

The results of the active search for loans during the decade of the fifties are shown in Table 3–2 for all member banks. It is notable that loans increased at an average annual compound growth rate of more than 10 percent and this rate was well in excess of those registered for deposits and capital accounts. Moreover, the growth rate in loans exceeded the growth rate in the economy as a whole, as measured by Gross National Product. At the beginning of the decade, loans amounted to about 18 percent of GNP; by the end of the decade they amounted to about 23 percent. Furthermore, this growth rate was attained during a period when large companies could finance their capital requirements on favorable terms in the external financial markets. As a result, their dependence on banks for anything but short-term funds was minimal. It would seem reasonable to conclude, therefore, that a major portion of the growth in commercial loans was the result of aggressive solicitation of developing companies.

As the decade of the sixties opened, much of the excess liquidity in the banking system had been extinguished. For all member banks the ratio of government securities to total deposits had

2. R. I. Robinson, *The Management of Bank Funds* (New York: McGraw-Hill Book Co., 1951), p. 94.

TABLE 3–2
MEMBER BANKS: SELECTED DATA
(In Billions of Dollars)

| | Loans | | | | | Deposits | | |
|---|---|---|---|---|---|---|---|---|
| Year | Commercial | Real Estate | Consumer | Other* | Total | Demand | Time | Capital Accounts |
| 1949 | 15.9 | 8.8 | 6.6 | 5.4 | 36.7 | 82.6 | 29.2 | 9.2 |
| 1950 | 20.5 | 10.5 | 8.3 | 5.9 | 45.2 | 90.3 | 29.3 | 9.7 |
| 1951 | 24.3 | 11.3 | 8.5 | 6.0 | 50.1 | 96.0 | 30.6 | 10.2 |
| 1952 | 26.2 | 12.2 | 10.4 | 7.0 | 55.8 | 100.0 | 32.9 | 10.8 |
| 1953 | 25.5 | 13.0 | 11.9 | 8.2 | 58.6 | 99.8 | 35.2 | 11.3 |
| 1954 | 25.0 | 14.4 | 12.1 | 9.6 | 61.1 | 103.3 | 38.0 | 12.2 |
| 1955 | 31.0 | 16.4 | 14.3 | 10.3 | 72.0 | 108.7 | 39.2 | 12.8 |
| 1956 | 36.3 | 17.8 | 15.8 | 9.5 | 79.4 | 110.2 | 40.9 | 13.7 |
| 1957 | 37.9 | 18.2 | 16.8 | 9.7 | 82.6 | 109.0 | 45.3 | 14.6 |
| 1958 | 37.4 | 20.0 | 17.0 | 11.3 | 85.7 | 114.2 | 51.1 | 15.3 |
| 1959 | 42.2 | 22.2 | 19.9 | 12.8 | 97.1 | 115.4 | 52.9 | 16.3 |
| Average Growth Rate (In percentage) | 10.2 | 9.7 | 11.7 | 9.0 | 10.2 | 3.5 | 6.1 | 5.9 |

Source: Federal Reserve bulletins (appropriate years).
* Includes agricultural loans, loans to carry securities, and other loans.

declined from about 47 percent in 1950 to about 26 percent in early 1960. In brief, to achieve a massive redistribution of assets from government securities to higher yield loans, most banks structured their commercial loan policies to encourage loan officers to be liberal and flexible in meeting loan requests. In addition, although some exceptions could be noted (primarily in areas where branches were prohibited), most large banks had established massive retail loan programs (mortgages and instalment loans). These programs involved heavy promotional expenditures and the development of large clerical staffs to service the credits. As fixed costs of these programs are generally high, a large volume of outstanding loans is required in order to obtain adequate returns. The result was that promotional programs to divert business from the traditional sources of such credit—the consumer finance companies—were widespread throughout the banking industry. These promotional efforts included assurances that loans would be accepted on a consistent basis through time and not turned on and off in response to variations in monetary conditions.

As a consequence, most banks had created a strong growth momentum in their loan programs. But with the elimination of excess liquidity, the momentum could be maintained only with an increased rate of growth in sources of funds. On a systemic basis, as indicated in Chapter 2, this would require some combination of a greater growth rate in the volume of legal reserves made available by the Federal Reserve, a change in the deposit mix toward time and savings deposits on which reserve requirements are lower, or seeking sources of funds (borrowings) not subject to reserve requirements. But aggressive solicitation of interest sensitive funds and minimal liquid asset positions necessarily made the system more and more sensitive to exogenous events. The system was, therefore, well suited to function smoothly and efficiently under easy money policies but became increasingly exposed to strain in the event of tight money policies.

### The "Easy" Years: 1960–65

The strong growth orientation of lending policies appeared entirely justified by the course of events in the first half of the sixties. National economic policies were consistently slanted toward the expansive side because of the sluggish economy in those years. Because of a generous supply of reserves made available by the Federal Reserve, total bank assets and deposits increased considerably. The growth bias is evidenced by the fact that, as shown in Table 3–3, loans increased significantly even during the 1960–62 period of relative economic stagnation. In those years the largest percentage increase was in the "other" category made up largely of consumer loans.

Then as economic conditions improved in 1963–65 the growth rate in loans increased considerably. Besides the steady infusions of legal reserves, Table 3–3 shows that the growth in assets also was made possible by a substantial change in the deposit mix in favor of time deposits, on which legal reserve requirements were (and are) substantially lower than those on demand deposits. Largely because of the significant reduction in the percentage of deposits absorbed by legal reserves, not only were member banks able to increase the loan-to-deposit ratio from about 57 percent in 1960 to 66 percent in 1965, but in addition, municipal holdings increased by more than $17 billion, which was only partially offset by a reduction of about $6 billion in the government security account. Investment policies, it is clear, also were becoming more aggressive during these years.

In short, even during a marked upswing in business activity, the banks were able to accommodate all apparent loan demands and still add modest amounts to their total holdings in the investment accounts. In fact, the empirical data for these years suggest that banks pressed ahead with innovative and liberal loan practices. Table 3–4 shows the distribution of loans by major categories for the large weekly reporting banks during 1960–65. The following observations might be made concerning these data: First, there were above-average increases in the real estate and consumer areas. These categories, as will be shown in the chapters on retail credit policies, are most likely to be extensively promoted and expanded when lending policies are aggressively oriented toward growth. By the end of 1965, for the first time in history, the totals of real estate loans and "other" loans (mostly consumer) together approximately equaled the total of commercial and industrial loans for the large banks.

TABLE 3–3
MEMBERS BANKS: SELECTED DATA
(In Billions of Dollars)

| YEAR ENDING | LOANS | SECURITIES | | DEPOSITS* | | TOTAL | LOANS/DEPOSITS |
|---|---|---|---|---|---|---|---|
| | | GOVERNMENT | MUNICIPAL | TIME | DEMAND | | |
| 1960 | 99.9 | 49.1 | 14.1 | 57.3 | 118.6 | 175.9 | 56.8 |
| 1961 | 106.2 | 54.0 | 16.7 | 67.1 | 125.0 | 192.1 | 55.3 |
| 1962 | 118.6 | 53.0 | 20.8 | 79.7 | 124.1 | 203.8 | 58.2 |
| 1963 | 131.7 | 49.3 | 25.2 | 90.9 | 123.6 | 214.5 | 61.4 |
| 1964 | 147.7 | 48.7 | 28.4 | 103.7 | 134.3 | 238.0 | 62.1 |
| 1965 | 167.9 | 45.0 | 32.6 | 120.2 | 137.0 | 257.2 | 65.3 |
| Average Growth Rate (In percentage) | 11 | neg. | 18 | 16 | 3 | 8 | |

Source: Federal Reserve bulletins (appropriate years).
* Excludes interbank deposits.

TABLE 3–4
LOAN PORTFOLIOS OF LARGE COMMERCIAL BANKS
(In Billions of Dollars)

| YEAR (AS OF MARCH 31) | COMMERCIAL OR INDUSTRIAL | AGRICUL-TURAL | TO CARRY SECURITIES | TO NON-BANK FINANCIAL INSTITUTIONS | FOREIGN BANKS | REAL ESTATE | OTHER* | TOTAL |
|---|---|---|---|---|---|---|---|---|
| 1960 | 31.0 | .9 | 2.8 | 5.8 | .8 | 12.9 | 14.6 | 68.8 |
| 1961 | 32.0 | 1.1 | 3.1 | 5.0 | .7 | 12.4 | 16.1 | 70.4 |
| 1962 | 33.0 | 1.3 | 4.5 | 5.6 | .7 | 13.6 | 17.0 | 75.7 |
| 1963 | 35.5 | 1.5 | 4.7 | 6.6 | .7 | 15.9 | 18.4 | 83.3 |
| 1964 | 38.3 | 1.5 | 6.0 | 8.2 | 1.1 | 18.4 | 20.6 | 94.1 |
| 1965 | 44.6 | 1.5 | 6.5 | 8.9 | 1.6 | 20.3 | 23.7 | 107.0 |
| Average Annual Growth Rate (In percentag) | 7.6 | 11.0 | 18.3 | 9.0 | 14.8 | 9.5 | 10.0 | 9.3 |

* Foreign government and consumer loans included in this category until 1967.

Second, financial institutions, principally consumer finance companies, were able to obtain fairly regular and sizable increases in their accommodations from the large banks. Because a significant proportion of such credits does not involve a close customer relationship, these institutions generally have a lower priority than do most borrowers in the commercial and industrial category. The significant increase in loans extended to financial institutions, therefore, reinforces the conclusion that large banks generally were actively soliciting loans during this period. Because there was no difficulty in meeting the demands, the decisions made in the previous decade to embark on aggressive expansionary policies in both old and new loan areas were entirely vindicated.

As shown by Table 3–5, interest rates generally were stable during this period. Some softening in rates took place in 1960–61 as monetary policy was eased in order to improve the growth rate in economic activity. Although subsequently rates moved up modestly as the economy responded to the expansive national economic policies, during 1965 interest rates in most areas were still at or below levels prevailing in 1959.

TABLE 3–5

SELECTED INTEREST RATES IN PERCENTAGES: 1959–65
(Averages for Year)

| YEAR* | GOVERNMENTS | | GOOD GRADE MUNICIPALS | | BANK PRIME RATE | EURODOLLARS† 3-MONTH MATURITIES |
|---|---|---|---|---|---|---|
| | 3-MONTH | 5–YEAR | 5–YEAR | 10–YEAR | | |
| 1959 | 3.32 | 4.26 | 2.95 | 3.35 | 4.50 | ... |
| 1960 | 2.88 | 4.13 | 2.90 | 3.30 | 5.00 | ... |
| 1961 | 2.30 | 3.69 | 2.50 | 3.05 | 4.50 | ... |
| 1962 | 2.73 | 3.71 | 2.30 | 2.75 | 4.50 | 3.73 |
| 1963 | 3.10 | 3.80 | 2.40 | 2.80 | 4.50 | 3.91 |
| 1964 | 3.51 | 4.08 | 2.75 | 2.95 | 4.50 | 4.35 |
| 1965 | 3.98 | 4.20 | 2.85 | 3.00 | 4.50 | 4.79 |

Sources: Salomon Brothers & Hutzler, *An Analytical Record of Yields and Yield Spreads* (New York, n.d.); Standard and Poors Corp., *Basic Statistics* (New York: 1959–65).

* Year-end data.

† Not reported until 1962.

Despite a sharp escalation in interest paid on time deposits because of the change in the deposit mix and some liberalization in Regulation Q, the dual forces of a substantial upward shift in the loan-to-deposit ratio and movement toward more aggressive investment portfolios enabled net income of member banks to increase at a reasonably favorable 6 percent average annual compounded rate. On balance, therefore, the first half of the decade of the sixties provided an environment wherein aggressive asset management policies applied to both the loan and investment accounts were highly rewarded, because liquidity problems were minimal. Portfolio risks were also minimized, because there was a steady improvement in business activity without sharp increases in interest rate levels.

## The "New Environment": 1966–75

In the decade that followed 1965, however, the economic context of asset management policies changed drastically. The relatively noninflationary economy of the preceding five years was replaced by a persistent escalation in the rate of inflation. Recurrent attempts to reduce the inflation rate through highly restrictive monetary policies dominated this decade along with recessions that followed each episode of tight money. The decade closed with the recession of 1974–75, which was the most severe since the Great Depression years.

During this period, as shown in Table 3–6, short-term interest rates advanced to unprecedented levels both in 1969–70 and again in 1973–74.[3] Moreover, cyclical fluctuations in short-term rates became considerably more pronounced. The major reason for more volatile interest rates has probably been a change in the focus of monetary policy from primary concern with appropriate levels of interest rates to active management of targeted growth rates in the monetary aggregates. Attempts to restrain inflation by restricting monetary growth necessarily required tolerance of

3. It is possible that during the liquidity crises which occurred before the advent of the Federal Reserve System short-term rates reached levels above those registered in these years. However, for the period since the Federal Reserve began to manage bank reserves actively during the Great Depression, there is no record of rates at at the levels witnessed in the 1969–74 period.

TABLE 3–6
SELECTED SHORT-TERM INTEREST RATES
(Yearly Range of Monthly Averages in Percentage)

| YEAR | FEDERAL FUNDS | PRIME RATE | COMMERCIAL PAPER (4–6 Months) | TREASURY BILLS (6 Months) |
|---|---|---|---|---|
| 1966 | 4.42– 5.77 | 5–6 | 4.82– 6.00 | 4.73–5.80 |
| 1967 | 3.79– 5.00 | 5½–6 | 4.65– 5.73 | 3.81–5.56 |
| 1968 | 4.60– 6.12 | 6–6¾ | 5.50– 6.25 | 5.14–6.01 |
| 1969 | 6.30– 9.19 | 6¾–8½ | 6.53– 8.84 | 6.15–7.79 |
| 1970 | 4.90– 8.98 | 5½–8½ | 5.73– 8.78 | 4.85–7.86 |
| 1971 | 3.71– 5.57 | 5¼–6½ | 4.19– 5.75 | 3.43–5.59 |
| 1972 | 3.29– 5.33 | 4½–6 | 3.93– 5.45 | 3.59–5.29 |
| 1973 | 5.94–10.78 | 6–10 | 5.78–10.23 | 5.53–8.70 |
| 1974 | 8.53–12.92 | 8½–12¼ | 8.66–11.72 | 6.87–8.85 |
| 1975 | 5.20– 7.13 | 7¼–10¼ | 5.79– 7.30 | 5.59–6.94 |
| †1976 | 4.77– 5.48 | 6¾–7½ | 5.23– 5.94 | 5.14–5.77 |

Source: Federal Reserve bulletins.
* Yields in secondary market.
† Range to June 1976.

wider fluctuations in interest rates than previously considered appropriate.

In addition, the removal of Regulation Q rate ceilings on CDs over $100,000 made a large portion of deposit costs both more expensive and more volatile, although the change removed the severe disintermediation effects consequent to higher interest rates which had occurred first in 1966 and again in 1969. During those years when open market interest rates advanced above the maximum allowed by Regulation Q, wholesale certificates of deposit (over $100,000) suffered severe runoffs as holders shifted to higher-yielding assets available in the money market. After 1970, however, rates offered on these CDs could be fully competitive and indeed in 1974 rates in excess of 12 percent for thirty- to sixty-day funds were not uncommon.

The data in Table 3–7 indicate the effects that ensued from the change in Regulation Q. In 1969 member banks suffered a significant decline in time deposits consequent to disintermediation, but in 1974 when interest rates on all money market instruments

TABLE 3–7
MEMBER BANKS: SELECTED DATA
(In Billions)

| YEAR | LOANS* | SECURITIES | | DEPOSITS† | | | CAPITAL ACCOUNTS | LOANS/DEPOSITS RATIO (In Percentage) |
|---|---|---|---|---|---|---|---|---|
| | | GOVERNMENTS | MUNICIPALS | TIME | DEMAND | TOTAL | | |
| 1965 | $167.9 | $45.0 | $32.6 | $120.2 | $137.0 | 257.2 | $24.9 | 65.3 |
| 1966 | 181.6 | 41.9 | 33.8 | 128.8 | 142.6 | 271.4 | 26.3 | 66.9 |
| 1967 | 196.8 | 47.0 | 41.5 | 147.4 | 156.6 | 304.0 | 28.1 | 64.7 |
| 1968 | 215.7 | 47.9 | 48.4 | 162.6 | 168.2 | 330.8 | 30.1 | 65.2 |
| 1969 | 235.6 | 39.8 | 47.2 | 149.6 | 173.9 | 323.5 | 32.1 | 72.8 |
| 1970 | 241.8 | 45.4 | 55.7 | 179.2 | 174.5 | 353.7 | 34.1 | 68.4 |
| 1971 | 262.8 | 47.6 | 65.2 | 209.4 | 182.8 | 393.2 | 37.3 | 67.0 |
| 1972 | 310.0 | 48.7 | 69.6 | 239.8 | 206.8 | 446.6 | 41.2 | 69.4 |
| 1973 | 365.3 | 41.5 | 72.0 | 275.4 | 210.9 | 486.3 | 44.7 | 75.1 |
| 1974 | 400.0 | 38.9 | 74.3 | 317.1 | 207.4 | 524.5 | 48.2 | 76.3 |
| 1975 | 387.5 | 61.2 | 74.1 | 328.9 | 211.4 | 540.3 | 51.7 | 71.7 |
| Average Annual Growth Rate (In percentage) | 8.7 | 3.1 | 8.5 | 10.6 | 4.4 | 7.7 | 7.6 | |

Source: Federal Reserve bulletins.

* Excludes Federal Funds sold.

† Excludes interbank deposits.

advanced to unprecedented levels, time deposits showed a large advance. It is notable that in 1969 significant reductions in the securities portfolio were necessary to meet deposit runoffs and also fund loan commitments, whereas in 1974 the net change in the securities portfolio was nominal. Thus the data suggest that prior to 1970 banks were subject to a severe funds squeeze during tight money periods and consequently had to restrict asset growth, including loans, to a significant degree. Subsequent to 1970, these periods resulted in a *rate* squeeze to the extent that interest-sensitive liabilities exceeded interest-sensitive assets, but funds remained available if a bank was willing to pay the price.

Over the entire period, loan portfolios increased at a rate significantly higher than that of deposits, with the result that the loan-to-deposit ratio in 1973–74 reached levels not experienced since before the Great Depression. Although during the recession of 1975 loan demand declined, the percentage increase in loans and municipal securities exceeded that of capital accounts, and in addition the moderate erosion in holdings of government securities continued. As a result, both asset liquidity and capital protection of risk assets showed some deterioration during the decade ending with 1975.

As the "new" environment gradually evolved, more intensive asset and liability management policies became evident; escalating money costs (resulting from both a shift in the deposit mix toward time deposits and high average rates paid) necessarily induced more aggressive asset-management policies. But the problem was that even high rates of earnings retention did not provide the capital growth needed to support the growth in risk assets. Therefore, unless the prices for bank equities improve considerably from 1976 levels so that banks or their holding companies can issue additional stock at reasonable cost, capital adequacy problems could conceivably constrain many banks in ther asset and liability management policies, if and when loan demand again shows a strong upward trend.

## Loan Portfolio Trends in Large Banks

Because our major concern is with the loan policies of relatively large banks, Table 3–8 shows the trends in the major categories

TABLE 3–8

LOAN PORTFOLIOS OF LARGE COMMERCIAL BANKS

(In Billion Dollars)

| YEAR (AT MARCH 31) | COMMERCIAL OR INDUSTRIAL | AGRICULTURAL | TO CARRY SECURITIES | TO NONBANK FINANCIAL INSTITUTIONS | FOREIGN BANKS OR FOREIGN GOVERNMENTS* | REAL ESTATE | CONSUMER | OTHER† | TOTAL |
|---|---|---|---|---|---|---|---|---|---|
| 1966 | 52.6 | 1.6 | 7.1 | 10.6 | 1.6 | 22.9 | . . . | 25.7 | 122.1 |
| 1967 | 62.0 | 1.8 | 6.7 | 9.6 | 2.5 | 27.1 | 15.8 | 10.6 | 136.1 |
| 1968 | 66.4 | 1.9 | 6.7 | 9.4 | 2.5 | 29.4 | 16.5 | 12.0 | 144.8 |
| 1969 | 75.0 | 2.0 | 6.6 | 10.4 | 2.6 | 32.6 | 18.8 | 13.8 | 161.8 |
| 1970 | 78.7 | 2.0 | 7.3 | 11.7 | 2.5 | 33.5 | 20.2 | 14.0 | 169.9 |
| 1971 | 81.2 | 2.0 | 7.3 | 13.3 | 2.1 | 34.6 | 21.6 | 13.8 | 175.9 |
| 1972 | 83.6 | 2.4 | 9.6 | 14.7 | 3.6 | 39.9 | 24.3 | 15.6 | 193.7 |
| 1973 | 100.0 | 3.1 | 10.6 | 22.2 | 6.4 | 47.5 | 28.7 | 18.7 | 237.2 |
| 1974 | 116.0 | 3.8 | 8.2 | 27.3 | 7.6 | 56.3 | 33.2 | 19.9 | 272.3 |
| 1975 | 125.8 | 3.4 | 6.5 | 29.5 | 6.5 | 59.5 | 33.9 | 18.3 | 283.4 |
| 1976 | 114.6 | 3.7 | 8.4 | 25.4 | 6.9 | 60.5 | 35.4 | 17.8 | 272.7 |
| Average Annual Growth Rate (Percentage) | 8.1 | 8.7 | 1.0 | 9.1 | ‡ | 10.1 | 9.4 | ‡ | 8.4 |

Source: Federal Reserve bulletins.

* Foreign Government included after 1967.

† Includes consumer loans and loans to foreign governments until 1967.

‡ Data not comparable during period.

of loans for the large weekly reporting banks during the decade ending in March 1976. As background for an investigation of current loan policies and programs in these banks, the following comments on these data would seem pertinent: First, although commercial and industrial loans have always represented the largest category, with about 45 percent of the total in most years, year-to-year variations tend to be more pronounced in this area. Indeed for the first time in many years these credits declined between the end of 1974 and 1976.

Second, the above-average rate of growth in loans to nonbank financial institutions and against real estate was somewhat surprising, because these categories had shown only average increases in 1960–65. It is often alleged that because the customer relationships tend to be more impersonal in these areas, they will have lower prority on bank resources during periods of monetary restraint. It is notable, however, that the major increase in real estate loans took place during 1972–74 when the Real Estate Investment Trusts managed to obtain an estimated $10 to $12 billion of credits from banks.[4] As REIT loans for the most part became and remain a serious problem for many banks, it may be conjectured that real estate loans may become less important in future years than suggested by the data in Table 3–8. Indeed, since early 1974 real estate loans have been relatively stagnant in amount so far as the weekly reporting banks are concerned.

Third, the data suggest that international operations of large banks have become increasingly important in the last decade or so. Loans to foreign governments and banks increased from trivial levels in 1966 to fairly significant levels in 1976. Moreover, many foreign credits are included in the commercial and industrial category, and some are structured through foreign affiliates and subsidiaries that are not included in the weekly data. Finally, the consumer loan category, which includes credit card operations, has grown to fairly substantial levels. Given the probable development of sophisticated electronic fund transfer systems and the increasing popularity of consumer credit cards, it seems probable that this area will enjoy considerable growth in future years.

4. *Wall Street Journal,* Jan. 5, 1976, p. 1.

## Long-term outlook for loan policies

Given the major innovations in asset and liability management that have marked the past two decades, simple extrapolation of past trends would seem to be a highly dubious means of projecting the future loan policies of commercial banks. Moreover, there is some evidence that loan portfolio problems in a number of banks resulting from the combined effects of aggressive loan policies, inflation, and the economic recession of 1975–76 may spur a redirection of policy.

In economic analysis, a significant turning away from the trends of the past is termed an "inflection point." Widely publicized alleged financial problems of some banks, the inevitable, strong political reactions to the problems, and the highly diverse earnings performance of the industry during the recession year of 1975 were specific events that suggested a possible "inflection point." Although some moderate variation in earnings might be expected because of diverse local economic conditions, in the case of commercial banks the major exogeneous economic factors that should have an impact on earnings results are more or less the same—the matrix of interest rate levels through time, the growth rate in the monetary aggregates, and the pattern of consumer and business loan demand. The only logical explanation for highly diverse earnings results, therefore, is that there may be significant differences in discretionary managerial policies.

And as shown by the data in Table 3–9, the diversity of performance in 1975 was very wide. The median and mode change in earnings both were in the positive 0–9 percent range, which compared favorably with the total corporate universe, which was negative in percentage change on average for that year. But despite the relatively favorable results for the industry, about 30 percent of the companies in the sample had earnings declines of 10 percent or more and an even more remarkable 21 percent of the companies had declines of 20 percent or more. On the other side, about 27 percent of the banks in the sample were able to generate earnings improvements of 10 percent or more.

Informed analysts of the banking industry seemed unanimous in their opinion that the highly aggressive loan policies followed

TABLE 3–9

EARNINGS PERFORMANCE OF BANKS

(Percentage Earnings Changes 1975 over 1974, Random Sample)

| | INCREASE | | DECREASE | |
|---|---|---|---|---|
| PERCENTAGE CHANGE | NUMBER | PERCENTAGE OF TOTAL | NUMBER | PERCENTAGE OF TOTAL |
| Over 30 | 6 | 4.8 | 20 | 15.8 |
| 20–29 | 3 | 2.4 | 7 | 5.6 |
| 10–19 | 25 | 19.8 | 11 | 8.7 |
| 0–9 | 41 | 32.5 | 13 | 10.4 |
| Totals | 75 | 59.5 | 51 | 40.5 |

Source: *Wall Street Journal,* issues Jan. 5–27, 1976.

Note: Sample includes only banks and holding companies whose earnings were reported in the *Wall Street Journal.* Almost all of these are large and publicly owned companies having sufficient public interest in their securities to justify publication in a national financial paper.

in previous year were a major cause of the 1975 earnings problems of a substantial minority of banks. For example, a survey of security analysts specializing in the banking industry elicited the following comment:

> Volatile earnings, while common in some industries, have been almost unknown to banking. From the end of World War II until the early 1970s, bank earnings never really declined . . . . There were a few flat years, but on average they grew 6 percent to 10 percent annually . . . . But all that has been changed in recent years by more aggressive (or lax, some observers say) lending policies, diversification into nonbank fields, and the steep recession. Together, these factors have sharply increased problem loans.[5]

The implication for management policies resulting from the experience was suggested by remarks of a senior executive of a large bank at an industry conference of loan officers:

> We should be concerned as to how we got here and, it is hoped, learn enough so we won't do it again. At least in my view, the biggest culprit in getting us into our current problem was the

5. *Wall Street Journal,* Oct. 27, 1975, p. 22.

> volume goal that we all seem to have worked so diligently to fulfill during the years 1971 through 1975 . . . . The trouble stems not so much from the recession as from the years of supercharged credit expansion that preceded the economic downturn.[6]

There is, therefore, considerable reason to argue that the events of 1975–76 may have caused an "inflection point" in loan policies. During the nine years ending with March 1975, total loans (as per Table 3–8) of the weekly reporting banks increased from $122.1 billions to $283.4 billion, which represented an average growth rate of about 10 percent per annum. Although the decline of 3.8 percent between 1975 and 1976 undoubtedly was caused, in large part, by a reduced demand for loans consequent to the recession, it is also entirely possible that a portion of the decline was due to more rigorous lending standards.[7] Subsequent chapters will discuss some specific changes that were introduced; it seems clear, however, that the general attitude had changed from that of seeking competitive growth at all costs to that of seeking sound and profitable loan programs. Consequently the average annual growth rate in loan portfolios during the next several years may be significantly below the average growth rate for the past twenty years. This is not to argue that policies are likely to become highly conservative across the board, but only to note that some areas—real estate development loans, for example—may be cut back and that further liberalization of credit standards is not probable for at least several years.[8]

6. John F. Holman, Executive Vice-President, Wells Fargo Bank, as quoted in the *Wall Street Journal,* Aug. 20, 1975, p. 1.

7. A lead article in the *Wall Street Journal* based on a survey of a number of banks supported this view: "It's important to look at Mr. Lientz [an individual bank officer] and the new way he does business because he is typical of the thousands of bank loan officers that companies around the country deal with every day. In general, borrowers are finding that [loan officers] have become far more circumspect of late in extending credit. Gone is the glad-handed, name-your-price approach of recent years. Instead, borrowers are finding that their balance sheets, and their management capability, are under much closer scrutiny than even a few years ago." *Wall Street Journal,* Mar. 12, 1976, p. 1.

8. Late in 1976 loan demand still remained weak and there were reports of aggressive solicitation of loans, but concessions in pricing terms were emphasized in these reports and not concessions in credit quality standards.

# 2

# DOMESTIC COMMERCIAL LOANS

# IV

## ORGANIZATION STRUCTURE

### Loan Departments

Except in a few banks which concentrate entirely on corporate accounts, the organizational structure of large banks includes at least four separate and distinct departments with lending responsibility. These are (1) commercial loans, (2) international loans, (3) real estate mortgage loans, and (4) consumer loans. In addition, in recent years the majority of large banks also have established leasing operations. In many cases, leasing is conducted through a separate subsidiary company for legal reasons, but for all practical purposes it may be considered part of the lending facilities of the bank.

The principle behind the departmentalization is that each type of credit requires very different policies to guide decision making; therefore each represents a natural area of specialization in the lending function. The commercial, international, and leasing departments are essentially concerned with business credits. Indeed, a given customer may have relationships in all three sectors. With some exceptions the organizational problems of all three tend to be similar in nature, although international and leasing credits usually have unique features which make it appropriate to handle them in specialized departments. The primary functional distinction, therefore, is between the wholesale credit structure (business loans) on the one hand and the retail credit structure (consumer-oriented loans) on the other.

This departmental structure is so basic that no particular comment or analysis of its logic is required. It is important to note, however, that the organizational problems in the retail loan departments are relatively routine. Consequently, only minor policy issues are involved in establishing the internal organization of these two departments. But the structure of the wholesale loan departments is an entirely different matter. In this instance, some clearly conflicting policy objectives create important organizational problems, and views differ about the most appropriate solutions. This chapter, therefore, is concerned with the major policy issues confronting management in the organization of the wholesale loan departments, the various views on their resolution, and the apparent advantages and disadvantages of each arrangement.

## Wholesale loans: Operational characteristics

The singular characteristics of a wholesale loan operation in a large bank which give rise to important organizational problems may be summarized as follows:

1. Borrowers have highly varied economic and financial characteristics and different financial needs. Therefore, each credit relationship has singular features which often require expert judgments to resolve. In addition, certain lending operations tend to be specialties in which a good deal of technical knowledge and experience is required.

2. Close contacts with borrowing firms are made at the senior management level. These individuals expect and demand service by bank personnel whose level and abilities are commensurate with their own, and who are empowered to render prompt attention to their needs.

3. As a result, a sufficient number of qualified officers must be available to give personal attention to a large number of borrowers; from fifty to a hundred loan officers may be required in a large bank.

4. In large banks customers are located throughout a wide geographic area, and their adequate servicing requires fairly regular personal calls. In addition, the number of customers in any area usually diminishes as the distance from the bank increases.

5. Because new lending officers are continually required for replacements and expansion, the training and experience of the loan staff are likely to vary over a wide range.

6. A relatively standardized set of complete credit information must be available on each major credit relationship to ensure that credit decisions are based on careful appraisals satisfactory to top management, internal auditors, and outside examiners.

7. The need for personal calls on borrowers often keeps loan officers away from their desks in the bank.

8. Because the banking statutes and court cases place special fiduciary responsibilities on top management, this group must exercise reasonable control over loan policies and major decisions. In this context top management may be defined as the chief executive officers and the board of directors.[1]

9. Many loans require significant allocations of resources, and these may require decisions as to the availability of funds and relative priorities that are to be established among various types of customers.

### Centralized versus decentralized structures: Decision authority

Some of the above characteristics clearly suggest the desirability of a decentralized organizational structure, while others suggest the need for centralization. The conflicts between several objectives usually lead to rather complex organizations, and a number of compromises are inevitable. The first four characteristics indicate that it would be desirable to delegate lending powers to a

1. With respect to the responsibility of directors, the following quotation is pertinent: "The directors are responsible for seeing to it that the loans a bank makes are within the statutory limitations. They should make sure at least that the larger loans are supported by adequate information as to the borrower's financial situation and the use to be made of the loan, and by the existence of a reasonable repayment plan. In some banks, directors have met trouble because they abdicated their functions to bank officers. When the bank gets into difficulty, the rule of reason determines whether the directors have any liability." (*A Bank Director's Job* [Washington, D.C.: American Bankers Association, 1970] p. 6.)

number of individuals. In that way the bank would maximize its ability to provide prompt service to a large number of customers over a wide geographic area, each with unique needs and problems. Assuming that each loan officer establishes a close personal relationship with his customers, mutual confidence and respect would be best maintained by allowing the individual loan officers to have a major voice in the final decisions instead of merely passing requests "upstairs" for action by superiors.

Moreover, it would be most difficult for a few senior officers to become expert in all the technical fields and also give adequate personal attention to customers in various parts of the country. But these same two requirements—technical knowledge and personal attention—also give rise to conflicting views concerning the most appropriate means of assigning customers to the various loan officers. The fact that industries vary widely in their economic and financial features suggests an allocation organization based on industry types. In that way the loan officers, alone and in associated groups, could become highly competent in evaluating the companies and structuring the credits to meet the unique financing needs of their industries.

On the other hand, the wide geographic distribution of customers suggests their allocation to loan officers be along territorial lines, particularly for areas some distance from the bank where the density of customers diminishes. The obvious advantage is more efficient use of traveling time. For example, several customers in different industries may be located within a given city; if industry allocation is followed, four or five officers may have to travel to that city, but if geography controls the allocation, only one need to go. Therefore, many more contacts might be assigned to a given officer under a territorial allocation, and the result would be more effective use of personnel. In addition, there is the opinion that when allocation is by industry type some customers object to a loan officer's becoming privy to confidential information while at the same time maintaining an intimate relationship with competitors. While all information obtained from customers is supposedly confidential, there is the possibility that something might be inadvertently be disclosed to competitors if a loan officer has close and continuing relationships with several competing firms.

Differences in views on this issue have resulted in a great variety of organizational arrangement. The typical compromise, however, has been to establish two or more loan divisions (metropolitan, state, and national) and then within each division to have several loan groups of five to ten officers. In the metropolitan division, where the customer population is dense, assignments are often made on a basis which is partly geographic but includes some other stratification methods as well. Similar economic characteristics, consumer durables say, are one means of stratification, but other means also are used. For example, large customers may be assigned to one or more groups and small customers to others. In addition, a few industry specialty groups may be established to handle all customers (both local and national) which have rather unusual economic features and have a volume of business sufficent to warrant the assignment of a group on a full-time basis. Table 4–1 shows the frequency of various specialty loan groups as reported by the respondent banks. In all cases, these banks had a specialized finance company group; the large number of major customers in this area and the applicability of highly specialized credit techniques to their evaluation provide the rationale for this group.[2] Real estate, investment bankers and brokers, and petroleum were specialty groups in about half the banks. Other specialized industry groups were reported by a few banks; in all instances they were based on unique industry features.

In the state and national divisions, loan group assignments typically followed geographic lines. The major rationale, of course, is that customer density is greatly reduced outside the metropolitan area and thus both efficiency in travel and calls per day are optimized by a geographic arrangement. A few respondents reported separate groups to handle only correspondent banks in certain geographic areas, but this arrangement was not typical.

Finally, a salutary development in recent years, which recog-

2. Other financial institutions, such as savings and loans and investment bankers, were also assigned to the finance company group if the volume of business in these other areas was not sufficient to warrant a separate group.

TABLE 4–1

INDUSTRY SPECIALTIES: LOAN GROUPS

| | INDUSTRY | FREQUENCY |
|---|---|---|
| 1. | Finance companies | 6 |
| 2. | Real Estate (mortgage bankers, REIT) | 4 |
| 3. | Investment banks (security dealers) | 3 |
| 4. | Petroleum (energy) | 3 |
| 5. | Commodities | 2 |
| 6. | Food processors | 2 |
| 7. | Transportation | 2 |
| 8. | Savings and loan | 1 |
| 9. | Utilities | 1 |

Note: From a six-bank sample. One additional bank reported all its loan groups, both local and national, on the basis of industry allocation. Another stated all groups within its metropolitan area structured on an industry basis but handled finance companies and investment banks in a separate group on a nationwide basis. This latter bank is included in the data in the table, but the purely industry-oriented bank is not.

nizes that the goals of banks extend to community improvement as outlined in Chapter 1, has been the formation of a special loan group within the metropolitan division to serve business activities in the inner cities. Such groups, often staffed by officers from minority groups, are authorized to make loans on more liberal terms and to offer more continuous assistance to borrowers than is customary on regular accounts. Most banks in the sample surveyed had established such a special loan group, and specific authority had been granted to these groups to extend credits on more liberal terms and with greater risk exposure than established policy guidelines justify.[3] In general, a break-even objective was considered reasonable for the special inner-city loan groups, although several banks indicated that a loss operation was probable for several years.

The fifth through ninth characteristics of the wholesale loan operation listed above suggest the desirability of some centraliza-

3. In some cases this group reported directly to top management or a committee thereof rather than to the division head. The reasons were to make sure that the unusual objectives of the group were fulfilled and because the relationships were perceived to have sensitive social and political overtones.

ton, or at least of a hierarchical form of organization. Under such a structure final decisions are made (or possibly reviewed and approved after the fact) by an upward chain of management operating in a consultative capacity with one another. The reasons are as follows.

First, because at any given time the commercial lending staff have widely varying training and experience, some review and approval of decisions made by inexperienced officers would be prudent. Logically, greater loan authority would be authorized as an officer proceeds to a higher level in the organization or reaches decisions in consultation with his peers. Second, the requirement that complete and reasonably uniform credit analyses should support every lending arrangement (beyond nomimal amounts) suggests that the credit analysis function be centralized in order to obtain standard and complete credit files.

Third, the fact that outside calls require loan officers to be away from the bank a considerable amount of time means that several officers should be familiar with the status of each account. If a customer makes inquiries concerning some problem, he expects a reasonably prompt response. Therefore, there is need for some centralized structure so that several officers are able to respond to specific problems that may arise on a customer's account. However, because the commercial loan operation is not a homogeneous operation, in the sense that the decision-controlling variables in each situation tend to be different, it is not possible for a given officer to have a detailed knowledge of a large number of accounts. The objective is to provide adequate personal attention to a wide variety of accounts and yet not overload any group of officers.

Fourth, the Board of Directors is charged under banking law with unique fiduciary responsibility for asset decisions, and under some conditions fund allocation priorities must be established. These features of banking clearly indicate the need for an organizational structure wherein major loan decisions receive some centralized attention. However, in a large bank the volume of such decisions may be several hundred per day. Therefore, compromise is essential. It invariably takes the form of delegating to individual loan officers responsibility for small credits where decisions are controlled only by policy constraints and audit reviews but requiring that one or more senior loan officers or a formal committee thereof approve large credit arrangements.[4]

## Wholesale loans: Normative organizational structure

In order to compromise the conflicting objectives, the general nature of the organizational structure that usually emerges is shown in Figure 4–1. The focal point for initiating loan decisions is the loan group as noted above, it typically consists of from five to ten loan officers. Officers within each group are responsible for maintaining regular contacts with their assigned accounts and formulating credit proposals with the assistance of the credit department. If a credit also includes international accommodation, then an appropriate officer from the international division would also be included in structuring the proposal. If a lease deal appears expedient, then an officer from the leasing company (department) would be included.

Organization into divisions and groups serves to accomplish the following objectives: First, it formalizes the means whereby senior officers can supervise and coordinate the work of less experienced personnel. These officers are responsible for providing continuous counsel to junior officers as well as regular reviews of their performance. In brief, the senior officers, and particularly the group head, have the important duty of supervising the training of junior personnel.[5] Second, the group becomes a discussion unit to formulate proposals on large and complex credits wherein it is desirable to have more than one view and opinion. Third, regular and direct contacts between top management and the large number of loan officers are exceedingly difficult to attain. The head of a loan division is responsible for implementing management policies and in this capacity becomes the natural line of

4. The chief executive officers are usually included in the membership of the major loan committees; but as the scope of banking services has expanded and operations have become more complex, the consequent burdens on the time of the executive officers have necessitated less participation in loan decisions. See McKinsey and Co., *Developing Future Bank Management* (Chicago: Association of Reserve City Bankers, 1968), pp. 21–22.

5. One bank indicated that the training function was a major duty of the group head. Most mentioned it specifically; a few merely implied the function by reference to a responsibility for "administration" of the personnel in the group.

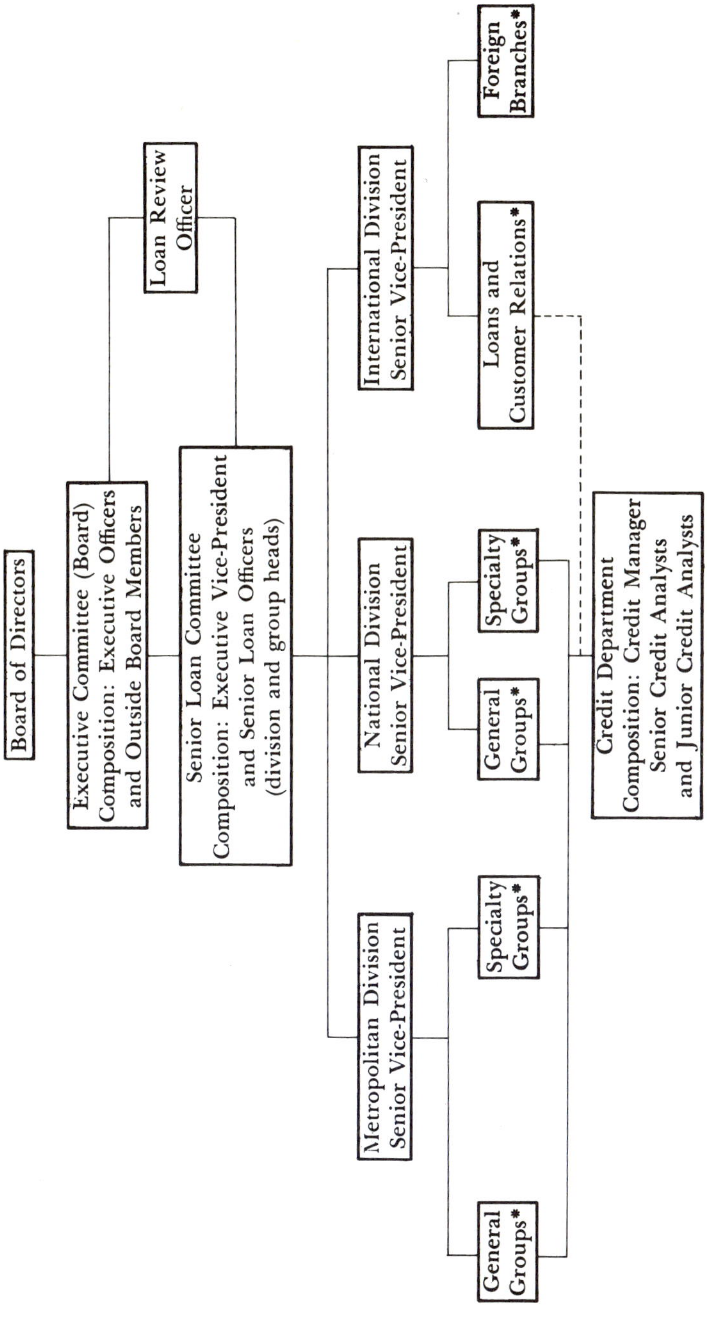


* Composition: Vice-Presidents, Assistant Vice-Presidents, Loan Officers or Assistant Cashiers.

**Fig. 4–1. Commercial loan organization.**

communication between the executive officers and the loan groups. Finally, the loan groups in some banks have become profit centers, and the group head is responsible for the development of a profit plan against which subsequent performance is evaluated. Loan groups, as profit centers, have a direct incentive to maximize performance and efficiency.

But while the division and group structure provides for some central control and coordination of the loan function, it is also necessary to coordinate the activities from the standpoint of credit policy and fund allocation. Such controls might be achieved by establishing rigorous budgets and standard criteria for decisions, but the difficulties of forecasting customer credit needs and the unique nature of most credit arrangements inhibit the use of these devices. Coordination and control can only be achieved in practice by some method of organization which will expedite loan requests, yet at the same time afford top management the opportunity to review or approve the major decisions. Thus it is typical but not universal to find one or more loan committees (composed of senior officers) that must give prior approval of major loan decisions, or alternatively in a few cases review the decisions after the fact.[6]

## The Credit Department

The operational functioning of the structure shown in Figure 4–1 may best be analyzed by starting with the credit department and working upward to the site of ultimate responsibility for all policies and decisions, the board of directors. The function of the credit department is essentially to provide information and credit evaluations; thus its personnel does not have loan authority as such. Credit departments were established as separate entities out of the recognition that formal credit files and objective credit analyses would greatly assist in rendering intelligent decisions on loan requests.[7] In large banks, therefore, the credit department

6. The role of the top executive officers might be compared to that of an appeals court. The analogy with the judiciary structure is based on the principle that neither appeals judges nor top management in banks take the initiative in decisions; their function is to review actions of others from an objective standpoint based on long experience and proved capacities. It is emphasized, however, that management should not use its review power to "second-guess" loan officers.

7. Charles Williams, ed., *The Credit Department: A Training Ground for the Bank Loan Officer* (Philadelphia, Pa.: Robert Morris Assoc., 1958), chap. 1.

has the duty of collecting in credit files all data and information considered pertinent to the present and future financial status of customers (and some noncustomers) with detailed information on all their past relations with the bank: deposits, borrowings, and other services. Since banks regularly exchange information and also provide credit checks for customers (though these tend to be perfunctory to avoid divulging confidential information), credit departments also maintain a correspondence section which handles these numerous requests.

There are two divergent views about the role of the credit department in the lending process. Some argue that the major tasks require only a modest degree of interpretive analysis and for the most part require only clerical skills. In this view the department is seen primarily as an agency for collecting information, including the analyses that may be required to provide background for loan decisions, such as receivable or inventory audits. In fact, perceiving the role of the credit department as that of clerical adjunct to the loan groups and stopping its responsibility at this point is by no means unusual. A number of banks operate on the theory that the decision-making function should reside entirely in the loan groups or committees and that maximum efficiency in the assembly and routine analysis of credit information can best be attained by a permanent staff largely of clerical grade.

An opposing view is that the credit department should go beyond more or less routine tasks and render interpretive opinions indicating whether various loans should be made and, if so, on what terms and conditions. This assignment is an important extension of the credit department's role in the lending process. It requires personnel of greater capacities and brings them into closer contact wth actual loan decisions. One argument for extending the duties to include documented recommendations on loan requests is that such an arrangement provides objective appraisals independent of the lending officers. Since the latter work closely with customers on a personal basis and also actively solicit business, they might place undue emphasis on the favorable aspects of credit requests. To avoid a biased input of information, the higher management echelons charged with approval and review of decisions may find a separate and objective opinion of considerable value. In fact, there is some tentative evidence that those respondent banks operating under a "strong" credit department structure had fewer loan portfolio problems during the recession of 1974–76 than those with "weak" credit departments.[8]

A second major reason for extending the duties of the credit department is that it can then perform an important role in the orderly training of prospective loan officers. Although personnel and training policies are considered to be sufficiently important to justify a separate chapter, it may be observed at this point that trainees can become acquainted with a wide variety of credit problems by being assigned to investigating and then writing interpretive analyses of the borrowing requests initiated in the various loan groups. If the credit department is limited to mostly clerical tasks, the effective training of future loan officers can be obtained only by formal assignments to the several loan groups. Under this arrangement, training experience may be more limited in its range and may perhaps provide less emphasis on the objective analysis of credit considerations.

In Figure 4–1 the credit department is shown as responsible to the domestic loan divisons. In some banks, the department also provides credit services for the international division, and thus trainees can obtain experience in appraising and structuring both domestic and international credits. In banks where the credit department performs mostly investigative clerical functions, however, there is usually little or no contact with the international operation.

## Loan groups: Decision authority

The focal point of personal contact with a customer is an individual loan officer within a given loan group. Therefore, primary responsibilty for initiating all credit arrangements rests with the officer assigned to the account, acting alone or in consultation with others in the group. But at the same time his authority to make a final decision is usually limited. Individual and

8. Based on loan loss data disclosed in annual reports and then the estimated incidence related to the nature of the credit department in each respondent bank.

joint (two officers) loan authorities are usually increased upward according to rank, since experience and proved abilities logically permit a greater exercise of individual judgment. However, one respondent rejected the automatic assumption that rank reflects capacity to make judicious loan decisions. In this case, the senior officers (division and group heads) operating as a committee assigned individual loan authorities based on their appraisal of each officer and the type of customer assigned to him. For example, if the customers were largely top-flight companies, the authority would be larger than if the lending area had greater perceived risks.

Loan authority limitations also tend to vary in some banks according to the type of loan. Authorities were higher on secured loans than on unsecured credits, and in some the authority is less on term loans (credits beyond one-year maturity) than on short-term credits.

Table 4–2 shows the dollar range of loan authorities on standard short-term commercial loans found in the several respondent banks; the ultimate authority is the legal limit, the maximum loan that a bank may advance to one borrower.[9] It might be expected that the larger the bank the larger the loan authority granted to a given officer rank. But no pattern was apparent on this score. For example, one bank which allowed vice-presidents an individual maximum authority of $200,000 was considerably smaller than another which limited the authority of such officers to only $25,000.

Apparently difference in views as to the appropriate resolution of the conflict in objectives discussed above was largely responsible for the variation in the structure of loan authorities. Some banks have concluded that the factors calling for centralized decision making should dominate; in these instances individual and loan group authorities tend to be low and major decisions are delegated to one or more loan committees. Others consider that a wholesale

9. In national banks the normal legal limit of loans to one customer is 10 percent of total capital and surplus, although certain specific exceptions exist. Most states follow the national law, but when there are differences they usually increase the limit to a higher percentage of capital and surplus. For example, in Michigan the legal limit is 20 percent of capital and surplus if two-thirds of the board of directors approve a loan.

TABLE 4–2
SCHEDULE OF LOAN AUTHORITIES

| | RANGE* | | |
|---|---|---|---|
| | MINIMUM | MODE | MAXIMUM |
| *Individual* | | | |
| Loan officers (ass't. cashiers) | $ 20,000 | $ 25,000 | $ 100,000 |
| Assistant vice-presidents | 25,000 | 50,000 | 300,000 |
| Vice-presidents | 25,000 | 150,000 | 500,000 |
| Group head | 50,000 | 500,000 | 5,000,000 |
| Executive officers† | 5,000,000 | | Legal limit |
| *Committees* | | | |
| Two officers‡ | 100,000 | . . . | 2,000,000 |
| Groups | 200,000 | . . . | Legal limit |
| Division | 500,000 | . . . | Legal limit |
| Senior credit | 1,000,000 | . . . | Legal limit |
| Executive committee | . . . | Legal limit | . . . |

* Based on unsecured loans; in some cases greater authority is given for secured loans.

† Variously defined as head of banking department, executive vice-presidents, president, or chairman. Only about half of the banks gave such authority.

‡ Authority of two officers generally increases as the rank of the senior officer involved rises to a higher level. If group or division head included, authority ranged up to legal limits in some cases.

loan operation requires decentralized decisions; as a consequence, major loan authorities are extended to the group and divisions, with loan committees given a review function only. At the extreme, one respondent bank operating under the decentralized approach indicated that their organization structure did not include a formal loan committee of any kind. At the other extreme, all loans over $1 million required advance approval of the executive committee of the board, although "emergency" authority for the legal limit was available to the chief executive officer.

## Loan committees: An evaluation

The banks following the centralized system emphasized that the restrictions are not imposed for the purpose of ensuring a conservative posture on loans. On the contrary, they reported that senior officers and loan committees tended to be more aware than junior officers of competitive pressures. In most large banks, senior managements seem to be highly sentitive to the need for favorable public and customer relations. This behavioral pattern suggests that customers may obtain better terms from a management committee than they would from an individual officer, although the tendency of some loan officers to identify personally with their customers makes this observation open to numerous exceptions. But the major reason advanced in support of the committee system was that it was the only feasible means of assuring consistent credit decisions within the bank. It was felt that there might be significant differences between groups as to credit judgments, and committee approval on major loan requests is necessary to eliminate possible inconsistency of treatment.

The obvious drawback to the committee system is the length of time that might be required to obtain a decision. But for several reasons this factor was held not to be important in practice. First, most large commercial customers usually do not need immediate action. The financial planning of most large companies anticipates credit needs and prospective loan requirements well in advance. Second, since the loan committee usually meets every day, the delay cannot exceed twenty-four hours except on very large loans which require executive committee approval. Finally, special authorities are granted for urgent situations, although even on urgent decisions a limited form of multiple action is sometimes required. For example, large "emergency" loans might require approval by any two or three senior officers available in the bank at the time, instead of the full loan or executive committee.

Three practical drawbacks to the committee system received mention. The first was that serving on loan committees absorbs an excessive amount of senior officers' time when the great majority of loans are subject to their approval. While attempts are apparently made to act quickly on clear-cut loans and to spend appreciable time only on the more difficult situations, sometimes a fair number of requests may for one reason or another fall in the latter category. A second problem is that some customers may be unfamiliar with the committee system of decisions. Consequently they may regard it as a somewhat impersonal approach. When this attitude is found, loan officers are supposed to emphasize that the purpose is really to keep management informed rather than to control decisions closely. Again, however, attempts to overcome this drawback may be only partially successful, since they largely depend on the tact and public relations skills of the individual officer. For example, some officers may perceive that they can avoid personal conflict with customers by blaming the impersonal committee for loan rejections or terms which are more restrictive than those originally anticipated. Customer relations clearly may be impaired by the inference that the committee system unduly inhibits loan decisions. Finally, some major customers inevitably realize that the loan officer assigned to the account has limited decision authority. As a consequence, they may prefer to have their regular personal contacts with senior officers of the bank rather than the account officers, and the senior executive officers of the bank may become the de facto loan officers for these customers.

### Executive committee of board

The role of the executive committe of the board of directors in the lending function varies widely. In banks following the decentralized approach, the committee has no role and merely receives reports on the loan portfolio from time to time. In others, prior approval of the committee is required on loans over a certain size. As mentioned above, one bank required advance executive committee approval of loans over \$1,000,000, but more typically the limit was set at loans over \$5,000,000. Since in major banks large loans often make up a very substantial proportion of the total outstanding dollar volume, the requirement provides for considerable centralization of loan decisions and the consequent composition of the loan account. The advantages ascribed to this practice are: (1) it provides screening of major risk asset acquisitions; (2) it enables the board to carry out its responsibility for asset policies more effectively; and (3) because directors may be held personally liable for neglect or negligence, it is prudent to have evidence of active participation in the lending process.

On the negative side, the executive committee normally includes outside directors—otherwise its composition might not be materially different from that of the senior loan committee—and therefore daily meetings are not expedient; even weekly meetings may impose some hardship on directors engaged in other occupations.

Thus final approvals of large loan requests may be delayed for a week or more if executive committee action is required, or alternatively the "emergency authority" granted top managment may be too frequently used. Moreover, it is held that sufficient supervision can be exercised through a periodic review of the major loan decisions. But because of the significant loan problems that emerged in some banks in 1974–76, there may be a tendency toward a more active participation of the board or executive committee in the lending operation. This may be achieved through more rigorous policy constraints to guide loan decisions, but alternatively greater attention to major individual loan exposures may also be considered appropriate either on an approval or review basis.

The full board of directors has so many areas of policy responsibility beyond loans that it cannot be expected to approve individual loan decsions except in moderate-sized banks where large loan requests are infrequent yet may, in dollars, amount to an important percentage of the total loan portfolio. The board's role in the lending function, therefore, is usually somewhat perfunctory. In most cases it is limited to formal approval of committee actions, with questions raised only on major credits which may involve policy issues. In addition, many boards review in some detail large past-due loans and those in a workout category, and management is of course responsible for explaining the actions contemplated on such loans.[10]

## Loan Review: Structure and Responsibilities

As statutory and case law have held that senior management and the board of directors can be held personally responsible for negligence in asset management wherein negligence includes lack of knowledge about, and failure to exercise appropriate supervision over, the loan portfolio, it is the policy of some banks to require board approval of large loan commitments and, in addi-

10. A partial list of other responsibilities of the board would include reviewing capital requirements and related dividend policy, examining major requirements for physical facilities, considering possible new services, and reviewing earnings progress, investment policies, and trust department policies. Selection and promotion of senior officers of course is also a major board function.

tion, to review delinquent loans of any magnitude with the full board or a committee thereof. In an organization structure oriented toward this type of centralized decision authority, an extensive independent loan review and evaluation process would seem less imperative than in a bank where decision authority is decentralized. In the latter instance, the loan review process becomes the only means whereby top management can discharge its fiduciary responsibility.

Therefore, in banks with decentralized structures, the loan review operation may be extensive, and although its functions are essentially staff in nature, it may have considerable influence over loan policies through its advisory recommendations to top management. Indeed in one such bank, the loan review group is lodged within the executive department, it is designated as responsible for credit policy, and is headed by the chairman of the executive committee, who also is a member of the board of directors. Some fourteen officers plus an extensive clerical staff are assigned to the operation.

The functions of a loan administration and review group typically includes some combination of the following activities:

1. Appraise the loan portfolio at specified intervals and assign quality grades to loans or categories thereof on some consistent basis.

2. Determine that credit decisions are in accord with approved loan policies. Any significant exceptions must be reported to management.

3. Review documentation and collateral procedures on loans to ascertain if credit information is sufficient and collateral is properly handled.

4. Follow status of large credit commitments and report problem loans to management. Comment on plans, or even initiate recommendations, for restructuring or working out serious credit problems.

5. Communicate the findings of the loan review officers regularly to line loan officers, groups, and divisions, with appropriate comments for modifications in future credit decisions.

Because loan administration involves a number of major issues, such as the appropriate response to Federal Reserve policies, a separate chapter will be devoted to policies in this area. The loan administration function may use inputs from the loan review process in reaching decisions, but conceptually the two are distinct.

Three versions of the role of a separate loan review section can be found. In the first, the role is limited to a semi-audit of loan documentation procedures and an investigation of the current status of major commitments with the findings reported to management. In the second, the role is expanded to include recommendations for handling problem loans and also may include evaluations of the performance of loan officers and groups. A third version makes the section responsible for monitoring the entire lending operation, including the initiation and the implemention of changes in loan policies. In the last version, the section can be viewed as the major interface between the board of directors (executive officers) and the line lending staff with the recommendations of the loan review staff carrying the implied weight of board action.

The first edition of this book[11] was written during the economic environment characterized in the preceding chapter as the "Easy Years" of 1961–65. At that time about half the respondent banks actually took the position that a formal loan review program was undesirable because it might inhibit "creative" credit decisions of loan officers and thus result in a loss of customers to competitors. For several reasons the attitude has changed, and without exception all respondent banks had a formal loan review process as of 1976. The reasons advanced were:

1. The rapid growth of loan staffs has resulted in less experienced officers making credit decisions, and as a result there is need for a closer monitoring of loan decisions.

2. The scope of loan activities has greatly increased to include longer term loans, international exposures, real estate development loans, and lease financing. Loan review reports

11. *Bank Lending Policies: Issues and Practices,* Michigan Business Studies XVI, No. 3 (Ann Arbor: Bureau of Bus. Research, Graduate School of Business Administration, The University of Michigan, 1964).

enable management to keep abreast of developments in these diverse areas.

3. The increased cyclicality of the financial markets and many industries since about 1970 requires greater attention to risk exposure and less attention to a growth orientation.

The first reason may decline in importance in the future as loan staffs will probably increase at a less rapid rate than in the past. However, given the economic context of 1970–76 as indicative of the future, it is probable that the loan review section will occupy an important role in the commercial loan operation.[12]

## Organizational Structure: Special Features

As might be expected, several modifications of the typical organizational structure have been found useful by various banks. For example, some banks establish loan authorities for officers in the personal accounts division. As the title of the division indicates, the principal responsibility is to supervise service on individual deposit accounts. At irregular intervals these depositors may desire to borrow against such collateral as marketable securities, savings accounts, and life insurance cash values. Granting loan authority to officers in the division is based on the view that most customers will prefer arranging such loans with their normal bank contact. Therefore, any officer in the division is authorized to make loans up to a specified amount, usually \$25,000 to \$50,000, against such liquid collateral, with after-the-fact approval by a senior officer. These loan authorities seem highly desirable because, although they involve some sacrifice of management control, such loans should involve minimal risk if they are properly made and they may improve customer relations.

A second special feature, first instituted in the 1969–70 period of severe credit restraint, has been the establishment of a special committee to decide fund allocations and priorities. The need for these procedures arose from the fact that loan demand in many banks exceeded their normal resource capacities. As a result, a

12. See C. Ellis, "Loan Review: An Organizational Dilemma," *Journal of Commercial Bank Lending*, Oct. 1975, pp. 28–30.

screening of requests beyond the regular credit evaluation was considered necessary. The following observation is illustrative:

> While credit judgments on loans still rests with the division and executive staff of the banking department, approval for allocation of funds for loans over $250,000 must be made by the head of banking department and Executive Vice-President or President.

In most banks, the secondary screening along these lines was applied only to new loans or increases in existing commitments. Its importance, however, is indicated by the fact that in several cases the president or chairman was involved in the decision.

Although the elimination of Regulation Q interest rate ceilings on large CDs after 1970 has reduced the impact of monetary restraint on fund availability for large banks, the need to monitor spreads between yields on increased loan commitments and the marginal cost of funds during periods of rapidly rising interest rates suggests the desirability of such a special committee. In addition, in some cases capital adequacy constraints may invoke limitations on the risk asset universe. In brief, any circumstance that might require limiting credit commitments to a level below that of effective demand under existing loan programs and policies would indicate the need for a fund allocation committee to supplement the normal decision-making structure.

Third, where branches are permitted, there is the policy question of the role that branch managers should have in loan decisions. Many small businesses and perhaps even some of moderate size may have their primary personal contact in a branch. Therefore, customer relations might be improved by giving moderate loan authority to the point of contact. On the other hand, the principal duty of most branch managers is supervision of operating functions, and for the most part their training and experience have not been oriented toward commercial loan decisions.

The usual solution for this problem is to establish a special branch loan group in the main office or regional headquarters. Each officer in the group is assigned to a specified number of branches and works closely with the branch managers in contacts with borrowers whose deposit accounts are serviced in the branches. Under this structure most branch managers do not have any significant loan authority but are usually consulted on customers' needs and problems. A potential drawback of this arrangement is that the branch personnel may tend to be less vigorous in their promotional efforts because they have no real participation in important decisions. To give branch managers the type of authority granted to the personal accounts division (as mentioned above) might have some merit; some branch loans have a minimal need for complex analytical procedures, and a reasonable degree of direct participation might make branch personnel more effective in customer solicitation.

It should be mentioned that it is typical practice to locate trained lending officers in major branches where the volume of business is large. In such cases the individual loan authorities granted in the main office usually prevail and on rare occasions have even been increased. Such a step would seem especially desirable in branches located in towns with distinct local features, since there is some sensitivity in such areas against real or imagined domination by the nearby metropolis.[13]

Finally, a special comment might be made on the techniques used to review rejected loan requests. According to several banks, junior loan officers may be inclined to feel that their rejection of marginal loan requests might expose them to less personal criticism than would more enterprising decisions. If approved, some marginal loans might become workout situations and represent visible evidence of error, while rejections would appear to involve fewer potential problems and consequently less exposure to personal criticism.[14]

Table 4–3 shows that the great majority of respondent banks required some supplemental review of commercial loan rejections.

13. The sensitivity is evidenced by the fact that in some communities where a major metropolitan bank has taken over the local bank by merger, a new independent bank has been organized by local interests.

14. Review of a large number of written analyses of loan cases made by practicing bankers in the course of their study at the University of Michigan School of Banking, a summer institute conducted by the Graduate School of Business Administration, leads to the inescapable conclusion that those with the least training and experience tend to make the most negative decisions. There was a strong implication that less personal jeopardy seemed to be associated with a negative decision, because the opinion was widespread that it was better to lose a customer than to make a "risk" loan on which there was a fair probability of future problems.

TABLE 4–3

POLICIES FOR REVIEWING LOAN REJECTIONS

| RESPONDENTS | POLICY |
|---|---|
| Bank A | Over $25,000, by division head |
| Bank B | By group head |
| Bank C | None |
| Bank D | By Senior Loan Review Committee |
| Bank E | By group head; large loans by Credit Policy Committee |
| Bank F | None |
| Bank G | By Division or Senior Credit Committee |

In general, the rejected loan had to be above a nominal amount before review was required, although junior loan officers were encouraged to discuss all proposed rejections with a senior officer. For larger rejections, some banks required review by either the group or division head. Alternatively, others indicated that committee review was the normative practice. Because customer rejections are a highly sensitive area and because experienced officers may be able to find a means of structuring credits to make them bankable, a formal review policy on proposed rejections of any magnitude would seem to be highly desirable.

# V

## PERSONNEL AND TRAINING

In the preceding chapter it was shown that the wholesale loan operation requires a significant number of officer level personnel who have the capacity to render recommendations and decisions on a wide variety of customer credit requests. While similarities between certain types of credits are to be found, each borrowing firm expects to have its credit arrangements structured to accommodate its particular needs and to have considerable flexibility to alter the nature and amount of borrowings as its financial requirements change through time. It is not unusual to have a firm approach its bank several times a year for some modification in the structure of its borrowing arrangements. Indeed it is these features of a wholesale loan operation that largely differentiate commercial banks from other financial intermediaries.

Moreover, the structuring and management of commercial loan portfolios cannot be conducted along the lines used in security portfolios, wherein diversification targets along industry and company lines can be established and achieved through impersonal decisions to buy and sell in the financial markets. A very few individuals can manage a security portfolio from a "portfolio universe" approach, in which each individual decision can be routine and subordinated to an analysis and evaluation of the portfolio as a whole on the basis of probability models and other quantitative analysis techniques. But in a commercial loan portfolio decisions are often based on customer needs rather than portfolio objectives; thus portfolio theory models are not realistically applicable to this sector of bank assets.

In addition the set of credit and other services offered corporate customers has become increasingly complex over the years as competitive pressures have intensified within the banking industry. The responsibilities of and challenges to loan officers have consequently increased over the years rather than diminished. One of the major problems most large banks have faced in attempting to provide these services is a recurring need to recruit and train a sufficient number of loan officers with the required capacities. In fact, the continuing development of high quality loan officers who possess the creative and analytical abilities to compete successfully for corporate clients is probably essential to achieving satisfactory long-term results for a large bank.

Two additional facts complicate the loan officers personnel problem. First, despite the extensive use of sophisticated computer data processing facilities, the preponderance of tasks performed in a bank are routine in character. The capacity to perform clerical tasks rapidly and accurately is sufficient for a large majority of the personnel, and therefore analytical abilities of a higher order are not sought in these employees. As a consequence, it is unlikely that many would be qualified for advancement to the loan officer ranks. In short the general personnel pool is not a viable source of candidates for the lending staff.

Second, the "pirating" of capable loan officers by corporate customers is a regular phenomenon. Because these officers work closely with top management of corporations in structuring financial requirements, they become natural candidates for financial management posts in these companies.[1] A customer relationship may of course be improved by a loan officer's becoming a member of the customer's management team. But the result is that the loan officer ranks need constant replenishment beyond that required to meet retirements and normal growth. While such opportunities should make the position of a loan officer trainee more attractive to an able young person, it means that a progressive bank must have an aggressive recruiting and training program to meet its recurrent needs for qualified loan officers.

One further observation, which can be inferred from the above discussion, should be mentioned. Because the loan officer staff is

1. Smaller correspondent banks that cannot afford formal recruiting and training programs may also look to large banks to staff their commercial loan department. For example, in Ann Arbor, the senior commercial loan officer of three of the four banks had originally been an officer in a large metropolitan bank.

usually the largest reservoir of managerial talents in a bank, a large proportion of top level executives tend to be drawn from the lending staff. While again this fact represents an opportunity for the individual, it poses a personnel training problem to the bank. The reason is that loan officers are essentially financial specialists and they are not required to engage in administrative management, wherein problems and decisions reach well beyond those encountered by a loan officer. Therefore, if the bank considers that a given individual has the abilities requisite for executive management, some arrangement to expand the scope of training beyond that required for loan officer duties becomes highly desirable.

## Recruiting Policies and Procedures

The major policy issues in recruiting potential loan officers may be identified as follows: (1) deciding where to concentrate efforts, (2) assigning responsibility for executing the program, and (3) determining salary and other benefits for the prospective trainees.

Policy decisions related to the first issue must take several alternatives into account. One possibility is to concentrate on recruiting experienced personnel from other banks. This policy has the apparent advantage of bringing in individuals with proved capacities and therefore entails less risk of unsatisfactory performance. Also, it may reduce the need for a rather unproductive training period. As noted above, it is the method typically followed by small and medium-sized banks. In their cases, since the need for loan officers is occasional, formal training programs are uneconomic and morale problems are minimal, because employees are hired for specific purposes in rather small numbers.

In a large bank, however, the practice of recruiting mainly from other banks has some very serious drawbacks. First, since there are no established channels for locating individuals with the desired capacities, there is a considerable risk of not finding enough candidates. Second, the policy cannot readily be combined with one that includes the recruitment of promising junior personnel. If the latter find that the bank is inclined to bring in senior staff regularly from the outside, they may quite logically regard such a policy as a serious impediment to advancement and decide that better opportunities can be found elsewhere.[2]

The result has been that most large banks have established formal recruiting and training programs to meet their needs for loan officers, Table 5–1 shows the policies of the respondent banks

TABLE 5–1
SOURCE AND BACKGROUND OF LOAN OFFICERS
(Respondent Banks)

| BANK | EDUCATION* | | | INTERNALLY TRAINED (Percentage) | EXCEPTIONS NOTED |
|---|---|---|---|---|---|
| | M.B.A. | B.B.A. | A.B. | | |
| A | Majority | Few | Some† | 90 | . . . |
| B | Some | Some | Few | 95 | . . . |
| C | Majority | Few | Few | 98 | Specialty officers |
| D | Majority | Few | Few | 99 | . . . |
| E | Majority | Few | Few | 95 | International division |
| F | Majority | Few | None | 95 | . . . |
| G | Majority | Some | Few | 95 | . . . |
| H | Few | Some | Some | 40 | . . . |

* Three banks mentioned that a few loan officers had degrees in law or from advanced schools of international finance and management in addition to degrees indicated.

† The bank encouraged trainees to do M.B.A. work in the evening program of a major university located nearby.

with respect to the recruitment of commercial loan trainees. It is notable that there is a clear preference for individuals with an M.B.A. degree. Most banks indicated that concentrating on graduate students resulted in obtaining recruits with greater maturity and usually with educational experiences that expedited the training process. However, some banks mentioned deficiencies in the orientation of M.B.A. programs. Primarily their criticisms related to a lack of rigorous courses in financial analysis and accounting. Several respondents tended to regard the trend in some graduate schools of business toward a highly theoretical approach to finance

2. The fact that it is established policy not to seek management level personnel from outside the bank is sometimes emphasized by banks in their recruiting programs. The record in this respect can of course be documented easily. Thus lateral or upward movement between large banks is rather unusual.

and accounting, based on abstract quantitative models, as a regressive development. Of course these alleged deficiencies were evaluated in terms only of the curriculum content considered optimal for potential loan officers. Nevertheless, one respondent indicated that it had become necessary to structure a formal course in financial analysis and acounting in order to bring some M.B.A. trainees up to the level of competence expected in these areas.[3]

Only one bank in this study indicated primary reliance on sources outside business schools; this bank was included to show the policies of banks of moderate size, and it had less need for new personnel than the others.

In the consumer credit and mortgage loan departments, the source of officer personnel was quite different. With only one exception, the respondent banks reported that half or more of the officers in these areas had either been obtained from the outside or had been transferred from other departments. Needs for officers are less recurrent here, even though the volume of loans may be considerable, because the credits are more routine in character. While officer supervision and control is necessary, individual credits can be handled for the most part by moderately skilled employees, and special programs for recruiting and training officer personnel in these departments are not considered practical.

One problem in maintaining consistent officer development programs is that they may be prime candidates for cutback during an austerity period, because their retrenchment does not have an immediate effect on the competitive position or earnings of the bank. In other words, such programs are long-range in nature and cutbacks only tend to have their impact on the bank with a five- or ten-year lag.[4] Because of the strong growth context of lending

3. In response to a query as to the important traits of a loan officer, the head of an executive placement firm made the following statement: "The desirable commercial loan officer must understand the financial nuts and bolts and must be able to verbalize the bank's capacity to provide services . . . . Academic and business credentials . . . plus the personality factor, would be needed in order to communicate effectively with corporate treasurers and understand their needs. Of course, a top commercial loan officer must also be a keen credit analyst." (Anthony Kane of Anthony Kane Associates as quoted in S. W. Elkins, "A Profile of the Loan Officer," *Journal of Commercial Bank Lending,* Sept. 1975, p. 53.)

4. T. Creedon, "Officer Development," *Journal of Commercial Bank Lending,* Sept. 1974, pp. 16–17.

activities during the 1960–73 period, this potential problem remained largely submerged for many years. But in 1974–75 some banks encountered flat or modest declines in earnings, and a policy to restrict or even eliminate recruiting of loan officer trainees was instituted. Perhaps the effects may be minimal if such a policy is limited to one or two years, but if it is maintained for long its ultimate consequences could be serious to the competitive position of the institution.

Though it may appear to be a minor issue, the question of where to lodge responsibility for recruiting loan officer trainees may be important to the success of the program. Two alternative policies are found. One is to give officers in the personnel department prime responsibility for visiting the schools and conducting the original interviews. The other is to delegate the original interview contacts to loan officers. The advantages cited for using professional personnel officers are: (1) they are trained specifically in interview techniques and therefore should be better equipped to evaluate prospective trainees; (2) they are more efficient interviewers because they can cover other needs of the bank at the same time; (3) loan officers can make separate appraisals when the prospective trainees visit the bank.

However, in selected graduate schools of business, most respondent banks have turned to using active loan officers operating under the direct supervision of senior management. The reasoning is that these officers are better able to discuss on a professional basis the challenges and responsibilities of loan officers and to answer technical questions of the students concerning the approach to lending decisions. Graduate students with professional education in finance and related areas appreciate a lucid discussion of these matters with a practicing officer in the field. There is an increasing tendency to assign, if possible, a young loan officer to interview at the school from which he graduated. The theory is that the graduating students can identify with such a person and will perceive at first hand an example of the success to be achieved by joining that particular bank.

While a strong on-site interviewing program is an important element in the recruiting process, it is also essential to have a well-organized and challenging evaluation program established for candidates invited to visit the bank. At this point, both the candidate and the bank are presumably seriously appraising each other, and representatives of senior management will normally become involved. One problem has been that visitation programs have been haphazardly arranged, and consequently often either senior management is not available or the candidate is required to stand idly by for long periods waiting for an interview. While immediate management problems must receive some priority, the candidates are likely to regard the bank as cold and disinterested if their visit is marked by delay and confusion. It has not been unusual for promising graduates to report being "turned off" by the reception they received at some banks.

One further salutary recent change in the recruiting policies of large banks deserves mention. A majority of the respondent banks reported having instituted an active effort to recruit members of minority groups, particularly black and female students as loan officer trainees. The following statement is illustrative of the existing policy of these banks:

> Especially heavy emphasis has been placed on bringing representatives of minority groups into our training program by recruiting at predominantly black universities and by transferring qualified black employees into the Credit Department from other areas of the bank. Presently approximately 10 percent of our trainees are black.

Because of this attitude, the opportunity for black and women students appears highly favorable in most large banks in the years ahead.

## Salary policies: Loan officer trainees

Although starting salaries are not of crucial importance in recruiting programs, a significant deviation from salaries available elsewhere can be a serious handicap. Whether rightly or not, many students view comparative salary offers as indices of relative opportunity and probable future treatment. Moreover, a number of graduates already have family responsibilities and feel that immediate sacrifices for possible future benefits are difficult to justify.

Table 5–2 shows the distribution of entry salary levels for M.B.A. graduates of the University of Michigan in 1976 for major types of employment. By and large it appears that salary policies of large commercial banks (which dominate formal recruiting in most universities) were reasonably competitive with alternative opportunities, although it is notable that the mean was slightly below the mean for all M.B.A. graduates. However, this difference

TABLE 5–2
SELECTED SALARY DATA: ENTRY POSITIONS
(M.B.A. Graduates, School of Business, University of Michigan, 1976)

| | Annual Amount | |
|---|---|---|
| Industry Areas | Mean | Range |
| Commercial banking | $17,200 | $14,000–20,700 |
| Management consulting | 20,000 | 16,100–28,500 |
| Investment banking | 20,000 | 17,000–25,000 |
| Public accounting | 16,900 | 16,000–18,200 |
| Financial service | 18,600 | 12,000–40,000 |
| All–M.B.A. average | 17,800 | . . . |

Source: Placement Office, Graduate School of Business, University of Michigan.

was probably due to the fact that banks were less willing than employers in certain other areas to offer out-of-line, high salaries for exceptional individuals. Specialized experience and educational backgrounds did not command a premium in banking to the extent indicated for management consulting, investment banking, and financial services.[5]

As a matter of interest, a survey of the graduates to determine the reasons for acceptance of entry positions resulted in the following conclusion:

> The compensation package is an important consideration in the employment decision. However, it is rarely the most important factor. The type of work, the opportunity for future development, and the general work environment continue to be the primary

5. A further breakdown of salary ranges showed that the high scale of the range was associated with two to four years of previous experience and also in a few cases with a technical educational background. *Salary Summary*, Placement Office, Graduate School of Business, University of Michigan, 1976.

reasons given by students for accepting or rejecting an offer of employment.[6]

## Training Policies

Major changes in training policies were instituted in most respondent banks during the decade of the sixties. First, formal programs to rotate trainees among various departments of the bank for a year or more were generally abandoned.[7] Second, there was increasing recognition that a lengthy assignment of trainees to clerical tasks in the credit department, such as statement "spreading" and responding to routine credit inquiries, is not necessary and may in fact cause frustration and an undue number of resignations. Third, some respondents indicated a deliberate policy to expose trainees early on to the more sophisticated areas of customer services, such as corporate financial services, management sciences, mergers and acquisitions, and international operations. Finally, the entire training period was significantly reduced, and participation in loan decisions was expected within a year or so.

Besides a concern with the turnover rate, two additional factors were then cited as inducing the policy changes. First, banks had been chronically short of loan officer personnel to handle adequately not only the growth in the number of customers but also the growing range of services offered such customers (such as computerized cash flow forecasts and international banking service). Second, in that era many loan officer candidates not only had graduate degrees but also had work experience in the armed services or in other firms; the average age of these individuals was between 25 and 30. It should be noted, however, that even then there was a wide difference of views concerning the scope and length of training programs. Some felt strongly that the period had been unduly telescoped and that too many junior officers were not equipped to make judicious credit decisions. Others held that the only significant change was to eliminate an undue amount

6. *Ibid.*

7. Short orientation exposure to other departments of the bank for periods of a few weeks to several months is still maintained in several cases. The stated purpose is to acquaint the trainee with the nature and costs of the services offered to customers.

of time spent on routine tasks. However, despite reservations of some, the training period was generally greatly reduced in most banks as competition for qualified graduates was intense and the growth in loan portfolios required a constant influx of new officers to service the accounts.

But conditions changed radically in the mid-seventies. Some major loan problems were ascribed to the lack of experience on the part of lending officers responsible for structuring the credits.[8] In addition, the overall demand for loan officer trainees slackened because of reduced loan growth at a time when the supply of M.B.A. students actually increased. Therefore, although it may turn out to be a temporary phenomenon if a strong recovery in loan demand occurs in future years, as of late 1976 a highly cautious attitude was notable in most respondent banks. In training policies, an extension of the training period and restricting decision authority for a longer period were considered the appropriate means of implementing the new attitude.

By and large, the heart of most training programs consists of two phases. In the first the trainee both obtains credit information and prepares credit analyses from data in the credit files to assist the officers in reaching loan decisions. During this phase, the junior analyst will probably work under the close supervision of experienced credit analysts. If the work is to be effective as a training device, a detailed review and evaluation of these analyses with the trainee would seem highly desirable. The problem is that such reviews are time consuming and may be perfunctory if the credit manager or loan officers are pressed for time.

The second phase is to assign the trainee, now a senior analyst, to one or more loan divisions as a loan officer assistant. In this capacity, the trainee may be given primary responsibility for several relatively small accounts. Under 1976 conditions, two to four years might be involved in the pre-officer training process.

On the whole, the restructuring of training programs to provide early challenges to prospective loan officers can be commended. This comment should not be construed as an argument for allowing inexperienced trainees to arrange credit terms and make final

8. While only one respondent was sufficiently candid to admit a mistake in this connection, allusions to the problem of inexperienced loan officers were frequent.

loan decisions after a short time in the job. But it does mean that the training process should emphasize challenging analytical work and supervised participation in loan decisions. Such experience represents the real substance of loan officer training programs and provides the challenges needed if the enthusiasm of the most capable trainees is to be maintained.[9] Greater time and effort on the part of loan officers is required under such a policy, and when work pressures are heavy this added duty may be a distinct disadvantage. But when, as some banks reported, about 20 percent of the loan officer trainees voluntaritly leave the bank, a high priority should logically be given to the training program.

### Promotion and Transfer Policies

The role and functions of the loan officer have expanded considerably as large banks have increased the scope of their customer services. For example, many banks now offer (for a fee) corporate financial services which include computer programs to forecast cash flows, asset needs, and prospective financing requirements. The result, as has been pointed out, is that loan officers now must have, in addition to capabilities required to make individual loan decisions, competence to act as a "professional financial consultant" and to render advice on the financial policies of customers. Strong educational backgrounds at the graduate professional level, therefore, have become increasingly important for loan officer candidates. But the higher capability requirements also suggest that the professional development of loan officers should be a continuing and selective process to a greater extent than has generally been true in the past.[10]

9. Periodic group seminars on credit analysis problems and techniques have been adopted by several banks in a further effort to challenge trainees and maintain their enthusiasm for the work. However, in some instances, trainees reported that the seminars repeated much of the content of their graduate courses at a rather elementary level. Seminar content and level of presentation should ideally be carefully worked out to avoid excessive repetition of basic finance and lending concepts usually obtained in the graduate academic program. Otherwise instead of enthusiasm the programs may induce boredom. For a detailed example of a formal credit training program both for trainees and for existing loan officers, see J. W. Wells, "Credit Training—A Systematic Approach," *Journal of Commercial Bank Lending*, Feb. 1976, pp. 18–29.

10. The Commercial Lending Division of the American Bankers Association has established a certification program for loan officers leading to the designation

TABLE 5–3

PROMOTION SEQUENCE: NORMATIVE TIME SPAN

| Designation | Time Range* |
|---|---|
| Junior Credit Analyst (Trainee) | 6 months to 1 year |
| Senior Credit Analyst (Assistant to Loan Officer) | 1 to 3 years |
| Assistant Cashier (Commercial Loan Officer) | 2 to 4 years |
| Assistant Vice President | 2 to 4 years |
| Vice President | indefinite |
| Group Head | indefinite |
| Division Head | indefinite |

* Assumption is M.B.A. degree on entry with strong program in finance and accounting.

Table 5–3 shows the consensus estimate of the normative time range for the promotional sequence of a commercial loan officer. Whether the time sequence is at the short or long end of the range depends on the needs of the bank, the capabilities and experience of particular individuals, and, as mentioned above, the loss experience on the loan portfolio. On average, about three years of pre-officer status can be expected and then perhaps six to eight additional years before the rank of vice president is achieved. Some individuals terminate upward advancement at the vice presidential level, where they have responsibility for a set of accounts but no administrative duties; the pyramid narrows considerably at that point, because there are far more account officers than openings at the group head level. However, the compensation and continuing challenges at that level are often superior to middle management positions in large nonfinancial corporations. Attainment of the rank of a group or division head will be the ultimate advancement level of most loan officers. These positions offer considerable challenge, diversity, and responsibility; they are well

of "Certified Commercial Lender." The candidates are required to sit for three examinations, although exemption from part three is granted for graduation from the Commercial Lending Graduate School. Among the objectives cited for the program is: "To encourage commercial loan officers in a continuing program of professional development." *Certified Commercial Lender,* brochure published by Commercial Lending Division, American Bankers Association, Washington, D.C. (no date).

paid and confer a high status in the bank. Attainment of this level can therefore be considered a highly satisfactory terminal career objective. A bank will have perhaps ten to thirty such officers, depending on its size.

But as indicated earlier, because the commercial loan staff typically has more individuals with high-level capabilities than most other departments, the half-dozen or so top executive officers are often drawn from this staff. However, a major problem may be encountered in this connection: even at a senior rank, a loan officer manages only a limited group of well-motivated individuals in a rather specialized activity, whereas top management has the responsibility for the planning, execution, and control of all the complex activities encountered in a modern major bank. A comprehensive study devoted to this problem concluded that even a highly competent professional banker may lack the training and qualities necessary for an executive management position.[11]

To meet the problem, the study first recommended that banks be competitive in attracting top graduates of leading business schools. Secondly, it was concluded that banks should establish policies that will select promising top management candidates at a fairly early stage in their careers and then provide a series of rotating assignments which involve general administrative responsibilities to expose these individuals to the type of management problems they would encounter in an executive capacity.[12] Some banks have adopted these policies, and it is probable that an increasing number will turn in this direction. One bank, for example, has adopted the policy of giving promising loan officers administrative experience by assigning them management responsibility for a regional group of branches. In this capacity, they encounter the managerial functions of strategic profit planning, cost control, and directing and motivating large numbers of people. Presumably the result is to make these individuals better prepared to take on the responsibilities of top management at a later date.

11. This study was prepared by a leading management consulting firm under the sponsorship of the Association of Reserve City Bankers. McKinsey and Co., *Developing Future Bank Management* (Chicago: Association of Reserve City Bankers, 1968), pp. 23–39.

12. *Ibid.*, pp. 33–37.

# VI

## TYPES AND CONDITIONS OF COMMERCIAL LOANS

### Characteristics of Commercial Loans

Most large banks are willing to assist a business firm in financing almost any conceivable asset required for operating the business. Alternatively the direct purpose of some loans may be to provide funds to meet maturing liabilities—trade accounts and income taxes, for example—wherein future asset liquidation or operating cash flows are expected to provide the means of repayment. The trend has been to structure credits to fit the unique financial requirements of the borrowers and not to force credits into preconceived patterns that may not fit a particular case. In fact, the major challenge to a commercial loan officer may well be structuring acceptable credits to firms that appear to have a viable economic outlook long-term but have immediate financial problems. Often the loan request of these customers may be greatly modified or indeed entirely changed in character in order to meet the financing needs while reasonably protecting the position of the bank. Therefore, it is difficult to distinguish sharply between the various types of commercial loans available at commercial banks. But most can probably be classified under one of the following headings: (1) open lines of credit, (2) transaction loans, (3) working capital loans, (4) revolving credits, (5) term loans and leases.

The first two classifications represent the traditional types of commercial loans, short-term accommodation to finance temporary needs for working capital or other requirements of a short-term nature. Fluctuations in working capital requirements quite often derive from a seasonal sales pattern, but they may also be caused by other events, such as production under project contracts. The latter include construction loans and financing of work under government contracts.

From the standpoint of the borrower, the open line of credit is perhaps the most attractive method of financing short-term requirements. In form it is merely a letter stating that the bank stands ready to grant loans up to a maximum amount during the coming year. Borrowings under the line are entirely at the discretion of the company concerned, and interest charges are applied against only the amount outstanding at any given time.[1] There is no enforceable commitment, however, and the bank has the legal right to refuse loan requests against the line. But it should be emphasized that this recourse would be considered only if something very serious happened to the status of the borrower or the bank. Honoring line commitments is a firmly established tradition in banking, and despite rumors that a few banks had reneged on line commitments during extremely tight money conditions no actual cases could be confirmed. The loss of status in the financial community would be considerable if lines were not met. Of course it is entirely legitimate to terminate a line at the expiration date when it is reviewed for renewal. But if the relationship has been handled satisfactorily, clear evidence of credit deterioration is ordinarily required to justify cancellation of a line.

A company can probably be considered to have made the financial "social register" when it receives bank accommodation on an open line of credit. In fact, in order to hold desirable customers against solicitation by competitors, it is good policy to review regularly the financial status of customers borrowing under less favorable arrangements. If their status has improved sufficiently in the judgment of the loan officer, then the customers should be offered an unsecured line credit at the volition of the bank. As

1. On the grounds that the commitment per se under a line of credit represents a valuable service, some banks have imposed a "facility" fee of 1/4 percent or so annually against the unused portion. This is a recent development and is relatively rare. Tight money conditions tend to result in more rigorous pricing policies as will be discussed in Chapter 8. Moreover, some argue that a "facility" fee represents consideration under a contract and turns the commitment into a legally enforceable obligation of the bank.

lines are extended to quality companies for short-term needs, it is normally expected that the borrowers will be out of debt to the bank during some part of each year. This expectation, however, may be open to negotiation should it become inexpedient to pay out during certain years.

Transaction loans are specific advances for short-term periods, although renewals are often granted if the circumstances indicate a continuing legitimate need for the funds. The name apparently derives from the fact that each loan is a separate transaction with the terms subject to negotiation each time the borrower requests credit accommodation. Transaction loans are appropriate when the need is for a specific amount and will recur relatively infrequently, or when for one reason or another the bank considers frequent review of the situation to be desirable. These loans, of course, may be secured by specific collateral, whereas almost all open lines are extended on an unsecured basis.

Working capital loans are similar to transaction loans in that the purpose is to acquire current assets or repay other debt incurred in acquiring such assets. They differ in the source of the need and the means of repayment. Whereas transaction loans are presumably made to finance temporary current asset needs and are usually repaid from the ordinary liquidation of the assets as the requirement runs off, working capital loans are made to finance permanent current asset needs and thus are usually repaid from cash flows over a longer period. Small and moderate-sized companies experiencing a rapid growth in sales with consequent expansion in current asset requirements are typical sources of these credits. Since seasonal financing may be required as well, these loans often fluctuate in amount; but their principal characteristic is a lack of complete pay-out for an indeterminate period, usually several years.[2] However, these loans are typically made against demand or short-term notes. In theory this arrangement gives the bank considerable leverage over the affairs of the borrower, but in practice borrowers often perceive that the feasible options of the bank may be limited. Therefore, because the term and even the ultimate amounts are often ambiguous, considerable

2. See M. J. Drake, "The Working Capital Loan," in *Business Loans of American Commercial Banks,* ed. by B. H. Beckhart (New York: Ronald Press, 1959), p. 146.

controversy exists as to the appropriate policy in this area. If allowed either by policy or by exception, these credits usually test the analytical and negotiating skills of loan officers.

Revolving credits may have the same financial purpose as working capital loans; in addition, they are often used for "bridge" financing of fixed-asset programs to be funded with long-term money at completion. The bank makes a legal commitment authorizing discretionary borrowing up to specified amounts for a period of two to three years. These authorizations are made under a written loan agreement in which the terms and conditions of the credits are formally set forth. Among the usual terms on revolving credits is an annual percentage "facility" fee on the unused portion of the commitment.

Term loans are also authorizations to borrow specific amounts for periods of several years, but their purpose more often than not is to finance acquisitions of fixed assets. The borrower may either "take down" the loan as needed over a period of months or alternatively obtain the entire sum at one time. The loan is then repaid on a regular amortization basis as specified in the loan agreement. Since both revolving credits and term loans are made under formal loan agreements for extended periods, special policy problems on these credits will be considered in a separate chapter. The present discussion considers only the basic policy issues related to obtaining any type of commercial loan, although it may be mentioned at this point that term loans are usually for intermediate credit needs of about five to seven years' duration. In general, banks have resisted providing long-term finance, although some exceptions have emerged, primarily in the leasing operation.

## Policy Issues

The relationship between banks and their commercial borrowers has the following characteristics: (1) there are usually close and confidential relations between the two parties; (2) credit arrangements are open to a continuing series of negotiations as the status and needs of customers change; (3) all or part of the borrower's regular cash balances are held on deposit with the bank; (4) the relationship is often multi-dimensional in that other bank services might be involved, such as pension fund management in the trust department; (5) the relationship may extend beyond the business and include personal services to executives of customer firms.

In addition, so far as the large metropolitan banks are concerned, the provision of correspondent bank services introduces a further area that credit policies must cover. In return for correspondent balances, large banks offer a number of services which may include loan participation in both directions. Because customer relationships become indirect under these arrangements, there are some special issues that deserve comment.

The significant policy issues which arise out of the several characteristics indicated above include: (1) the kinds of information required to support loans; (2) the purposes for which loans will be granted; (3) the appropriate response to continuous and perhaps escalating credit commitments; (4) pricing of loans based on the variables of customer relationship, risk, cost of money, and the type of credit arrangement; and (5) the appropriate terms on correspondent accommodation loans. In addition, as banks have the option to require specific collateral to secure loans, which may take a wide variety of forms, policies on collateral requirements are important.

**Information requirements**

Without exception banks should maintain credit files on all business borrowers. In addition many construct files on all business depositors, whether or not they are borrowers. The files accomplish several purposes: (1) they provide an accurate historical record of the essential features of the customer's relation with the bank; (2) they are the source of data for evaluating credit needs and risks and thereby reaching credit decisions; and (3) if properly used, they provide a summary record of all verbal communications which may be pertinent to the relationship.

The first purpose is achieved entirely by the clerical accumulation of information available from internal sources, and no significant policy issues are involved. The relevant information includes the statistical record of deposits, the amounts and types of previous loans or commitments, and the repayment record compared with the terms of the credit arrangements.

The files' second purpose, providing a data base for credit

decisions, is perhaps the most important; here policy decisions are required to define the nature and amount of information considered essential to substantiate credit judgments. First, there is the question of financial statements. For all lines of credit and transactions loans, the usual policy is to require comparative balance sheets and related income statements covering about three years. As an exception, if the borrower adequately secures the loan with marketable collateral, some respondents would waive the requirement of financial statements. On term loans, most banks indicated that they desired additional operating data, such as income statements for at least five years, plus cash flow analyses and forecasts. However, if the company is of moderate size and lacks a sophisticated accounting and financial staff, the bank may undertake the task of estimating cash flows, if that information appears necessary for reaching a decision.

Although all the respondent banks required financial statements of all commercial borrowers, their policies with respect to audit verification were more variable. Table 6–1 shows their normative policies on audit requirements by size and type of credit. At the one extreme, two banks stated their policy was to require audited statements for all loans beyond very modest amounts. Waivers of the policy required specific senior officer or group approval. At the other extreme, one bank required audited statements only when the amount exceeded $1 million on short-term commitments. In general, however, it would seem that until commitments exceeded about $500,000, audit requirements are negotiable. Somewhat surprisingly, requirements were only moderately more rigorous on extended maturity loans.

Because cost of full financial audits are not trivial, it would seem reasonable to allow waivers for commitments up to about $500,000. (If adequate collateral is available, then of course the waivers might be extended to larger commitments.) Loan officers should be personally acquainted with each borrower, and should have a good impression of the reliability of the management and its accounting procedures. It is true, however, that a problem might arise when credit demands escalate because of the firm's growth. If financial audits have been customarily waived, then it becomes difficult to remove the waiver when the level of the

TABLE 6–1

FINANCIAL AUDIT REQUIREMENTS
(Frequency by Size and Type of Loan)

| Frequency by Type | Amount of Commitment: Under $250,000 | $250,000–$500,000 | $500,000–$1,000,000 | Over $1,000,000 |
|---|---|---|---|---|
| *Term Loans and Revolving Credits:* | | | | |
| Always | 2 | 4 | 5 | 8 |
| Frequently | 3 | 3 | 3 | ... |
| Sometimes | 2 | 1 | ... | ... |
| Rarely | 1 | ... | ... | ... |
| *Lines and Transaction Loans:* | | | | |
| Always | 2 | 3 | 4 | 8 |
| Frequently | 2 | 3 | 3 | ... |
| Sometimes | 3 | 1 | 1 | ... |
| Rarely | 1 | 1 | ... | ... |

Note: The financial audit *requirement* was interpreted by some respondents as an indication of a strong policy *preference* but subject to negotiation on credits under $500,0000.

commitment increases without the customer's interpreting the new requirement as a lack of trust in his integrity. The only means of solving the problem is to convince the customer that, given the expansion of the firm to a scale beyond that which can be easily monitored, a financial audit would be in his own best interests. Alternatively, if the commitment has been on a secured basis, the possibility of shifting to an unsecured open line basis might be advanced with the condition that the financial statements be audited.

The techniques for obtaining qualitative information do not involve significant policy questions. Usually the primary source is personal visits to borrowing firms. Some discussions of mutual problems may take place at the bank; but it is standard policy to require that bank personnel make at least one visit per year to all borrowers' offices or plants, and more frequent visits are encouraged. Although loan officers are not technical management experts, general impressions as to operating methods, the condition and quality of the assets, the character of management, and other relevant factors can be obtained only through such visits. In this connection, it is typical policy to require that every visit or phone conversation with a customer pertinent to the business relationship be followed with a memorandum to be placed in the credit file outlining the nature of the conversation and the conclusions reached, if any. This practice is highly desirable to make sure all relevant information is contained in the credit file. Documentation of oral information can avoid serious problems; to rely on memory to supply details of a conversation several months earlier would not be acceptable. Circumspection in comments may be recommended because, while credit files are nominally confidential, they are subject to subpoena in court cases.

In addition to direct contacts with the borrower, outside sources of general information are regularly used. Reports from such agencies as Dun and Bradstreet are often obtained; these reports offer considerable background information, although some respondents raised questions about undue reliance on the agencies' conclusions. Finally, the bank may contact suppliers and customers of borrowing companies. There is no prevailing policy on this score. Some banks indicated that such checking was fairly frequent, particularly on new accounts or on smaller companies; other stated that such inquiries were rarely made, because agency reports on these matters sufficed. Moreover, even banks which used these sources agreed that the inquiries had to be circumspect to avoid possible adverse repercussions on the subject company. However, the information might be a highly valuable indication of the quality and competitive position of the product line. If product sales are concentrated to a few customers, then some impression of customer satisfaction with the products becomes very important.

## Purpose of credits

Although some banks may waive their usual requirement of financial statements when adequate collateral is provided, all respondents flatly stated that the purpose of the loan must be indicated in all cases. The inference is that, even if risks in any ultimate sense are minimal, some loans may be rejected because there may be policy constraints against the proposed uses of the proceeds. A few such constraints are imposed by law. Therefore assurance must be obtained that the purpose of a loan does not violate any legal restrictions, such as margin requirements. But even beyond this obvious requirement, prevailing opinion is that the purpose must also meet standards of appropriateness.

During tight money periods, the "purpose" constraint has often become more rigorous, because some uses of funds may be construed as unproductive at such times. For example, loans to finance corporate takeovers have sometimes been placed in the *verboten* category during such periods, on the ground that their priority should be below that of financing assets required to further economic output. But purpose-screening in response to changing monetary conditions is properly a part of the dynamics of loan administration, and for that reason it will be considered in Chapter 12. Here we shall consider only the basic tests which are applied to determine the eligibility of a request for bank credit—basic, in the sense that if they are not met the credit arrangement will be rejected even under easy money conditions.

One frequently mentioned test was that banks should not finance "speculative" business loans. The problem, however, is that differences of opinion are possible as to what is speculative. According to one view, a credit is speculative unless it is reasonably required to finance the efficient conduct of a business operation.[3] But again problems of interpretation arise. For example, a firm may have the opportunity to purchase raw material inventories at a bargain price but only if an excessive amount is acquired. Alternatively, inventory purchases beyond normal needs in anticipation of a possible labor strike at a supplier may be cited as the purpose of a loan request. Possibly a program to expand fixed assets may be instituted that will provide capacity well in excess of probable product demand at the time of completion; expectations of continued increases in the costs of such assets are advanced to justify the program. Some banks might argue that

3. Loans to individuals to carry securities are often made but are considered outside the commercial loan area; loans to brokerage houses to carry security positions (inventories) are commercial in nature but are not considered speculative because they are necessary and inherent to the business.

the financing in these instances is speculative in character; others might conclude that the credits are justified on the grounds that their probable contribution to the success of the business outweighs the risk involved. Therefore, while this test may screen out some clearly inappropriate credits, it cannot be applied without considerable judgment and discretion.

A second proposed test is that the proceeds should be used in a manner which gives rise to the probable means of repayment. Loans to acquire assets which are to be liquidated in the ordinary course of business or which will probably contribute to the earnings potential are considered appropriate; otherwise, it is argued, the purpose should be questioned.[4] But if the means of repayment seems reasonably assured from other sources, and if the customer relationship is otherwise satisfactory, most banks will grant the credit. For example, a corporation may want a loan to acquire a highly marginal operation, although the earnings potential of the acquisition is very dubious and it is doubtful if the assets acquired will give rise to the means of repayment. But if earnings from other sources appear clearly adequate to service the loan, it would seem reasonable to grant the request.[5] These can be regarded as special cases, however, and the policy can be adjusted to indicate that alternative sources must provide for an orderly repayment program.

In a third test of purpose some policy statements indicate merely that the purpose should be "constructive" and that loan requests should be appraised in that light. When interpretation is requested, the typical answer is that the application of a loan should provide benefits to the customer either through improving his productive capacity and profit prospects or solving some other problem that may impede the progress of the firm. In either case, it is assumed that a repayment program can be reasonably de-

4. The loan may be made to replace liabilities—trade credit, for example—previously assumed in order to acquire such assets; in this case the loan still meets this test because it is considered to be indirectly related to the asset acquisitions.

5. If the operation is entirely unrelated to the principal business of the borrower, then a case can be made that the purpose is not acceptable on the ground that it is an "investment," not a "productive" purpose. Moreover, if it is beyond the management expertise of the borrower, operating losses can result in a severe drain on cash flows from the established operations of the firm.

signed. While a statement along these lines does not provide a clear benchmark for screening credit requests, it would seem to be useful in a general sense. The company must show what constructive results are probable from a given credit arrangement, presumably in relation to the risks involved, and both the bank and the customer may benefit from that inquiry.

### Repayment program

On open lines of credit an annual pay-out of thirty to sixty days is considered a normal expectation because the normative purpose of such lines is to finance temporary or seasonal working capital requirements of quality companies. In some cases, particularly on finance company lines, pay-outs are obtained by rotating lines from one bank to another, and there is no significant reduction in total short-time borrowings.[6] Although rotation is an artificial means of meeting pay-out requirements, it is condoned on the grounds that the line continuation can be reviewed each year during the pay-out period.

However, although they are not frequent, there are situations in which companies find it inexpedient to meet the pay-out requirement. Utilities, for example, often use line borrowings to finance construction in progress, and when the projects are completed the borrowings are retired through long-term financing.[7] But sometimes capital market conditions may suggest a delay in a bond or stock issue necessitating continuance of line usage. In other companies, rapid growth in sales may increase capital requirements to a point where line usage becomes continuous.

A policy issue arises, therefore, as to the appropriate set of alternative actions when lines have no pay-out periods for a year or more. Some banks take the position that if the reason for the

6. Finance companies with access to the commercial paper market also may increase open-market borrowings to reduce borrowings under lines. However, it is still true that, through the rotation of the use of multiple lines and commercial paper, long-term capital needs are financed with short-term borrowings.

7. The general policy is that lines are granted for this purpose only to companies whose ability to obtain long-term financing in the capital markets is unquestionable. Otherwise, the "bridge" financing may be provided under a revolving credit commitment wherein there is a formal loan agreement with detailed protective covenants.

lack of payment can be justified (growth) and if the credit position of the company remains sound, lines will be renewed for several years despite the absence of pay-outs. This alternative has the virtues of simplicity and good public relations. Its drawback is that some companies may come to regard line borrowings in effect as long-term credits—which is not their purpose. Therefore, the following policy position given by one respondent bank would seem to be a more appropriate alternative:

> Normally [in the absence of pay-outs] lines will not be renewed, but one of the following actions is taken in its place: transfer to a secured basis or fund with a term loan.

This position may be subject to some ad hoc exceptions for two reasons: (1) the situation seems remediable within a year or so, and (2) the relationship has been and probably will be highly profitable to the bank on a long-term basis. The basis for the first exception should be ovbious; there is no point in a major restructuring of the basic credit relationship which may be reversed in a year or so. The basis for the second is essentially competitive: a request to restructure may induce the customer to "shop" its banking affiliation, which, under the assumption given, presumably the bank would like to avoid. But if the character of the financing needs has clearly changed, then even the customer might be persuaded that restructuring the relationship to reflect the new circumstances would be in the best interest of both parties.

The recommended policy on short-term unsecured transaction loans might well be similar to that on lines. The source of repayment should be indicated at the time the loan is granted. Renewals for a reasonable time may be considered; but at some point, if renewals are chronic for the original or increasing amounts, transfer to another arrangement should be made. Usually a secured working capital loan is the alternative, although a revolving credit or term loan is also a possibility.

Perhaps the most difficult problem of repayment policy arises when continued growth or, alternatively, a lesser rate of earnings than expected, not only prevents the company from meeting expected loans payments, but forces it instead to escalate its credit requests. A condition of this sort most often occurs in relatively new and in moderate-sized companies where unexpected events drastically change the proposed financing program. If earning progress is satisfactory, some banks indicated that their policy was to more or less overlook a growing and possibly excessive amount of bank debt. Others flatly stated that they ask such companies to find alternative sources, such as a finance company, that can afford to follow such credits closely because they charge considerably higher rates. Possibly some banks became too lax with respect to such situations during the easy years, and indeed, given the adverse loan-loss experience of many large banks in 1974–76, policies may be more restrictive toward constant and escalating bank debt in the future.[8] On the other hand, an excessively rigid posture may result in the loss of customers who offer the bank a potentially profitable relationship. An ad hoc policy on these credits would therefore seem appropriate, with regular reviews of progress, rates, collateral sufficiency, and other terms of the arrangement.

## Correspondent Banks: Special Policy Issues

Because statutory limitations of most states restrict branch extensions to areas close to the home office, there are a large number of small–to–moderate-sized unit banks throughout the country.[9] It is economic for these banks to have the large metropolitan banks perform a wide variety of services in return for deposit balances or fee charges. These services include providing facilities for check collections, purchasing or selling Federal Funds on a daily basis, providing foreign currencies, and—perhaps most important—assisting in credits extended to customers of the smaller banks. When some or all of these services are supplied, a correspondent banking relationship is established.

8. The large loan losses of several large banks in the 1975 W. T. Grant bankruptcy (wherein lines were increased to meet operating losses) is perhaps a good example of the policy problem. This company had been a good customer of these banks for a number of years, and as a consequence there was a natural reluctance to force it into bankruptcy even in the face of serious earnings problems beginning at the end of 1973.

9. The federal statute governing national banks specifically permits the state statutes to govern branching privileges. These vary from allowing statewide branching in California to allowing none at all in Illinois. Most states permit branching within a radius of twenty to thirty miles from the home office.

As shown in Table 6–2, the principal reason for correspondent service in the loan area is to enable small banks to meet short-term credit requests in excess of their legal limits. In addition, assistance is sometimes rendered on term loans, either because the loans exceed legal limits or because technical assistance on structuring the credits is considered desirable. Also on a few occasions block purchases of consumer and mortgage loans have been made in order to relieve excessive portfolio positions, but in recent years, which have been dominated by tight money conditions, such purchases have become exceptional.

TABLE 6–2
FREQUENCY OF CORRESPONDENT ACCOMMODATION LOANS

| TYPE OF ACCOMMODATION | FREQUENCY | | | |
|---|---|---|---|---|
| | REGULARLY | SOMETIMES | RARELY | NEVER |
| Line of credit (overlines)* | 6 | 2 | . . . | . . . |
| Transaction loans* | 7 | 1 | . . . | . . . |
| Term loans | . . . | 5 | 3 | . . . |
| Consumer loans (block purchases) | . . . | . . . | 8 | . . . |
| Block purchases of mortgages | . . . | . . . | 3 | 5 |

* Generally described as that portion which exceeds the legal limit of the correspondent bank.

In the commercial loan area, the reasons for correspondent accommodations imply the possibility of a delicate policy problem, and a few of the more candid loan officers specifically mentioned its existence. A smaller bank's recurring need to call on a large bank in order to provide adequate credit service to some customers is, in effect, good evidence that these customers have outgrown their present banking affiliation. Under such circumstances, it would seem logical for these companies to transfer their principal banking connections to large city banks. Yet the small banks are naturally reluctant to lose a substantial portion of the deposits of these customers, and thus they take a dim view of larger banks' actively soliciting direct connections. While the general policy is to avoid direct solicitation of correspondent banks' customers, it often becomes evident that ultimately such companies will seek other banking connections of their own volition and that compromise arrangements may be in the best interest of all concerned.

There are other policy issues with respect to the appropriate terms of accommodation loans. First, the majority of respondents held that overline commitments (seasonal lines of credit in excess of the correspondents' legal limits) should be extended on a last-in, first-out basis (LIFO). This approach, as its name suggests, calls for the large bank to enter the picture only after the correspondent has extended its legal limit to borrowers, then to obtain the first repayment from the subsequent liquidation. Because the purpose of such loans is to enable small banks to handle temporary customer needs beyond their own capacity, the LIFO policy would seem entirely logical. It tends to reduce the credit risk to the large bank and to concentrate it in the smaller bank which has the direct deposit relationship. However, banks in one state indicated that the regulatory authorities prohibit the LIFO arrangement. There is also some question about the legal enforcement of a LIFO arrangement if default occurs when both banks are in the credit. Moreover, on term loans, where the purpose of the accommodation may also include help in structuring and administering the details of loan agreements, a LIFO arrangement is usually not practicable.

Views varied to some extent on a second issue—the level of correspondent deposit balances appropriate to justify a given amount of accommodation commitments. Most banks stated that balances were definitely a factor in determining the amount of such loans; one bank in fact indicated a rather firm policy of limiting total overline credits to five times the average balances in the previous twelve months.

There is a good reason for having a policy on supporting balances for accommodation loans which differs from that on direct customer credits. Clearly, in evaluating an appropriate deposit balance, the size of the correspondent bank must be one factor, in addition to the total amount of loans on which assistance may be requested. For example, it would not seem reasonable to request a relatively small bank to maintain balances out of proportion to its size because there happens to be a need for an occasional heavy overline commitment to a large company in its area. On the other hand, chronic requests for significant amounts of accommodation overlines or term loan participations may put a strain on the resources of the large bank, and, unless adequate balances are maintained to support these requests, a negative attitude may be justified.

Finally, some small correspondents sometimes request accommodation in the reverse direction and desire to purchase loans for income purposes. As a result, some large banks have established "loan pools," consisting primarily of short-term prime credits, and participation in the "pool" is sold to correspondents. The technique in a sense resembles an open-end investment company. The credits are based on demand loan rates (brokers' loans) and are redeemable at any time. In essence, the operation makes a convenient source of secondary reserves available to small banks at favorable rates. By and large, there is a reluctance to sell any "risk" loans to correspondents, because if problems develop subsequently, the latter tend to assume there is an implicit guaranty of the credits by the selling bank.[10]

10. Sale of participations in long-term loans is inhibited by the fact that the courts have held such sales as subject to Rule 10b–5 of the Securities and Exchange Commission, which requires full disclosure of all material facts, usually through a detailed prospectus. For a discussion of a case on this point, see *Journal of Commercial Bank Lending* 51 (Aug. 1969): 58–59.

# VII

## TERM LOAN AND LEASING POLICIES

Term loans are defined as those with an original maturity of more than a year, which in the ordinary course of business must be repaid out of cash flow from operations rather than from the normal liquidation of a current asset.[1] A second singular feature of term loans is their structure, which is a commitment under a formal loan agreement quite similar to an indenture on a public offering of bonds. Therefore, the classification is restricted to credits extending for more than a year and based on formal loan agreements.

On some proposed credits there may be justifiable uncertainty as to the exact amount of the financing and as to the timing and means of payment. For example, if a customer undertakes a plant expansion project wherein at completion there also will be a need to finance working capital requirements, both the amount and the timing of his financing needs may be uncertain. To cover this situation, a "bridge" financing arrangement becomes appropriate. The bank sets up a firm loan commitment for a period of perhaps two to five years and the company can borrow against the commitment at its convenience. When the project is completed, a term loan or perhaps open market financing is expected to fund the total amount of the advances under the commitment.[2]

1. J. William Middleton, "Term Lending—Practical and Profitable," *Journal of Commercial Bank Lending* 50 (Aug. 1968): 31. In exceptional cases, special sources of repayment such as market refunding or prospective sale of excess fixed assets may also be included.

2. The following arrangement illustrates this type of financing: "A revolving credit arrangement permits a subsidiary to borrow a maximum of $200 million (revolving credit portion) and an additional $400 million (standby portion) with interest of 115 percent of prime rate. The agreement provides for a commitment fee of ½ percent per annum on any unused borrowings under the revolving credit portion, and a ½ percent fee on the initial borrowings under the standby portion. Any loans outstanding on the earlier of March 31, 1978, or 30 days after completion of the trans-Alaska pipeline, may be converted to a term loan payable over approximately five years with interest of 119 percent of prime rate." (Standard Oil Company, an Ohio Corporation, *Annual Report for 1975,* p. 24.)

The formal type of loan commitment developed to recognize uncertainties of this nature is known as a "revolving credit." In essence, the revolving credit enables the customer to use a fluctuating amount of bank financing over an intermediate period of, say, two to three years and then to make such arrangements as appear feasible when the uncertainties are resolved. From a functional point of view, this type of credit arrangement is more or less a combination of a line of credit and a term loan.

As a substitute for term loans, most large banks now offer lease financing for certain types of capital equipment. In some instances, leasing operations are conducted through a separate subsidiary of a holding company, although national banks may engage in direct leasing and some state jurisdictions also permit direct leasing.[3] When a subsidiary conducts the operation, the assets and liabilities resulting from the leasing program show up only on the consolidated statement of the holding company and not on the statement of the bank per se. Nevertheless, the activities of the leasing subsidiary are in fact usually either conducted as part of the commercial lending operation or closely associated with it. On the assumption that this type of financing is, therefore, essentially within the framework of commercial loan policies and given its growth, leasing policies will be covered in a separate section of this chapter.

## Financial functions: Purposes

The role of term loans, leases, and revolving credits can be related to three types of borrowers. First, they provide medium-term financing to moderate-sized companies that ordinarily do not have access to the public markets. Second, because of the personal relationships and supporting balances, large corporations may find leases or term loans more liberal as to debt-equity pro-

3. By statute the Board of Governors of the Federal Reserve has been empowered to determine the allowable activities of subsidiaries of bank holding companies. Under Regulation Y, section 225.4, covering nonbanking activities, holding companies are specifically permitted to own companies engaged in leasing transactions. However, Regulation Y includes a number of detailed constraints on the transactions, and their effect on leasing policies will be considered in the separate section below devoted to this area.

portions than financing obtainable on the open market.[4] Third, revolving credits, as noted, are attractive to corporations desiring project financing of which a part or all may be refinanced with term loans or public financing. For the most part, policies on these credits have been extended to cover almost any legitimate asset acquisition. The most common purposes are the financing of plant construction and all types of equipment, or to increase permanent working capital.[5] There are, however, some types of requests that raise policy questions as to their legitimacy. Table 7–1 shows the attitudes of the respondent banks toward certain special purposes that arise from time to time.

Acquisition loans, for example, represent a controversial area. In some cases, an acquisition may merely be an alternative way

TABLE 7–1
SPECIAL PURPOSES OF TERM LOANS
(Respondents' Policies)

| Frequency | Purpose of Credit | | | |
|---|---|---|---|---|
| | Acquisitions* | | | |
| | Control Interest | Minority Interest | Nonbusiness Asset† | Retire Portion of Equity* |
| Regularly | 4 | 2 | 1 | 2 |
| Some times | 3 | ... | 1 | 4 |
| Rarely | 1 | 6 | 6 | 2 |
| Never | ... | ... | ... | ... |

* During periods of credit restraint, some respondents indicated loans for these purposes were singled out for drastic limitations.

† Described, for example, as the purchase of real estate not needed in the business.

4. As a specific example, Georgia-Pacific Corporation at the end 1973 had $631.4 million of long-term debt financing against an equity of $774.3 million. The heavy debt resulted in a credit rating of Baa (medium quality) by Moody's and probably was responsible for the fact that $182.1 million of the debt was in bank term financing and $152.5 million had been obtained from insurance companies. The company reported that 15 percent supporting balances were maintained against all bank loans and rates were 110–115 percent of prime. (Georgia-Pacific Corp., *Annual Report*, 1973, p. 24.)

5. Funding of current debt or refinancing of long-term debt held by either the public or other financial institutions is considered an appropriate purpose; in these instances the immediate purposes may be to improve the working capital position, to obtain an improvement in terms, to anticipate maturities, or some combination of these.

to acquire productive assets for normal expansion purposes, and its financing would not pose policy problems. In other cases, however, the acquisition may be in essence only an aggressive investment proposition wherein the operations acquired bear no reasonable relation to those of the acquiring firm. For example, one bank cited a case in which a beer distributor, an excellent customer, requested a term loan to finance the acquisition of a radio broadcasting company. For competitive reasons, it is difficult to reject such requests if the prospective cash flows and balances of the parent company support the credit. However, if the acquisitions encounter difficulty, tensions may arise. The customer may request additional funds to finance operating losses, and he may also evidence some reluctance to divert cash flows from profitable operations to service the principal and interest requirements on an unprofitable investment loan. A general policy to avoid such loans would therefore seem appropriate, with exceptions in unusual cases.

Most respondent banks as shown in Table 7–1 had a policy of discouraging term loans to finance nonbusiness assets, but again exceptions for good customers were noted for competitive reasons. The issue here is comparable to that in the investment type of acquisitions, although some proposals for acquiring nonbusiness assets have the added feature of providing "luxury consumption" for the principals of the borrowing firm. Prospective purchases of yachts, airplanes, and recreation land fall into this category, and unfortunately the tax laws have tended to encourage such requests. Again, however, if the prospective cash flows from other sources seem adequate, it is difficult to turn down these requests despite their lack of a constructive purpose.

Finally, the use of term loans to retire equity capital raises an interesting policy question. Because the effect is to reduce the capital base subordinate to creditors while at the same time increasing outstanding debt, one view holds that this purpose is inherently an unsound financial practice. The other view, held by a majority of the respondent banks, is that extending loans to buy one or more ownership interests may be appropriate, especially if these interests are lodged in an estate or with inactive individuals. On the whole the latter view seems the more reasonable, although there should be other factors in the credit which make it particularly favorable.

**Role in loan portfolio: Trend and outlook**

Term loans, leases, and revolving credits have come to occupy a very important role in the loan portfolios of large banks. Respondents reported that such credits within the rough classification of commercial loans typically amounted to 35 to 45 percent of outstanding dollar amounts, although during periods of credit restraint the proportion has declined somewhat. The reason is that term credits absorb resources for longer periods and therefore tend to be screened more closely under credit-rationing conditions than are short-term commitments. The extended maturities also mean that these loans are subjected to a more extensive analytical process than are short-term commercial loans, and the terms are more complex. On the average, therefore, each term loan credit requires a more sophisticated and extended investigation. In many instances credit packages extended to customers include a mix of both seasonal and term funds. In fact it is not unusual for revolvers or term credits to emerge from a funding of a portion of a seasonal accommodation that for one reason or another becomes inexpedient for the company to pay out annually.

The reasons for the important role of term credits in bank loan portfolios can be inferred from their financial functions noted above, but a few additional points are worth noting. First, up until 1975 there had been a general assumption that national economic policy would be oriented to the prevention of serious and prolonged recessions, even at the expense of tolerating some inflation. At the same time, corporate financial planning had become more sophisticated through the use of elaborate forecasting models designed for computer application. As these models often assumed the probability of an upward trend in cash flows without serious variations around the trend (because of national economic policy assumptions), the historic constraints on the use of debt leverage were relaxed. But, while increased use of debt in capital structures seemed appropriate, bond rating services tended to maintain a conservative posture. As acceptance of new issues in the public markets depends on such ratings, private placements of debt with financial institutions, including bank term loans, became major sources of debt to increase the leverage position to the desired levels. Second, cash flows have been front-ended and corporate taxes deferred by the accelerated depreciation and investment credit provisions in the tax laws. Therefore, amortization of debt to finance plant and equipment expenditures could be scheduled at a more rapid rate, with the result that more financing of these items seemed expedient within the maturity limits of term loans than had been possible before the advent of these tax deferrals.[6]

However, the national economic policy assumptions came into serious question during the recession of 1974–75. The following comment is illustrative:

> Our economy has become more volatile. Each of the past two business cycles has been more violent than the preceding one. Increasing dependence upon debt—especially short-term debt—contributes to this volatility. Leverage, of course, works on the downside as well as the upside. Moreover, confidence is crucial to a credit system, and confidence is not enhanced by volatility.[7]

The fact that problem loans and loan losses reached levels unprecedented since the Great Depression reinforced the opinion that credit policies across the board had been excessively liberal. Favorable cash-flow projections became suspect, and instead concentration on the adequacy of cash-flows during adverse cyclical periods became more important in credit decisions. But the memories of many bankers appear to be notoriously short; the admonitions on liquidity exposure following the credit crunch of 1969–70 were widely ignored during the easy money policies of the subsequent two years. Therefore, whether cautious credit policies will be maintained under future conditions of monetary ease is problematical.

Indeed there is the view that in the years ahead a "capital shortage" may develop with the following consequences:

6. Freed and Hunn, *Journal of Commercial Bank Lending* 52 (Mar. 1970): 24–25.
7. H. G. Warner, "Changing Patterns of Corporate Finance," *Journal of Commercial Bank Lending* 58 (Oct. 1975): 5.

> . . . Looking ahead, observers of the financial scene are uneasy about the ability of equity markets to provide the necessary amounts of business capital, particularly for medium-size and smaller firms. Similarly, the capital crunch will continue to make it difficult for all but corporations of very large size, and with the highest possible ratings, to count upon fulfilling their long-term debt requirements in the bond market.
>
> If this is the picture before us, it would seem to me inevitable that commercial banks not only will be faced with strong, recurring demands for short-term credit . . . but, more importantly, will also be pushed toward providing longer-term credit for these corporations, particularly for medium-sized and smaller firms.[8]

The ability of promising firms of moderate size to obtain tailor-made credit packages from commercial banks is perhaps the singular contribution of commercial banks to the financing process of the private sector. Therefore, although risk tolerance must be held within reasonable limits, a positive policy attitude toward such credits would seem desirable. In the past, these customers have often become excellent customers as they have progressed and prospered.

A flexible approach towards such companies is required because rapid growth frequently escalates capital requirements. Instead of regular amortization, these companies often request refundings of term credits or working capital commitments at successively higher amounts. An indication that this course of events is typical is the fact that a special term has been coined to characterize such loans; they are called "evergreen," suggesting that they may have to continue indefinitely during the growth period. In general, it is probable that these credits offer the greatest challenge to the talents of lending officers.

## Maturity and Amortization Policies

### Term loans

Conventional wisdom on banking policies long held that because the liabilities of banks were preponderantly short-term in character, assets should also be limited to short-term commit-

8. C. H. Golembe, "Commercial Lending: Where Do We Go From Here?," *Journal of Commercial Bank Lending* 58 (Jan. 1976): 61.

ments. But with the development of modern monetary policy concepts it became apparent that a significant proportion of even demand deposits were "hard core" in nature and that, as a result, banks could prudently extend credit for somewhat longer periods. Given the long history of orientation to short-term credits, however, most banks established maturity limits of two to three years on term loans when they first entered the area. Then after World War II the aggressive search for loans to obtain higher yields than on government obligations led to an extension of maximum term loan maturities to about five years. The generally prosperous decades that followed led to further liberalization of maturity policies until by the early seventies, many banks would consider ten- to twelve-year commitments.

Recently, probably as a consequence of the dramatic increase in problem loans during 1974 75, some moderate retrenchment in maturity policies has seemed evident. As Table 7–2 shows, as of 1976 the normative policies of the respondent banks limited

TABLE 7–2
TERM LOAN MATURITY POLICIES
(Respondent Banks)

| FREQUENCY | MATURITY | | | |
|---|---|---|---|---|
| | 5 YEARS | 7 YEARS | 10 YEARS | 12 YEARS |
| Regularly | 7 | 4 | ... | ... |
| Sometimes | 1 | 4 | 3 | ... |
| Rarely | ... | ... | 5 | 2 |
| Never | ... | ... | ... | 6 |

term loan maturities to between five and seven years, although most were sufficiently flexible to permit maturities to be extended to ten years in special cases and a few would consider twelve-year maturities. The data on maturity policies thus indicated that the majority of term loans are made to accommodate financial needs that can be covered by cash flows within several years. It seems clear, therefore, that term loan policies are oriented toward providing intermediate term credit and not long-term funds.

However, the toleration of "evergreen" credits through successive refundings at equal or higher amounts than the original loan suggests that in some instances long-term funds may in fact be advanced to some customers whose progress justifies continued confidence on the part of the bank. Although escalating credit requests are presumably screened carefully, only one respondent bank indicated that refinancing of these credits was encountered only rarely; most indicated that extensions of maturity and additional advances would be considered on an ad hoc basis. The justification is that refinancing of term credits is often related to new conditions and needs. The process may be viewed as a series of loans, each of which is amortized from cash flows over an intermediate term. Amortization policies, therefore, must be considered in connection with maturity limits, because, if periodic and complete amortization of term credits is a normal requirement, then these credits may be viewed as truly of intermediate length in nature. However, if amortization requirements are nominal, then it is probable that a substantial proportion will be de facto long-term credits, because restructuring of the unamortized portion will be the only acceptable option open in most cases at the purported original maturity. It is a delusion to consider that somehow a substantial amount of funds will suddenly be available in the typical company that has had a history of constant asset expansion.

In the case of large companies, public financing might be considered as a possible take-out source of the unamortized portion of a term loan; but, as indicated above, large companies that rely on term credits often do so in order to increase their debt leverage to levels that are not readily acceptable in the public markets. In some instances, private placements with life insurance companies that will accept high debt levels in return for higher yields may offer a means of refunding an unamortized term credit. But unless the take-out is arranged in advance, this option may be either not readily available or not desirable to the customer because of the rigorous terms that insurance companies usually impose in such a situation.

Table 7–3 shows the estimated frequency in the respondents' term loans portfolios of the alternative amortization options on term loans. It is clear that full amortization on a straight-line basis over the life of the loan was regarded as the preferable policy.

However, most would consider an amortization schedule of less than the full loan which results in a so-called balloon at the final maturity, although there was a clear preference for the balloon to amount to less than 50 percent of the original credit.[9] In most instances if the balloon maturity is of any magnitude, its purpose is really to allow the bank to restructure the credit at the nominal maturity as considered appropriate, and in fact the effective maturity must be realistically regarded as considerably longer than specified in the original loan agreement. A "bullet" maturity loan is of course one wherein no payments are made on principal until the final maturity; without exception policies were to avoid such commitments unless an alternative source of funding appeared reasonably probable at the expiration of the term period.

TABLE 7–3
AMORTIZATION FREQUENCY: TERM LOANS
(Respondent Banks)

| AMORTIZATION OPTIONS | IMPLEMENTATION | | | |
|---|---|---|---|---|
| | FREQUENTLY | SOMETIMES | RARELY | NEVER |
| Straight-line | 8 | ... | ... | ... |
| "Balloon" maturity: | | | | |
| 50% of loan or more | ... | 1 | 5 | 2 |
| Less than 50% of loan | ... | 4 | 3 | 1 |
| Delayed: | | | | |
| 2 years or less | 3 | 3 | 1 | 1 |
| Over 3 years | ... | ... | 6 | 2 |
| "Bullet" maturity (no amortization) | ... | ... | 5 | 3 |

Finally, the responses indicated that most banks will consider delayed amortization in which the delay is two years or less. The concept here is that it may require a year or so before the assets financed with the loan become productive; in the interim all

9. A balloon maturity may be accompanied by an "earnings recapture clause" which requires that if earnings exceed a certain prescribed level in any year, then a proportion of such earnings must be devoted to a payment on the loan in addition to the contractual amount. In this way, if the company lives up to expectations, then the balloon might be automatically eliminated. The problem is that strong growth in earnings often requires additional asset commitments that make it inexpedient for the company to divert cash flow to the repayment of the loan.

cash flows may be needed to provide supplemental finance to the project. Under these conditions, the loan may be structured for an eight-year maturity (say) to be amortized in full over a seven-year period beginning one year after the original extension of the credit. Given the hypothesis that credits should be individually structured to fit the cash-flow situation of each customer on a realistic basis, the policy to permit delayed amortization in certain cases seems appropriate.

### An evaluation

In evaluating term loan maturity and amortization policies, two questions might be raised. First, are the limits reasonable in the light of customers' financial requirements and alternative options to meet these requirements? Second, are the limits appropriate from the standpoint of prudent asset management of a commercial bank?

With respect to the first question, there is no doubt that until the mid-sixties a maturity gap existed in the financial markets. Long-term lenders, such as life insurance companies, avoided commitments of less than ten-year maturity, while banks were generally reluctant to go beyond five years. However, as shown by Table 7–2, most large banks have maximum maturity limits of about seven years. Moreover, because of recurrent wide variations in interest rate levels, long-term lenders have decided that somewhat shorter maturities are acceptable. The substantial number of publicly offered bond issues with maturities of from five to seven years that have been sold in recent years is evidence of this change in policy. Of course, if fluctuations in interest rates should moderate, preferences of long-term investors may change back to a ten-year minimum. But even so, prevailing maturity limits suggest that banks are prepared to meet the requirements of good quality companies up to approximately the ten-year point.

The situation is less clear with respect to the term needs of moderate-sized companies that are below prime quality. In these instances banks are reluctant to go much beyond five years, and these companies usually lack access to the long-term institutional market. Delayed amortization, or nominal amortization with additional contingent payments based on earnings, are means of alleviating the problem to some extent, as are indeterminate working capital loans based on assignments of receivables and possibly inventories. But long-term debt financing remains a problem for many of these companies, and further liberalization of maturity and amortization policies might appear desirable from their viewpoint.

However, it is necessary to consider whether such liberalization would be consistent with prudent asset management. The first argument advanced against a more liberal maturity and amortization policy is that it would reduce asset liquidity. But because liquidity is obtained either from short-term marketable assets, from borrowings, or from purchased deposits in the form of CDs, the traditional argument that long-term loans are inconsistent with liquidity requirements no longer seems relevant. The second argument advanced against further liberalization is that it might increase portfolio credit risks to undesirable levels. Credit uncertainties obviously increase as the time horizon expands, and short maturities with full amortization quickly reduce the credit exposures on term credits. Moreover, the typical long-term lender often takes equity participations and also can afford to be more objective and selective in credit decisions than banks, which must take account of other factors, such as supporting balances, in their decisions. Therefore, particularly in view of the apparent increased volatility of the economy in recent years, from a risk standpoint there would seem to be considerable justification for limiting maturities to about five years on term credits extended to companies of marginal credit quality.

As a result, prevailing maturity and amortization policies do not seem unduly conservative in most large banks. It has been suggested that banks should liberalize their policies as to both risk and maturity limits and seek to offset the consequent lower quality credits with some form of equity participations.[10] It is doubtful, however, that many banks would be willing to introduce policies which would reduce the quality of the loan portfolio to a signifi-

10. The legality of equity participations is clouded. As a consequence, until specific statutory or regulatory approval of such arrangements is forthcoming, it is doubtful if many banks will consider them as a viable option in their pricing policies.

cant degree in view of recent credit problems that brought loan losses well beyond anticipated levels.

## Loan Agreement Policies

### Purposes

Because of their extended maturity, both term loans and revolving credits are made on the basis of a formal loan agreement that usually sets forth a number of positive requirements and negative restrictions on the borrower. Most banks use a long printed form, which is filled in to fit the particular case. Hence the term "boiler plate" is applied to many covenants that are contained in the loan agreement.

While there are several reasons for requiring detailed loan agreements, it should be emphasized that a proliferation of legal promises cannot assure payment of a term loan. Put another way, a weak credit cannot be converted into a strong one by specific promises to do certain things or refrain from doing other things. Unless independent collateral values are present, all creditors are likely to suffer losses if serious economic misfortune overtakes a company; contractual constraints may be of some assistance in forcing liquidation or reorganization before complete catastrophe ensues, but such drastic remedies are usually very unpleasant for all concerned. On the other hand, detailed protective covenants in a very strong credit would seem largely redundant; they do no harm, but the prospect of their being applicable is extremely remote.

However, the convenants may have a salutary effect in many intermediate situations. In these cases the premises are: (1) the general economic risks bearing on the companies during the life of the loan are acceptable to the bank; (2) companies that need substantial amounts of term money are often under some financial strain; (3) such companies may inadvertently or voluntarily engage in practices or execute transactions which appear desirable from their point of view but which may jeopardize their ability to repay the loan; and (4) as the bank must live with these borrowers for a period of years, provisions designed to restrain such practices or transactions are desirable.

The third premise is the one that is both crucial and debatable.

On the surface it may seem curious that the interests of the bank and the borrower could possibly diverge on certain policies, since both are presumably interested in maintaining a strong and profitable entity. However, a borrowing firm's evaluation of reward and risk may be quite different from the bank's. The firm's management could with good reason decide that certain types of transactions entail considerable risk but that the possibility of large rewards to the stockholders (often themselves) justifies a positive decision. The bank, however, is precluded from participation in the potentially large rewards on these transactions, and it very likely would find the risk on its loan materially increased. For example, large expenditures on fixed assets to expand productive capacity at the expense of financial liquidity might seem a justified risk to the company but not to the bank.

In effect, therefore, protective covenants have as their major purpose the prevention of management decisions which might impair the liquidity or solvency of the borrower or jeopardize the claim of the bank against the earnings and assets. A second and closely related purpose may be to establish specific guides for financial planning by setting forth definite limitations on the major types of discretionary expenditures. To accomplish these objectives, a number of detailed and specific covenants may be incorporated into the loan agreement. A third purpose of the agreements is to require the approval of the bank for major changes in the structure of the firm, such as its merger or sale. Finally, the covenants may provide for action in the event of certain contingencies, such as accelerating prepayments if earnings should increase substantially.

## Guideline objectives

Before reviewing policies with respect to the various optional provisions in loan agreements, some general guidelines for their structuring might be considered. The following might be suggested:

1. Besides the standard affirmations, covenants should be limited to those clearly appropriate to each situation. This means that specific covenants setting forth detailed financial

constraints are only included in those situations where financial planning seems inadequate and close controls seem desirable.

2. The covenants should avoid undue complexity and be "stated in terms that are well defined and measurable."[11] Ambiguity must be avoided in all instances.
3. The covenants should not establish specific financial constraints which are so rigorous that technical default is a reasonable probability. Future events, financial requirements, and cash flows cannot be predicted with precision.
4. A corollary of (3) is that the covenants should be structured to allow for the normal seasonal and possibly cyclical variations of the borrower.
5. Within reasonable limits, the covenants should be phrased in terms that will accommodate the normative growth prospects of borrowers. However, because growth often results in financial strains, it may be difficult to balance risk limitations with the growth objectives of borrowers in practice.

### Specific terms of loan agreements: Covenant options

The standard affirmations in loan agreements usually are that the borrower will not pledge, sell, or merge the assets of the business without permission of the bank, that the financial statements reflect the known assets and liabilities of the firm, and finally that periodic financial statements will be furnished the bank during the term of the loan.[12] Table 7–4 shows the major covenant options used in term loans and revolving credits, and these standard affirmations are normally included in all loan agreements; the exceptions may be instances of prime credits where only minimal loan agreements are used.

11. C. S. Zimmerman, "An Approach to Writing Loan Agreement Covenants," *Journal of Commercial Bank Lending* 58 (Nov. 1975): 7. In this connection, Mr. Zimmerman points out, for example, that a covenant requiring that "borrower will maintain an adequate cash flow" is unacceptable because it cannot be measured.

12. *Ibid.*, p. 5.

TABLE 7–4

TERM LOAN AGREEMENTS: FREQUENCY OF SPECIFIC COVENANTS BY RESPONDENT BANKS

| Covenant Provisions | Frequency of Inclusion | | | | |
|---|---|---|---|---|---|
| | Always | Frequently | Sometimes | Rarely | Never |
| *Liquidity and solvency* | | | | | |
| Working capital floors | 6 | 2 | ... | ... | ... |
| Debt limits | ... | 7 | 1 | ... | ... |
| Lease obligation limits | ... | 6 | 2 | ... | ... |
| Neg. pledge clause | 6 | 1 | 1 | ... | ... |
| Min. net worth requirement | ... | 2 | 3 | 3 | ... |
| *Financial planning guides* | | | | | |
| Fixed asset expenditure limits | ... | 6 | 2 | ... | ... |
| Dividend restrictions | 3 | 4 | 1 | ... | ... |
| Salary restrictions | ... | ... | 4 | 2 | 2 |
| Inventory and receivable control | ... | ... | 2 | 4 | 2 |
| Audit requirements and interim financial statements | 8 | ... | ... | ... | ... |
| *Maintain structure of firm* | | | | | |
| Limit sales of assets | 4 | 3 | 1 | ... | ... |
| Limit merger discretion | 3 | 4 | 1 | ... | ... |
| Limit discretion on acquisitions | 1 | 5 | 2 | ... | ... |
| Limit sale of principals' stock to others | ... | 2 | 4 | 2 | ... |
| Maintain existing management | ... | 2 | 3 | 3 | ... |
| *Contingent events* | | | | | |
| Earnings acceleration clause | 1* | 2 | 4 | 1 | ... |

* Specified "always if balloon payment is involved." This provision is also known as "earnings recapture" clause.

Beyond these standard affirmations, only the working capital floor seemed to be an automatic covenant. The working capital floor automatically limits the excessive diversion of internal cash flows to discretionary expenses or illiquid assets, and the assumption of current debt for these purposes. In the instances where customers evidence adequate financial controls, this provision makes all further specific financial constraints redundant, because in order to meet the floor requirement, discretionary expenditures must be closely related to available cash flows.

But some firms, either by design or inadvertently, may not recognize the effects that certain decisions can have on the level of working capital, particularly moderate-sized firms. Therefore, specific restrictions on certain discretionary expense and asset items are often considered desirable to supplement the working capital floor. In this connection, fixed-asset expenditures and dividend payments are most frequently subject to specific limits, whereas restrictions on salaries, inventories, and receivables are seldom incorporated into loan agreements. Salary tends to be a personal and sensitive consideration; thus salary restrictions often involve public relations problems. Usually they are included only in the case of closely held firms where there is evidence that salaries have been substituted for dividends, or in cases where executive bonuses appear to have been excessive. In other words, the inclination is to *not* limit salary payments unless there is a compelling and specific reason for doing so.

The working capital floor does not inhibit the assumption of excessive amounts of long-term debt or of obligations under leases. Therefore, while Table 7–4 shows that limits are often applied to these items, it is somewhat surprising to find that they are used less frequently than working capital floors. Lease obligation limits may be particularly desirable because the acquisition of assets through lease arrangements can circumvent fixed-asset limits and conceivably could represent a major drain on future cash flows. Minimum net worth requirements are used less frequently, because in essence, dividend restrictions can adequately cover the possibility of partial liquidation. Operating losses, of course, can trigger a violation of a net worth covenant whether or not a dividend restriction exists; but if such losses are considered a reasonable probability, either avoiding the credit or requiring adequate collateral would be the most feasible options.

Covenants to restrict the sale of principals' stock and maintain existing management are applied only to those cases where the success of the firm seems clearly identified with a few individuals. The usefulness of these covenants is also debatable because they offer no safeguard against the contingencies of sickness, death, or retirement that may arise during the period of a term credit.[13] Thus it is not surprising that policies of respondents were divided as to the frequency with which they included such restrictions in loan agreements.

The major contingency covenant is the earnings acceleration (recapture) clause, which requires that a certain percentage of earnings, usually above a certain base amount, be devoted to the repayment of the loan. More specifically, the inclusion of this covenant would seem particularly desirable in loan agreements with cyclical companies where earnings forecasts are subject to a wide margin of error. The immediate outlook may indicate favorable near-term earnings prospects, but subsequent prospects may be highly uncertain. Therefore, a rapid reduction of the risk exposure would seem highly appropriate in these cases. Several techniques can be used in connection with an earnings acceleration clause. A balloon maturity is one option, and it also can be applied against the most remote maturities. However, some loan officers commented that not infrequently waivers on this requirement were requested because of pressing needs for capital funds if in fact a significant growth in sales and earnings does materialize.

## Violations of agreement: Alternative remedies

The literal language of loan agreements conveys the distinct impression that violations are likely to result in immediate legal action against the unfortunate delinquent borrower.[14] However,

13. If the success of a business clearly depends on one or possibly two individuals, a covenant that requires life insurance of a substantial amount (perhaps equal to the loan) on these individuals payable to firm can be included. (*Ibid.*, p. 10.)

14. The following language is typical:"[if there is] any breach or failure of the company to perform any other term or condition of this agreement binding upon it, and [if] such breach or failure shall continue unremedied after ________ days

without exception the respondent banks regarded litigation as an extreme remedy to be invoked only in case of a continued and serious adverse trend or in special situations, such as those where fraud seems to be involved. The basis for this view is that it is in the interests of both parties to negotiate an acceptable solution for the violation and to maintain the firm as a going concern.

In general, the prevailing policy is to consider two alternatives: (1) an outright waiver of the covenant following a discussion of the problem with the borrower, or (2) a formal amendment of the loan agreement. There was a consensus that very probably the action resulting from a technical violation of a specific financial covenant (no fraud or default on interest or principal payments) would be a waiver. Depending on circumstances, the waiver might be made with very little question, or it might follow a formal meeting with the borrower to review the situation and work out a corrective program. The de facto policy on violations suggests that many protective covenants are, in effect, advisory rather than legally binding in the usual sense. As their purpose is often to serve as benchmarks for general financial planning, the waiver policy seems reasonable; but at the same time it has the possible drawback of encouraging borrowers not to take the covenants seriously.[15]

Formal amendments of the loan agreement in response to violations, or upon request from the borrower in anticipation of violation, are also considered normal practice. The amendment may be minor, such as moderately increasing fixed-asset expenditure limits; less frequently it includes major changes, such as extending maturities or even increasing the amount of the loan. For important changes, the borrower might also be expected to make concessions—such as complete elimination of dividends, the providing of collateral to support the loan, or an increase in the interest rate.

---

[specified] notice shall have been given the company by the bank, then, in any such event, the notes and all other indebtedness then existing of the company to the bank shall become forthwith due and payable on demand of the bank."

15. The majority of respondent banks admitted that waivers were made "relatively frequently." Several loan officers commented that some customers made a chronic practice of violating one or more of these terms, and that waivers were almost routine, particularly on asset-limitation covenants.

In this connection a significant difference between banks and other institutional lenders can be noted. Because loan officers as a rule maintain close contacts with their customers, often acting almost as regular financial advisers, they generally seek every conceivable means of bringing a borrower through periods of difficulty without permanent damage to his earning capacities. Thus flexibility in adjusting terms of loan agreements to changed conditions is regarded as an axiom of policy. In contrast, life insurance companies and pension funds use basically the same approach to long-term direct loans as to purchases of bonds in the market. There is seldom any expectation of a continuing regular relationship or of ancillary business. As the relation by the nature of the case is impersonal, these institutional investors have an understandably strong preference for avoiding frequent negotiations for changes in the terms of loan agreements. This difference in policy views was cited as an important reason why participations with such lenders have never become an important financing device, despite the complementary feature of relative maturity preferences.[16] A major advantage of term loans as a financing device is that borrowers obtain greater flexibility in their administration than with loans obtained from other financial institutions.

## Leasing Policies

Regulation Y of the Federal Reserve restricts subsidiary leasing companies to the extension of financial leases and it specifically prohibits operating leases. An operating lease (alternatively called a service lease) allows the lessee the use of an asset for a brief or unspecified period of time. The lessor owner provides maintenance and insurance, and it is often expected that a number of users will lease the asset over its service life. Monthly or daily auto leasing arrangements typify the operating lease.

In essence the financial lease is a substitute for a term loan arrangement. In fact, if the lessee has an option to buy the asset

16. One loan officer firmly maintained that in a participating deal with an insurance company his preference was for a complete absence of protective covenants. In this way, subsequent difficulties on adjustments were avoided, and acceleration of the long maturities held by the insurance companies did not become a potential problem because of technical violations.

at depreciated book value at the expiration of the lease term, the deal closely resembles a secured term loan, for it is expected that final ownership will end up with the lessee. In addition, during the term of the lease, the lessee must bear all the risks and costs of ownership (insurance and maintenance) and usually these lease obligations are noncancelable except with the payment of a large penalty.[17]

From a credit standpoint, the legal arrangement of a financial lease as compared to a loan has both an advantage and a disadvantage for the bank (lessor). On the positive side, because ownership resides with the bank, it is somewhat easier to repossess the property in case of default than under a mortgage structure, where foreclosure proceedings must be followed. On the negative side, the lessor does not have a full creditor claim against the lessee such as exists under a loan; beyond the amount derived from a repossession sale or re-lease, the legal remedy for the deficiency is a damage suit for nonperformance, which may be difficult to establish after repossession has taken place. This lack of full creditor rights probably has led some regulatory jurisdictions to disallow direct leasing by banks per se. The practical effect is that lease deals are most attractive to a lessor where the property is not highly specialized but has attractive alternative-use value to other companies. So far as borrowers are concerned, leasing rather than term loans becomes attractive when the tax shelters of investment credits and accelerated depreciation have more value to the lender than to them.[18] Also, as amortization of a lease may be related to the useful life of specific equipment, a somewhat longer maturity may be available on a lease transaction than on a term loan.

17. The close relationship between most financial leases and the incurrence of debt is now recognized in accounting principles whereby such lease obligations must be capitalized and shown as debt equivalents on the financial statements. And under Regulation Y it is specified that leasing company subsidiaries of bank holding companies are restricted to situations where "the lease is to serve as the functional equivalent of an extension of credit to the lessee of the property." Board of Governors of the Federal Reserve System, *Regulation Y,* June 24, 1974, Section 225.4, paragraph 6 (a) (i).

18. Some major airlines, UAL for example, engaged in lease financing of a significant portion of their flight equipment because earnings had been nominal and as a consequence the tax benefits would not benefit them.

## Financial leases

Under Regulation Y a financial lease is defined as one where

> at the inception of the initial lease the effect of the transaction . . . will yield a return that will compensate the lessor for not less than the lessor's full investment in the property plus the total cost of financing the property over the term of the lease, from (1) rentals; (2) estimated tax benefits; (3) the estimated residual value of the property at the expiration of the lease, which in no case shall exceed 20 percent of the acquisition costs of the property to the lessor.[19]

Under these constraints, the lease arrangement can also be described as a "full payment" lease.

Table 7–5 shows the existing policies of the respondents with respect to financial leases. Most relied on internal generation of lease financing, but with some this included active solicitation of noncustomers. For example, one made the following comment: "We use direct mail campaigns (generated from selected mailing lists) and ads in trade magazines and local newspapers to promote awareness of our leasing activities." In an active leasing operation, the leasing company is regarded as a separate profit center entity and not as a service activity to supplement the commercial loan operation. Under these conditions referrals by brokers of leasing deals are also regarded as acceptable; only a minority of our respondents would reject all broker referrals as a matter of firm policy.

Although the tolerance for terms of longer than ten years appeared greater on leases than on term loans, maturities of between five and ten years dominated financial lease transactions.[20] Full payout without regard to estimated residual values was

19. Board of Governors of the Federal Reserve. *Regulation Y,* Section 225.4, paragraph (6) (iv). In the case of short-term leases of less than seven years, a guarantee by the lessee or a third party covering 60 percent of the required total return at expiration of the lease is also allowed. This provision is similar to a balloon maturity on a term loan.

20. Computers, industrial machinery, and transportation equipment (air, rail, and truck) were most frequently mentioned as items covered by lease transactions. Respondents divided on the attractiveness of medical equipment and specialized mining and oil drilling equipment. Furniture and fixtures and restaurant equipment were specifically mentioned as undesirable for financing leasing. Some of the attractive items generally have useful lives of ten years or more.

TABLE 7–5
FINANCIAL LEASE POLICIES
(Respondent Banks)*

| DESCRIPTION | FREQUENTLY | SOMETIMES | RARELY | NEVER |
|---|---|---|---|---|
| *Origination* | | | | |
| Generated internally | 6 | 1 | ... | ... |
| Referred by brokers | 1 | 2 | 2 | 2 |
| *Original leasing term* | | | | |
| Up to 5 years | 2 | 2 | 3 | ... |
| 5 to 10 years | 5 | 2 | ... | ... |
| Over 10 years | 1 | 2 | 3 | 1 |
| *Payout calculation* | | | | |
| Residual value included | ... | ... | ... | ... |
| Residual value not included | 7 | ... | 3 | 4 |
| *Purchase options* | | | | |
| Stated at outset | 2 | ... | ... | ... |
| Fair market value at expiration | 6 | 1 | ... | 5 |

* One of the eight respondents did not have a leasing company subsidiary in the holding company structure and was located in a jurisdiction where direct leasing by the bank was prohibited.

normally required, but of course the implicit interest rate could be adjusted to reflect expected residual value. It was somewhat surprising to find purchase options heavily oriented to fair market value at expiration rather than based on depreciated cost, because the first approach makes the return calculation less certain at the outset. However, under expectations of consistent inflation, there might be reason to anticipate that a fair-market-value approach to purchase options would bring higher net returns on average than would an approach based on depreciated cost.

## Leveraged leasing

Leverage leases may be defined as financial leases wherein the lessor-owner borrows a significant portion of the cost of the property from a third party. This party takes the property as collateral, has first claim on the lease payments, and may have some outside guaranty, but typically does not have recourse against the lessor-owner for a deficiency in case of default.[21] But of course if default occurs the equity of the lessor is the first to be eliminated in a restructuring transaction.

However, if the package of expected returns from the tax benefits, residual value realizations, and interest rate charges exceeds the borrowing costs of the third-party loan, the returns to the lessor can be greatly magnified. Because the transactions are rather complicated and involve greater structuring costs, leveraged leasing is generally limited to big ticket items of $500,000 or more. Only one respondent with an active leasing operation had a firm policy of not engaging in leveraged leasing. This fact suggests that this type of arrangement has become more common in recent years.

Table 7–6 shows the special policy terms applied to leveraged leases; origination, payout calculation, and purchase option policies were the same on these as for straight financial leases covered in Table 7–5. The responses suggest that a large portion of the acquisition cost of the property is often borrowed from third

TABLE 7–6

LEVERAGED LEASING POLICIES

(Respondent Banks)

| POLICY TERMS | INCIDENCE | | | |
|---|---|---|---|---|
| | FREQUENT | SOMETIMES | RARE | NEVER |
| Percentage of Equity in Property: | | | | |
| 20 or less | ... | 2 | 1 | 3 |
| 21 to 30 | 2 | 3 | 1 | ... |
| 31 to 40 | 2 | 3 | ... | 1 |
| Length of Term: | | | | |
| 5 years | ... | ... | 1 | 5 |
| 5 to 10 years | ... | 2 | 1 | 3 |
| over 10 years | 3 | 3 | ... | ... |

Note: Six respondents included; one of the eight banks studied made no leases and another had firm policy against leveraged leases.

21. E. R. Packham, "An Analysis of the Risks of Leveraged Leasing," *Journal of Commercial Bank Lending* 57 (Mar. 1975): 4.

parties; only a 20 percent equity was held in some transactions, and between 21 percent and 30 percent equity was common. However, in general respondents indicated that between 25 percent and 35 percent was the normative equity position.

It is notable that typical maturities on leveraged lease transactions were significantly longer than those on either term loans or straight financial leases. Apparently maturity terms in excess of ten years dominate in this area. One reason is that real property deals (land and buildings) are more frequent here; these are essentially substitutes for commercial mortgages, which often run beyond ten years. Moreover, as already mentioned, leveraged leases are only expedient for big ticket equipment items, and it would be expected that such items would have an average useful life greater than that of lower-cost equipment, such as a truck or standard machine tools.[22]

22. In general, respondents indicated that all lease transactions were limited to a minimum of $5,000 to $10,000 and that even this size was not desirable. Regulation Y places no limit on a maximum amount of a financial lease made by a subsidiary leasing company; note the bank legal limit constraint does not apply to a leasing company. Regulation Y limits maturities of lease transactions to 40 years, but this is hardly regarded as restrictive, except perhaps in a few real property deals.

# VIII

## COMMERCIAL LOANS: PRICING POLICIES

### The Prime Rate Convention

For many years the focal point of pricing policies on commercial loans has been the so-called prime rate convention. It originated during the Great Depression when short-term money market rates declined to less than $\frac{1}{2}$ percent because of the combination of a highly expansive monetary policy with a very limited demand for short-term finance. At such nominal rates, a commercial loan operation could hardly be justified. Therefore, money center banks established a minimum rate for prime quality customer loans that would provide some net return on equity after operating costs were deducted. The original prime rate was established at $1\frac{1}{4}$ percent and it remained largely unchanged until after World War II.

When loan demand increased in the late forties and then active monetary policies were reestablished, the prime rate began to change more often, but for the entire decade of the fifties it changed only sixteen times, mostly in an upward direction. In general the historical record shows that a change in the Federal Reserve discount rates often triggered a change in the prime rate, although a few independent movements could also be observed. Even in the decade of the sixties, when monetary policy became considerably more active, the prime rate moved only eighteen times, with an unprecedented four changes in 1968 when monetary policy became highly restrictive. The mechanism of change essentially was that a large bank, usually in New York, would announce its intention to move the rate. If other banks followed, then the new rate became effective; if they did not, then the initiating bank would retract its proposed change.

The system seemed to work fairly effectively so long as interest rates fluctuated within moderate limits, but when vigorous attempts to restrain the inflationary boom in 1969–70 resulted in a surge of money rates to unprecedented heights, flaws in the logic and nature of the system became evident. In the first place, the prime was an administered rate dominated by the large money center banks. In the second place, as changes were relatively infrequent, they received considerable attention in the news media including the national television networks. Even though the system was based on monetary conditions, its political vulnerability should be evident; populist demands to remove the power of large money center banks to determine the cost of money to business throughout the country became fashionable.

Political pressures to restrain the upward movement of interest rates centered on the prime during the monetary "crunch" of 1969–70 and in effect put the money center banks in an intolerable position. As a result of media publicity, prime rate changes had to be explained to Congressional committees, and the following statement indicates the dilemma that resulted from political pressure to hold the prime below market rates:

> Our loan accounts were already at an all-time high, credit demands were increasing alarmingly, and as the commercial paper rate in early June [1969] approached 8 percent, companies that normally finance themselves in that market turned to us for accommodation under their lines of credit at the prime rate of 7½ percent then in effect. Moreover, additional heavy borrowings were in prospect over the mid-June corporate income tax date. Meanwhile, despite the fantastically high rates we were paying for Eurodollars and Federal funds, our own sources were rapidly becoming exhausted.
>
> Faced with this powerful combination of market forces, we raised our prime commercial lending rate by one percentage point in order to induce potential borrowers to use the commercial paper market and other sources of financing in preference to bank loans.[1]

The statement suggests that the economics of the prime rate are that it should be moderately above marginal costs of deposit and

1. Statement by Alfred Brittain III (President, Bankers Trust Company, New York) before the U.S. Congress, House Committee on Banking and Currency, *The Increase in Our Prime Rate* (Washington, D.C., 1969), p. 3.

perhaps borrowed funds and also at least equal to or slightly above the rates available to major corporate borrowers in the commercial paper market.

Two alternative solutions to the problem subsequently emerged, although the differences between them have turned out to be more in form than in substance. The "floating" prime rate represented the first solution. Innovated by National City Bank of New York in 1971, the ninety-day commercial paper rate plus an appropriate spread automatically sets the prime rate, with changes made weekly. The second solution was to retain the administered rate but to change it more frequently. More frequent movements, it was felt, would reduce the interest of the media in reporting changes and indeed this has turned out to be the case. During the extremely tight money conditions of 1974, the prime rate advanced to unprecedented levels. Yet probably because changes occurred weekly for several months, the mass media (television particularly) did not consider most changes newsworthy.[2]

However, the so-called "floating" prime rate has retained some administrative features and the administered prime rate, as might be expected, has usually moved concurrently with any significant change in the "floating" rate. Administration of the "floating" rate has been in the form of recurrent, although not frequent, changes in the formula. For example, in early 1976 it was reported that Citibank decided that the spread between the commercial paper and the prime rates should be 1½ points rather than 1¼ points, which in turn had been increased from 1 point in April of 1975. The reason advanced for the change in the formula is notable because it clearly suggests the interface between the two prime rates:

> A spokesman for Citibank said the formula was changed because the old one was "producing a prime rate that the rest of the [banking] market didn't see as appropriate." Because of the formula, Citibank generally has led in prime rate changes. "It was an irritant

2. The financial journals of course reported every change in the prime rate, but it did not receive much attention in television news or on the front pages of daily newspapers until 1970–70. For the record, the changes in the prime rate in the 1945–74 period were obtained from *An Analytical Record of Yields and Yield Spreads* (New York: Salomon Bros., 1974), pp. 195–97.

to the rest of the world to have to make decisions they didn't want to, . . ." the Citibank spokesman said.[3]

For the most part, it appears that the problems encountered in 1969–70 with the politically visible prime rate have largely been eliminated with the new approaches. However, certain disadvantages have been cited. First, some skeptics argued that large borrowers in the commercial paper market, such as General Motors Acceptance Corporation, might have considerable influence over the rates they offer on such paper. As these borrowers also use bank lines at the prime rate, it has been charged that indirectly major customers are able to price their own loans at unduly low rates by astute management of their commercial paper offerings. However, during the 1974–76 period, commercial paper rates fluctuated widely in response to supply and demand conditions and there was little evidence of "control" by major borrowers. Second, weekly changes in the prime rate under the "floating" formula approach probably have increased operational costs in the loan portfolio. Computations of interest accruals on all loans priced in relation to prime (the great majority) must be scheduled on a weekly basis rather than monthly as has been customary. But on balance the policy of setting the prime rate on the basis of a clear, functional relationship with open market rates has been a great improvement over past policies wherein changes sometimes appeared quite arbitrary in nature.

## Factors Influencing Pricing Differentials: Commercial Loans

As brought out in Chapter 3, the liability mix of large banks has changed radically in the past decade or so. A significant proportion of liabilities has become interest sensitive in nature. On some, such as Fed Funds purchased, rates vary each day. Then, as most large CDs are written for 30 days to six months, rollovers to retain the funds must offer the prevailing rates in the market. As a consequence, pricing policies of large banks now start with the premise that rates on commercial loans of any significant size, including term loans, should move up and down (float) with

3. *Wall Street Journal,* Jan. 26, 1976, p. 15.

changes in the prime rate. Differentials over the prime rate are usually based on a set of factors than can be listed as follows:

1. The amount of supporting balances offered in relation to the credit commitment, or in a few instances the amount of other profitable services supplied to the customer.
2. The perceived credit risk on the loan in relation to others in the portfolio; in some instances risk classes are established to indicate the appropriate differential.
3. Costs of servicing, usually in the form of collateral management.
4. The term of the loan; policies invariably are to charge higher rates on long-term loans to a given borrower than on any short-term commitments.
5. The negotiating ability of the borrower; although policy is always to offer similiar rates to similar borrowers, because each loan is subject to individual negotiation, moderate variations inevitably arise that usually relate to the negotiating ability of the borrower.

Supporting balance policies are complex and far from uniform between banks, but they are at least subject to quantitative measurement techniques. Risk appraisals of course are somewhat subjective in nature and the pricing differentials here are often intermixed with collateral servicing costs because the risk-reducing attributes of the collateral must be evaluated concurrently with the servicing costs to be incurred. The effect of extended maturity on pricing policies will be considered separately, and the last factor, although not by nature a matter of policy, must be included in any rationale of pricing differentials that might be found in commercial loan portfolios.

### Supporting balances: Concept and issues

*Concept.* The concept of supporting balances in commercial loan policies rests on three assumptions: (1) that all business customers must maintain demand deposits in some bank, because such deposits are the principal medium of exchange used in commercial transactions; (2) that companies would naturally turn to their banks of deposit for credit accommodations; and (3) that the amount of a proposed credit arrangement should bear some relation to the size of the deposit balance.

The first two of these assumptions are not questioned, but the third has been subject to constant controversy both within and outside the banking community. One controversial aspect of this assumption relates to the alternative means of computing the size of the deposit balance maintained by a company, because the measurement of supporting balances can be approached from several different points of view. Figure 8–1, a diagram of a hypothetical seasonal deposit and borrowing pattern, has been constructed to show the nature of the alternatives. In the diagram it is assumed that a company must finance increased inventories and receivables associated with a high seasonal level of output and sales in the fall of each year, and that the bank grants a line or loan in the amount of $40,000 to assist in meeting the seasonal requirements.

Several possible alternatives for measuring the supporting balances offered by this firm emerge from the pattern. First, it can be observed that the average balances for the period preceding the loan request were about $10,000. Second, the minimum balance during this same period was $6,000 at the end of August, and the maximum was $15,000 at the end of February. Third, balances for the entire year averaged $12,000, somewhat more than for the debt-free period; this higher average was largely the result of the build-up in deposits immediately before the repayment of the loan. Fourth, during the interval when the loan was outstanding the minimum balance in September and November was only $3,000, a consequence of the substantial needs for working capital in those months.

Some economists conclude that supporting balance requirements make firms borrow in excess of their needs. This conclusion, however, implicitly or explicitly assumes that measurement is based on the minimum balance during the time the loan is outstanding.[4] If this minimum is in fact the basis of measurement, and if we suppose for the moment that a 20 percent supporting balance represents the normal policy objective, then a loan of

4. E.g., see T. A. Gudiness. *Journal of Commercial Bank Lending* 52 (May 1970): 33.

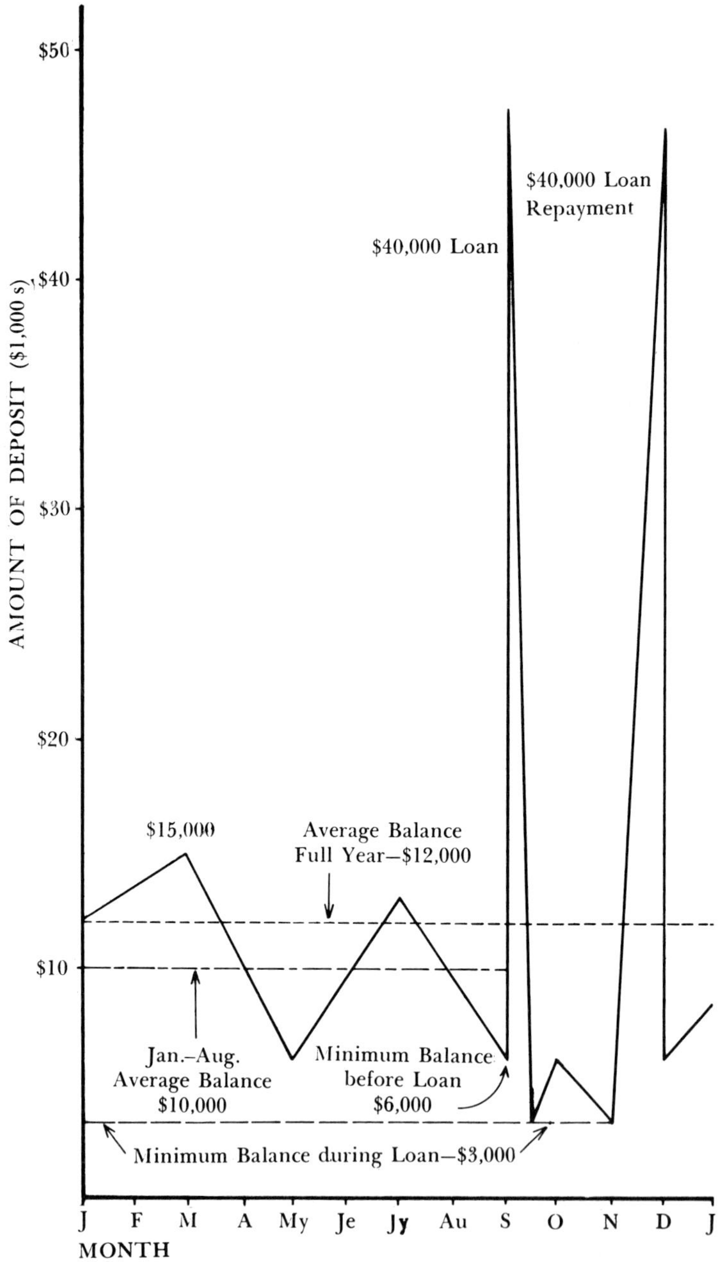


**Fig. 8–1. Hypothetical annual deposit and borrowing pattern (based on a $40,000 line of credit or loan).**

$40,000 presumes a tacit understanding that the borrowing firm will not reduce its deposit balance below $8,000 during the period when the loan is outstanding. A firm that could in fact operate temporarily with an absolute minimum balance of only $3,000 would be forced to borrow $5,000 more than it really needed under the circumstances. Critics hold, with justification, that when minimum balances are used to compute supporting balances, the policy is nothing more than an indirect means of increasing the interest rate on the effective amount of the loan.

*Measurement.* As a matter of actual fact, however, not one respondent bank measured supporting balances in this way (except on lines of credit extended to finance companies), and all specifically denied that minimum balances were considered in any way. The average balance for several years, and particularly the average for the most recent entire year, was universally stated to be the basis of measurement. This interpretation, it might be added, is the only one in full accord with the logic of supporting balances. In the hypothetical example the supporting balance would be viewed as $12,000; and temporary declines during the debt period to an assumed operational minimum of $3,000 would not be regarded as a violation of the balance requirement. Indeed several banks regarded such a decline as a normal expectation. Therefore the concepts of supporting balances per se indicate that hidden charges to borrowers need not exist in practice except on finance company lines.[5]

However, the opportunity cost of maintaining demand deposit balances on which, by law, interest may not be paid) has greatly increased in recent years as rates on short-term, highly liquid assets have become very attractive. Therefore, most companies of any significant size have adopted formal cash management procedures to minimize demand deposit balances. As a consequence, whereas a decade or so ago average demand deposit balances of

5. Large finance companies traditionally seek lines from as many as twenty to forty banks and the relationships are formally structured and impersonal for the most part. In this instance the approach more closely resembles security investment decisions than customer loan decisions. The only difference is that, in order to retain the business of the finance companies, it is understood that the lines will be renewed despite monetary conditions, if the financial position of the company remains up to acceptable standards, whereas securities of course can be liquidated at maturity or before with no subsequent consequences.

perhaps 15 percent of line or loan requests did not seem excessive, current cash management procedures may make it possible to operate comfortably with balances averaging 10 percent or less of line or loan requirements.

*Percentage objectives.* Given these circumstances, many companies have pressed their banks to modify policies with respect to supporting balance objectives. The preference of course was to obtain the same rate, prime if possible, with lower average balances than before. The response of banks has made pricing policies more complex but also more flexible. Table 8–1 shows the normative policy objectives of the respondent banks with respect to supporting balances. One bank, however (not included in the table), limited its response to the following statement:

> Our pricing policy assumes that all credit commitments will be supported by compensating balances on the basis of 10 percent of any credit commitment and an additional 10 percent for any usage under a credit commitment. The bank is indifferent as to whether or not the above balances are maintained or if they are appropriately converted to a fee at the same yield with no reduction due to the effect of reduced reserve requirements.[6]

The above statement of policy clearly represents an attempt to standardize pricing but only with respect to a single variable—the average amount of customer balances. The data for the other banks in Table 8–1 suggest that supporting balance requirements are somewhat negotiable. Average balances of about 15 percent of commitment appeared to be the normative expectation, but variances between 10 and 20 percent were not uncommon. Moreover, it appeared that some would consider pricing loans completely independent of normative balance targets, but these situations were regarded as very exceptional in nature. In other words, a fee or rate adjustment relative to prime might rarely be substituted for zero or inadequate balances. However, the basic policy assumption remained that commercial loan accommodation should be limited to depositors.

6. In Table 8–1 this response was interpreted to mean that commitments were structured frequently on a 10 percent plus 10 percent basis but it could not be classified elsewhere in the data.

TABLE 8–1

SUPPORTING BALANCE POLICIES: NORMATIVE PERCENTAGES

(Seven Respondent Banks)

| Type of Borrower and Requirement | Estimated Frequency of Use | | | |
|---|---|---|---|---|
| | Frequent | Sometimes | Rarely* | Never |
| *Finance companies:* | | | | |
| None (price adjusted) | ... | 1 | 4 | 2 |
| Specified percentages† | 7 | ... | ... | ... |
| *Other commercial loans:* | | | | |
| None (price adjusted) | ... | 1 | 4 | 2 |
| 10% | 1 | 4 | 1 | ... |
| 15% | 7 | ... | ... | ... |
| 20% | 2 | 3 | 2 | ... |
| *Other reported policies:* | | | | |
| 10% + 10% | 2 | ... | ... | ... |
| 15% + 5% | 1 | ... | ... | ... |

* Includes one response for both finance companies and other loans that bank considers incremental amounts only on a price adjusted basis, but most of line or loan must have balance support.

† Defined as a percentage of the line commitment when not in use and a different percentage when line is in use. Credit status and negotiating strength of finance company determines actual requirements, but 10 percent against commitment plus another 10 percent when in use is typical.

But there is a second policy issue in the area of supporting balances. This relates to the method of determining the amount available to support credit accommodation. One view is that credit support balances should represent only "free" balances after deducting an amount necessary to cover activity costs on the account, uncollected funds, and the legal reserve requirement. Otherwise, it is argued, "double counting" results, in the sense that the same balances might be applied to cover servicing costs and also credit support. The other view is that the percentage balance norms should include adequate compensation for all services and that an unbundling through a specific allocation to each service is not required. Table 8–2 shows that the majority of respondents accepted the first view as to appropriate policy but that the second view received considerable support as well.

TABLE 8–2
SUPPORTING BALANCE POLICIES
COMPUTATION OF AVERAGE BALANCE AVAILABILITY
(Eight Respondent Banks)

| METHOD OF COMPUTATION | YES | NO |
|---|---|---|
| Collected balances only | 7 | 1 |
| Amount to cover account servicing costs deducted | 5 | 3 |
| Legal reserve requirement deducted | 2 | 6 |

Given the recent (1975) requirement of the Securities and Exchange Commission that companies subject to the reporting requirements of the Securities Exchange Act of 1934 must disclose supporting balance requirements on all outstanding credit commitments, it would seem probable that for these companies (mostly large and publicly owned) the computation of supporting balances will increasingly reflect the unbundling approach. Moreover, computer programs make possible the rapid daily calculation of the necessary information; Table 8–3 shows the computer program format used by one respondent to calculate "free" balances that are normally required to support a loan commitment.

*Policy implementation.* Although a trend toward more rigorous and standardized supporting balance policies seemed evident as of 1976, policies still seemed flexible in some banks on the basis of one or more of the following factors: (1) the prevailing competition for loan and deposit accounts; (2) the negotiating strength of the customer, (3) the local or national character of the account, (4) the estimated growth potential of the borrower, and (5) the relationship, if any, between the borrower and other departments of the bank.

The first of these factors suggests that norms for supporting balances may change through time because of temporal changes in the supply of available bank credit relative to loan demand consequent to changes in Federal Reserve monetary policy and general economic conditions. For example, most banks referred to balance requirements as "more insistent during periods of tightening" or "less stringent because of competition" under easy money conditions. In the private sector, policy adjustments to

TABLE 8–3
SUPPORTING BALANCES: ANALYSIS
(Computer Program Format)

| | | |
|---|---|---|
| Ledger balances (daily averages) | | $100,000 |
| Less: | | |
| Float (daily averages) | | 20,000 |
| Average collected balance | | $ 80,000 |
| Less: | | |
| Activity cost requirements (6 percent earnings assumption) | $20,000* | |
| Reserve requirements on balances to cover activity costs (10 percent average) | 2,000 | $ 22,000 |
| Net "free" balances available (average) | | $ 58,000 |

* Activity cost on annual basis $1,200; $20,000 required at 6 percent to cover such cost.

meet competitive conditions may be considered axiomatic; the flexibility of the banks on this score, therefore, seems entirely consistent with their long-term objectives.

The other factors suggest that supporting balance norms may vary as between different customers at the same point in time. Indeed the responses shown in Table 8–1 reflected such variances in the case of several banks. The second and third factors—negotiating power and local vs. national character—may be considered together, because in a sense they represent conflicting pressures. One view is that banks should be more "firm" with the large national companies to maintain adequate balances. Two reasons are given for this view. First, nationwide firms usually generate less ancillary business (trust services and individual accounts, for example) than local firms; second, they have financial specialists who are well aware of prevailing balance policies throughout the country. The other view can be summarized in the pragmatic observation of one respondent: "National companies can sometimes maintain lower balances than you might like, and competition precludes much action on your part."

The estimated growth potential of the borrower received mention in two ways in connection with departures from the normal expectation of past supporting balances of 15 percent of credit commitments. First, there was the view that "a projection of prospective balances to be carried in the future" should be considered in evaluating a customer. Second, because of the normal financial strains incident to rapid growth, some banks expect rapidly expanding companies to be "light" on balances during this period. Assuming that credit exposure is within acceptable limits, special consideration for superior growth prospects clearly seems to be a desirable policy, because these customers may ultimately contribute significantly to the deposit growth of the bank.

Policy on the question of waiving normal balance expectations on credit commitments because the customer offers profitable business to other departments of the bank was varied. Some banks granted concessions if the related business was substantial and profitable, but others flatly indicated that their policies did not include such concessions. In banks maintaining a large retail operation in the form of instalment loans, it has not been unusual for balance requirements to be waived on floor-plan loans for volume auto dealers who provide the bank with substantial quantities of instalment paper. Special consideration is also sometimes given to firms maintaining their pension accounts in the trust department. In effect, these considerations suggest that the entire framework of the relationship with the bank may be considered in reaching credit decisions, and that a strong position in one respect may offset a less profitable position in another.

## Fees and Premiums

There are two means by which banks obtain returns on commercial loans in excess of the prime rate applied to the specific number of days of the amount of actual usage. The first is to charge a percentage fee on the unused portion of a commitment. The justification is that the customer obtains value from his ability to borrow up to a specified amount at any time for a term convenient to his needs although with a maximum limit. From the bank's point of view it can be argued that the obligation to lend against commitments at any time requires maintaining standby sources of liquid funds that otherwise might not be required. Experience indicates that a large proportion of customers tend to maximize their usage when it is least convenient to the bank in terms of fund availability—in other words, during tight money periods. In fact loan administration policies now typically include regular monitoring of total commitments against usage through time with a view to forecasting probable percentage usage. However, past experience has not proven a reliable guide to the future, and the reported results of this exercise have not been favorable.

### Commitment fees

Table 8–4 shows the reported fee policies of the respondent banks. Historically, banks have not imposed fees against the unused portions of open lines of credit. But in 1974 when monetary policy became highly restrictive, it seemed appropriate to discourage increases in lines and to reduce them if possible. As a consequence, a few banks imposed fees in a selective fashion, primarily in those cases where balance adequacy was marginal. But the responses show that most banks do not regularly impose fees against line commitments. However, as noted above, one bank would consider incorporating balance inadequacies into a rate premium through a fee. In concept, the amount of the fee would be equal to the difference between the return potential based on normative balances and that computed on actual average balances. For example, if, under existing policy, balances should be $100,000 on average but only average $80,000, then a fee of $20,000 times the prime rate might be applied for a given year. But it appears that this approach to pricing was not in general use as of 1976.

On revolving credits customers obtain a contractual commitment for periods of two to five years usually. In this instance, commitment fees on the unused portion are regularly imposed and the average is about ½ percent. However, the percentage tends to vary through time with monetary conditions; ¼ percent may be typical during easy periods and ⅝ percent to ¾ percent during tight periods. The bargaining strength of the borrower is also a consideration.

Term loans are made for a specific amount for several years, but customers may delay takedown for a month or more after the firm commitment has been made. Policies on imposing fees covering the period between commitment and takedown seemed to vary considerably. Presumably if the takedown were to be delayed

TABLE 8–4
COMMITMENT FEE POLICIES: FREQUENCY
(Eight Respondent Banks)

| TYPE OF LOAN | USE OF FEE | | | |
|---|---|---|---|---|
| | FREQUENTLY | SOMETIMES | RARELY | NEVER |
| *Lines of credit* | | | | |
| ¼ to ½% | 1 | ... | 4 | 3 |
| ⅝ to 1% | ... | ... | 3 | 5 |
| *Revolving credits** | | | | |
| ¼ to ½% | 6 | ... | 1 | 1 |
| ⅝ to 1% | 3 | ... | 3 | 2 |
| *Term loans* (until takedown) | | | | |
| ¼ to ½% | 2 | 1 | 3 | 2 |
| ⅝ to 1% | 2 | 1 | 3 | 2 |

Note: Commitment fees are alternatively described as facility fees.
* Applied against unused portion only.

several months, there would be more reason to impose a fee, but such cases are relatively infrequent; thus the response indicated fees generally were imposed only sometimes or rarely.

## Pricing premiums

Prior to about 1973 premiums were typically stated in fractional steps of absolute points over the prime rate. For example, a loan might be priced to float at a constant 1 point above the prime rate. Gradations in premiums were usually in ¼-point steps, although ⅛-point gradations were sometimes used. This method of quoting rate premiums is still used, but policies to quote premiums in terms of percentage of prime have perhaps become more typical among large banks.

The difference between the loan rates that result from the alternative methods of quoting premiums is shown in Table 8–5. Under the percentage-of-prime method, the absolute spread becomes greater as the prime rate rises, and the difference in spreads also varies in absolute amount with the amount of the premium. (At a 6 percent prime rate the difference between 1 over and 110 percent is .4, but at the same prime rate the difference between

TABLE 8–5

FLOAT PREMIUMS: COMPARISON OF POINTS OVER VS. PERCENTAGE OF PRIME

(At Various Levels of the Prime Rate)

| | Rate Premium Comparison | | | | | |
|---|---|---|---|---|---|---|
| Prime Rate | 1 Over | 110% | 2 Over | 120% | 3 Over | 130% |
| 5% | 6% | 5.5% | 7% | 6 % | 8% | 6.5% |
| 6 | 7 | 6.6 | 8 | 7.2 | 9 | 7.8 |
| 7 | 8 | 7.7 | 9 | 8.4 | 10 | 9.1 |
| 8 | 9 | 8.8 | 10 | 9.6 | 11 | 10.4 |
| 9 | 10 | 9.9 | 11 | 10.8 | 12 | 11.7 |
| 10 | 11 | 11.0 | 12 | 12.0 | 13 | 13.0 |
| 11 | 12 | 12.1 | 13 | 13.2 | 14 | 14.3 |
| 12 | 13 | 13.2 | 14 | 14.4 | 15 | 15.6 |
| | Range of Points: Low to High | | | | | |
| 7 | 7 | 7.7 | 7 | 8.4 | 7 | 9.1 |

3 over and 130 percent is 1.2.) Thus the percentage-of-prime method produces rate premiums which in absolute terms are more volatile than the prime rate itself. The virtue of this result is that a larger proportion of fund sources have been high-cost, interest-sensitive borrowings and CDs when interest rates generally are at a high level.[7] At such times banks must aggressively purchase money to fund loan commitments and the only available sources are highly interest sensitive in nature.

Particularly if the purpose of the rate premium is to act as a substitute for supporting balances, the percentage-of-prime approach seems logical because the opportunity cost sacrifice on inadequate balances increases as interest rates in general advance. On the other hand, if the purpose is largely to cover collateral servicing costs, then the "points over" approach seems sensible as these costs do not vary with fluctuations in interest rates. In other words, the costs of monitoring collateral adequacy is the same whether the prime is 5 percent or 12 percent.

7. In recent years, Congress has recurrently considered legislation to remove all interest rate ceilings on deposits over a period of years. If the proposed legislation becomes law, an even larger proportion of deposit funds will become interest sensitive.

## Short-term credits: Rate frequencies

Table 8–6 shows the estmated rate frequencies of the respondent banks by types of accommodation in the short-term credit areas. Term loan rates have some unique policy problems so they will be considered separately below. As expected, all respondents reported that open lines of credit frequently carried the prime rate. However, as some banks now allow large high-quality companies to obtain lines with inadequate balance support, rates of 110 percent to 120 percent of prime were not considered unusual on lines. But rates in excess of 120 percent of prime were very unusual on lines of credit.

Greater variance in pricing policies seemed evident on trans-

TABLE 8–6
ESTIMATED RATE FREQUENCIES AT RESPONDENT BANKS
(By Types of Credits)

| TYPE OF LOAN | RATE UNIVERSE | | | | |
|---|---|---|---|---|---|
| | PRIME | ½–1 OVER (110%) | 1–2 OVER (120%) | 2–3 OVER (130%) | MORE THAN 3 OVER (OVER 130%) |
| *Lines of credit* | | | | | |
| Frequently | 8 | 2 | . . . | . . . | . . . |
| Sometimes | . . . | 5 | 5 | . . . | . . . |
| Rarely | . . . | 1 | 2 | 5 | 2 |
| Never | . . . | . . . | 1 | 3 | 6 |
| *Transaction loans* (Short-term) | | | | | |
| Frequently | 1 | 4 | 1 | 2 | . . . |
| Sometimes | 4 | 3 | 7 | 1 | . . . |
| Rarely | 2 | 1 | . . . | 5 | 7 |
| Never | 1 | . . . | . . . | . . . | 1 |
| *Working capital commitments* (Secured by receivables) | | | | | |
| Frequently | . . . | 1 | 5 | 4 | . . . |
| Sometimes | . . . | 2 | 3 | 3 | 2 |
| Rarely | 1 | 4 | . . . | 1 | 4 |
| Never | 7 | 1 | . . . | . . . | 2 |

action loans. The reason may be that some banks apparently assume that any company eligible for the prime rate will prefer a line to a specific loan while others will structure individual loans to such companies. By and large the rate premiums also have a wider spread than those on the line category. These loans may be secured and thus involve collateral servicing costs, and in addition their size and credit quality tend to vary over a wider range. The pricing spectrum seems to fall mainly between 110 percent and 130 percent of prime (1 to 3 over in points), depending on an assessment of these variables in each situation. In the case of secured working capital commitments, many represent continuous borrowing for several years and most typically carry considerable risk. Therefore, a premium of 2 to 3 over prime (120 percent to 130 percent) seemed typical, but again other premiums would apparently be considered in some circumstances.

### Term loans and revolving credits: Rate frequencies

Because revolving credits and term loans always presume continuous borrowing for periods of more than a year, it is generally agreed that these commitments should automatically be priced at some premium above the prime. As the length of the term increases, presumably rate premiums should increase. In addition, the credit risk evaluation of a company becomes more uncertain as the repayment period is extended through time; thus one would expect that a term loan to a given company would carry a higher rate than a short-term credit commitment, with the possible exception of a few blue chip situations.

Table 8–7 indicates that the pricing policies of the respondents generally were in accord with these expectations. On good quality commitments (where adequate supporting balances are assumed), premiums in points of between ¼ and 1 above prime appeared to be the normative policy. However, higher premiums were not considered unusual, although the practical maximums seemed to be about 2 points on revolvers and 3 points on term loans. The fact that term loans may have much longer final maturities than revolvers explains the difference between the two. Because banks on occasion consider term commitments to promising companies with inadequate balances, somewhat higher rate premiums were

TABLE 8–7

RATE UNIVERSE: ESTIMATED FREQUENCY

(Term Loans and Revolving Credits; Respondent Banks)

| | Revolving Credits | | | | Term Loans | | | |
|---|---|---|---|---|---|---|---|---|
| Rates | Fre-quent | Some-times | Rare-ly | Never | Fre-quent | Some-times | Rare-ly | Never |
| Floating | | | | | | | | |
| Prime | 3 | 2 | 2 | 1 | 1 | ... | 2 | 5 |
| ¼ to 1 (110%) | 7 | 1 | ... | ... | 7 | 1 | ... | ... |
| 1–2 (120%) | 1 | 5 | 1 | 1 | 4 | 4 | ... | ... |
| 2–3 (130%) | ... | ... | 7 | 1 | ... | 4 | 4 | ... |
| Over 3 (over 130%) | ... | ... | 3 | 5 | ... | ... | 3 | 5 |
| Fixed | ... | ... | 5 | 3 | ... | 1 | 4 | 3 |
| Cap | ... | ... | 4 | 4 | ... | ... | 3 | 5 |

Note: Response requested on current policy on new loans rather than on universe of existing loans in portfolio; in latter case "cap" and fixed rates would have been more frequent.

indicated for rare situations. On the other side, several banks reported that they frequently extended revolving credits at the prime rate. Particularly on "bridge" financing of top flight companies, wherein the revolver is extended against a series of project expenditures and then this loan is ultimately repaid from a subsequent term credit when the project is completed, the prime rate is not unusual.

It is clear that banks now avoid fixed rates on both revolving credits and term loans. The historical development of policy in this connection is interesting. Up until the mid-sixties, fixed rates were not unusual on these commitments. The policy to allow such rates was based on a view of the world which presumed that interest rates would fluctuate around a reasonably level trend and that setting a fixed rate in relation to the historical average would be acceptable. However, for a decade or so the trend of interest rates has been sharply upward, and under these conditions fixed rates for future periods of five to ten years have considerable opportunity cost risk. Therefore, only in rare instances would a few banks consider a fixed rate on these commitments and then the premium over prime had to be about three to four points. And other respondents reported that their policy was never to consider a fixed rate in this area.

The "cap" rate concept on term loans was innovated in the early seventies as a compromise between a floating rate and a fixed rate. Under this pricing arrangement, the rate varied with the prime at a prescribed premium but a maximum average rate (cap) is established in advance for the life of the loan. Aggressive competition for customers essentially led to the introduction of the cap rate, because customers may see a real advantage in the ability to compute the maximum limits of the cost of capital represented by a term loan. A senior officer of a major bank made the following comments on the arrangement at the time it was popular:

> We deserve an added premium for the cap–it is insurance for the borrower. Loans priced at standard market rates with low caps thrown in, we feel are giveaways. Such loans may have their place, but we should see them for what they are–an attempt to buy business. But reasonable caps with adequate balances–where the bank has done its homework, when the bank gets a specified premium for the cap–can be good loans. What the right cap is depends, of course, on credit judgment, maturity, and balances–it is not easy to decide. . . . Will we still see cap loans in five years? The next period of tight money could finish them off, or they could endure.[8]

This comment proved to be prophetic. In 1974, the prime rate reached a peak of 12¼ percent and averaged almost 11 percent. In 1972, when cap rates were introduced, the prime averaged about 5 percent and the previous record peak was 8 percent, registered in 1969–70. Thus, cap rates set in 1972–73 based on historical prime rates turned out to have a high degree of "income risk." As a consequence. Table 8–7 shows that the respondent banks had a highly negative attitude toward including cap rates in their pricing policies. But in late 1976, when loan demand was weak, reports of term loans structured on a cap rate basis again emerged; some apparently regarded the device as an attractive competitive mechanism in weak loan periods. But considerable margin for forecast error may also be included in the determination of an appropriate cap (maximum average) rate, as apparently was not the case in 1972–73.

8. C. E. Schmidt, Executive Vice President, First National Bank of Chicago, "Lending '73," *Journal of Commercial Bank Lending* 55 (Mar. 1973): 4.

## Comparative Pricing Analysis

As brought out above, several trends have resulted in more complex pricing policies with respect to commercial loans. To repeat in summary, these trends are: (1) an increasing reliance on interest-sensitive sources of funds acquired at competitive market rates; (2) an increasing range of interest rate fluctuations with an upward secular trend; (3) the preference of some major customers to obtain credit commitments that are not scaled proportionately to demand deposit balances.

Given these developments, it would seem desirable to analyze effective returns obtained from alternative pricing arrangements. In order to obtain a fairly precise indication of returns based on the supporting balance approach, the following formula seems useful:[9]

$$Y = \frac{R}{1 - [(1-RR)\ (FCD)]}$$

where

$Y$ = Yield on loan
$R$ = Nominal rate on loan
$RR$ = Average reserve requirement on demand deposits
$FCD$ = Free collected balances as percentage of loan or of average usage per year under line.

To illustrate, if a loan is made at a prime rate of 8 percent, the average reserve requirement is 16 percent, and free collected balances are 15 percent, then the computation would be as follows:[10]

$$Y = \frac{8\%}{1 - [(1-.16)\ (.15)]} = 9.1\%.$$

Table 8–8 shows the comparative effective yields that would result from the normal pricing alternatives wherein the balance-

9. Source is G. R. Severson, "Determining Pricing Alternatives," *Journal of Commercial Bank Lending* 56 (Nov. 1974): 3.

10. These numerical assumptions seemed reasonably realistic for large banks as of 1976 when reserve requirements on demand deposits were 13 percent on demand deposits between \$100–400 millions and 16½ percent on such deposits over \$400 millions. Also as shown in Table 8–1, 15 percent supporting balances were normative for the respondent banks.

supported effective yields are based on the numerical assumptions given for the illustrative computation. It is clear that effective returns on a prime rate commitment supported by 15 percent balances and one entirely without balance support are closely equalized by a rate of 115 percent of prime applied to the latter.

TABLE 8–8

COMPARATIVE YIELDS: PRICING ALTERNATIVES

(At Various Levels of Prime Rate)

| | Effective Yield | | |
|---|---|---|---|
| Prime Rate = R | Balance-Supported | 115% of Prime* | 1.5 Over Prime* |
| 5% | 5.7% | 5.75% | 6.5% |
| 6 | 6.8 | 6.90 | 7.5 |
| 7 | 8.0 | 8.05 | 8.5 |
| 8 | 9.1 | 9.20 | 9.5 |
| 9 | 10.2 | 10.35 | 10.5 |
| 10 | 11.4 | 11.50 | 11.5 |
| 11 | 12.5 | 12.65 | 12.5 |
| 12 | 13.7 | 13.80 | 13.5 |

* Assumes zero balances held by borrower.

However, using the equivalent "points over" of 1.5 points results in effective yields which do not closely scale with the balance-supported returns. Therefore, to provide an equalized alternative for customers at all levels of the prime, a rate premium based on a percentage of prime is necessary. This means also that split pricing of commitments to the same customer is possible. For example, if a customer's free collected balances average $100,000 and 15 percent balance support is considered normative, then the prime rate may be justified on an approximate $660,000 credit. A rate of 115 percent of prime on significant usage beyond this amount results in equalized returns on both portions of the credit accommodation.

Finally, on some types of credit, the return may include commitment fees on the unused portions. To obtain the annualized yields on the funds actually advanced under these commitments, the additional return consequent to the commitment fee must be computed. The formula to derive this return factor on an after-the-fact basis is as follows:[11]

$$EA = \frac{CF\ (1-U)}{U}$$

when

$EA$ = Additional percentage return
$CF$ = Commitment fee on unused portion
$U$ = Utilization (equal to average loan outstanding for year divided by commitment).

For example, if the commitment fee amounted to ½ percent and the average annual usage was $400,000 under a $1,000,000 revolving credit commitment, then the additional annualized yield would be:

$$\frac{5. \times (1-.4)}{.4} = \frac{.30}{.4} = .75\%.$$

As average annual percentage usage of a commitment cannot usually be estimated very accurately in advance because it is strictly the customer's decision, the pricing effects of commitment fees as compared to premiums over prime are difficult to assess when structuring a credit. But if actual usages are likely to be low relative to commitments, such as usage under standby lines to support commercial paper issues, then commitment fees may provide a significant addition to returns. This practice may be justified on the ground that these commitments per se represent a significant service to the customers at some cost to the bank in the form of increased liquidity problems because of potential high usages at unforeseen times. In the past, high usage under such standby lines has come during extremely tight money periods, when the commercial paper market may be congested, and of course this is the least convenient time for usage so far as the bank is concerned.

11. G. R. Severson, "Determining Pricing . . ," p. 3.

# IX

## SECURED LOANS: POLICIES AND PROCEDURES

A secured loan may be defined as a loan wherein the bank contractually establishes a claim beyond that of a general creditor of the borrower. In the typical case, specific assets or a combination thereof are legally pledged so that in case of default the bank has the right to institute legal proceedings to take over the pledged property and liquidate it to satisfy its claim with precedence over all other creditors. Under this definition, however, a secured loan does not require a specific pledge of assets; if, for example, a third party guarantees payment, then the claim extends beyond that of a general creditor and, as a consequence, the loan enters the secured category.

### Alternative Policy Concepts

The first policy issue in connection with secured loans is that of establishing the conditions under which the bank will require a source of repayment beyond that of a general creditor. At one extreme is the view that all loans should be secured except in unusual circumstances. This view is based on the concept that a security interest of some sort necessarily improves the position of the bank, and that some asset is normally available to secure the loan. Small banks, in particular, often seem to follow the policy of requiring practically every commercial loan to be supported by specific collateral of some kind. Three reasons for this policy may be cited: (1) by and large such banks have few top-flight credit customers; (2) information derived from small businesses and farmers tends to be sparse; (3) loan officers in small banks may have a limited ability to conduct sophisticated credit analysis. Given these conditions, it follows that most loans will be made on a secured basis.

In contrast, in the short-term commercial loan area at least, unsecured credits tend to dominate the portfolios of large banks.

The policy assumption is that commitments should first be considered on an unsecured basis and collateral required only when the credit quality is inadequate. Moreover, the general view is that loans should not be made where there is a strong possibility that payment can be made only through involuntary liquidation of a secured position. Collecting a loan through legal proceedings is expensive and involves an inordinate amount of loan officers' time. Therefore, in theory at least, a secured position is taken as a secondary source of support to limit ultimate loss rather than as the primary means of repayment.

The unsecured arrangement is considered preferable because it is more economical for both parties. The assets of most firms are not in a form which makes them convenient collateral. Although there are contrived devices available for pledging conventional business assets, the effective use of these devices often involves high servicing costs, so that, even though rates are higher on secured loans using these devices, the additional return may be more than offset by the greater servicing costs.

The same cost factors, of course, are relevant to loans of more extended maturities. As a result, the same preference for unsecured arrangements would appear appropriate, and indeed most term loans to strong credits are extended on an unsecured basis. However, a greater proportion of term loans than of short-term transaction credits are secured for two reasons. First, such loans are often associated with specific fixed asset acquisitions, and it seems logical to take a security interest in the assets so financed with the proceeds of the loan. On short-term loans, the direct connection between specific asset acquisitions and the proceeds of the loan may be less clear. Second, risk factors become increasingly more difficult to assess as the time span lengthens. For example, competition, management problems, and possible cyclical fluctuations are more significant risk elements on term credits to be repaid from earnings than on loans to be repaid from a near-term liquidation of assets. Therefore, despite a general preference for unsecured credit arrangements, the upward trend in the relative importance of term loans and in other continuous borrowing arrangements has resulted in greater emphasis on collateral policies and techniques.

These comments, however, relate to credit commitments where convenient collateral does not arise from the ordinary operation of the business. Where such collateral is readily available, it is standard policy to require security regardless of the risk involved. Loans to investment bankers, stock and mortgage brokers, and commodity dealers fall into this classification. In these cases, assets in the form of standard negotiable instruments emerge from the firms' regular activities, and there is little if any cost involved in assigning a security interest in such assets. In discussing the reason for collateral requirements in these areas, some banks mentioned their typically heavy liability positions in relation to equity and thus an implied risk feature. But because marketable collateral was an automatic requirement, it appeared that no real attempt was made to determine whether the security interest was in fact necessary. Routine collateral requirements on commitments which generate easily hypothecated assets have the practical advantage of enabling prompt service with a minimum of investigation. Paradoxically, collateral in these situations can be viewed as a means of reducing servicing costs by eliminating extensive credit analysis procedures.

Collateral may also be required in two special instances related to options extended to borrowers. First, some customers may be reluctant to divulge information considered essential to substantiate loans on an unsecured basis, or unable to provide the information because they lack adequate records. Under these circumstances most banks will allow the pledge of clearly adequate collateral ito justify a waiver of the requirement of financial statements. Unless there is some reason to doubt the integrity of the customer, the practice seems reasonable. Second, in rate negotiations, a collateral option may enter the picture. If the customer happens to own some marketable collateral either within or outside the business, a rate lower than that on an alternative unsecured loan may be available. A reduction in risk and in costs of investigating the credit justify the policy of offering rate concessions in these instances. It was generally agreed, however, that both of these special reasons for collateral loans were rather rare in actual practice.

Finally, several banks specifically singled out loans to individuals or professional people as a category where security is often required. The only specific reason offered for the policy was that "it is much more difficult to police application of funds and changing fortunes of individuals." Along these lines, the possibility of significant income tax assessments, which would have a priority over an unsecured loan, was mentioned as a source of uncertainty on loans to professional individuals, such as doctors or dentists. The heavy prior claim of the federal government on the earning power of individuals seems, perhaps deplorably, to have forced banks to be quite cautious with regard to such loans, and in a sense even to discriminate against professional people in their lending policies. As a matter of fact, unless the deposit relationship is satisfactory, some banks often refer professional loans to the consumer credit department, where close policing is routine, but where rates are about twice as high as those on regular commercial loans.

## Accounts Receivable Loans

As mentioned above, except on loans to high-quality companies, there is a bias towards requiring specific collateral for commitments to finance relatively permanent asset needs. Temporary borrowings may also be included, but the dominant characteristic is a "core" of bank credit even at seasonal lows. Most banks are willing to consider continuous borrowing commitments, because the financing is often associated with growth situations where an upward trend in sales requires increases in receivables and inventories greater than can be financed with retained earnings. Ultimately, retained earnings are the typical source of repayment, although occasionally other sources of permanent capital may be found. When the asset core to be financed is primarily working capital in the form of receivables or inventory, both of these become the logical source of the collateral. On the whole, receivables are considered preferable because their stated values, unlike those of inventories, represent firm dollar claims.[1] Also,

1. In distress situations, the collection of receivables may be difficult, however. Returns of goods and claims of unsatisfactory performance of services seem to escalate when it is realized that a company is in or close to bankruptcy. As explained later, an appropriate margin between the amount of a loan and the

inventories often include a wide variety of physical goods marked by differences in quality, state of completion, and perhaps location.

The policies of the respondent banks on receivable assignments are shown in Table 9–1 and they can be summarized as follows: First, negotiations must be conducted to establish both the nature of acceptable receivables and the percentage to be advanced against them. To be acceptable, the accounts should be reasonably current, therefore, a list of receivables and an aging schedule showing the length of time each has been outstanding are usually required.[2] Delinquent accounts, such as those unpaid for 90 days or more when the regular credit terms are 30 days, are eliminated from the list of eligible receivables unless there is evidence that ultimate payment is likely.

As indicated, the typical commitment (usually with a maximum total limit) is 70 to 75 percent of acceptable accounts; but because the nature of receivables may vary widely, policies allow for a negotiating range. The most preferable situations are those in which receivables are based on sales to a moderate number of high-quality companies and evidence shows that merchandise returns are not a problem. Under these conditions, a loan commitment of up to 90 percent of the accounts might be made. On the other hand, if small accounts dominate the receivable portfolio or if there are other reasons to question the quality of the accounts, the advance might be limited to 50 percent or less of the acceptable accounts.[3]

On most receivable commitments, funds are usually advanced or repaid on a revolving basis. If acceptable accounts increase, then advances up to the established limits can be drawn; if they

---

amount of receivables is required for this reason, but even so, defaulted accounts receivable loans often seem to payout at less than full amount because of the attrition in collections.

2. In preparing an aging schedule, the technique of "cross-aging" is recommended. That is, if several shipments have been made to a given customer at different times, and all invoices covering such shipments are unpaid, the entire receivable is aged on the basis of the oldest invoice. The rationale is that there is no reason to believe that a recent shipment represents current debt if the customer is delinquent on prior shipments.

3. Several banks reported a definite bias against accepting service receivables as collateral. In fact, one bank stated receivable loans are made against "sale of merchandise only, except in rare cases." Medical receivables supported by insurance or government guarantees may represent an exception.

TABLE 9–1
POLICIES ON RECEIVABLE ASSIGNMENTS
(Respondent Banks)
N = 8

| POLICY | NUMBER OF BANKS USING |
|---|---|
| *Ratio of loan to acceptable receivables** | |
| 70 percent | 2 |
| 75 percent | 5 |
| 80 percent | 1 |
| *Audit requirements* | |
| Bimonthly | 1 |
| Quarterly | 2 |
| Semiannually | 4 |
| Not performed | 1 |
| *Continuous borrowing under assignment†* | |
| Allowed | 6 |
| Not allowed | 2 |
| *Percentage of loans under dominion of funds* | |
| Under 20 | 7 |
| 21–50 | 1 |
| Over 50 | . . . |

* Average.
† Two years or more.

decrease, then pay-downs are required. In order to police the arrangement properly, recurring audits, usually of a surprise nature, are desirable. But because such audits represent a significant servicing cost, it is necessary to effect some tradeoff between maintaining adequate supervision of receivables commitments and keeping servicing costs at reasonable levels. There are no generally accepted rules to govern this tradeoff, and audit policies are therefore subject to considerable variation.[4]

As most states have adopted the Uniform Commercial Code (UCC), the legal requirements to establish a receivable assignment have been simplified. The options generally available are (1)

4. Several banks reported that more frequent audits would be required under receivable commitments in large or weak credits than under the average commitment. According to one view, however, banks generally have been remiss in both their audit requirements and in their evaluation of accounts receivable collateral. *See* R. S. D'Agostino, "Accounts Receivable Loans—Worthless Collateral?" *Journal of Commercial Bank Lending* 52 (Mar. 1970): 34–42.

a general and continuous assignment, or (2) an assignment under a dominion of funds. Under the first option, one or two standard forms are prepared and a record filed in the appropriate public office to protect the assignment against unsecured creditors. A general and continuous assignment means that existing and future receivables come under the lien, but cash collections are available for general use in the business. While the borrower might promise to maintain an adequate security margin, there is no continuous control over the collection and replacement of the collateral. But because servicing costs are minimal, a majority of the respondent banks indicated that most receivable assignments were structured under this arrangement.

Dominion of funds, the second option, provides closer control over the cash collections. Under this approach, the borrower is required to deposit such collections in a "cash collateral account," and the bank releases funds from the account upon receiving proof of the generation of new acceptable receivables. As a result, unless fraud is committed, there can be no dissipation of the proceeds from the collection of the collateral assigned under the loan. Given the simplicity of establishing security interests under the UCC and the rather consistent court decisions supporting the lien position against intervening claims when properly filed, the general and continuous assignment has become standard policy on account receivable loans.[5] When there is a compelling reason to finance a weak credit, such as a restructuring of a deteriorated credit that cannot be paid out, then the dominion of funds approach is considered. Otherwise the servicing costs imposed on both the bank and the borrower are likely to be excessive in relation to the additional security.

It is not uncommon for borrowings under receivable assignments to remain continuously outstanding in fluctuating amounts for several years. The general view is that the revolving nature

5. In 1969 the U.S. Court of Appeals for the Seventh Circuit in the case of Grain Merchants of Indiana, Inc. v. Union Bank and Savings Co. held that receivables put under a continuous assignment within four months of bankruptcy did not represent an invalid preference transfer in conflict with provisions of the Bankruptcy Act. The issue has been litigated in subsequent cases and generally the lien position has been upheld. It is true, however, that under a dominion of funds arrangement, this legal uncertainty does not arise, because each pledge of receivables is construed as a new loan.

of the collection and repledge process justifies continuous borrowing in many instances. The following statement of one bank concerning its policy on such loans is illustrative:

> Theoretically, we continue because of growth in the company (or they become entitled to unsecured credit); however, most honestly we have stayed with many companies who do not grow at all.

A minority of respondents expressed a policy view against continuous borrowings under receivable commitments for a number of years, but even in these instances policies seemed highly flexible: for example, the following statement of one such respondent:

> We prefer to restrict [such] loans to situations where prospects are that unsecured credit may be justified within two years, but we do have such loans running for a longer period.

The observation suggests an important final point: If a customer does show the progress anticipated, it is good policy to offer a change to an unsecured basis rather than wait for the customer to request it; these customers are natural targets for competitors, who can solicit their business on the grounds that they deserve unsecured credit.

## Commodity and Inventory Loans

So far as policy issues are concerned, loans secured by inventories can be divided into two types. First, there are advances made to commodity dealers and brokers to finance the purchase, transportation, and storage of raw materials—largely agricultural—in anticipation of subsequent sales to manufacturers. Loans to manufacturers to finance the storage and processing of staple commodities are placed in the same category, because the technical problems are largely the same. In the second category are credits extended to manufacturers and retailers of nonstandardized products against the specific pledge of their inventories.

Loans of the first type are largely concentrated in geographic areas where agriculture processing facilities or commodity markets are located. Moreover, the relative role of agricultural production and processing has declined as the economy has become more affluent, and these loans have not been among the growth elements in most portfolios—in contrast to, for example, receivable and term loans.

**Commodity loans**

Since the financing of staple commodities is a limited and specialized operation, only a brief comment on its nature and related problems seems necessary: These loans require considerable technical knowledge of the various commodity markets, and they are usually assigned to a special group of loan officers. In addition, warehouse receipts covering the storage of most staple commodities can be conveniently assigned, which means that collateral requirements may be routine.

The major pitfall associated with these credits has been the assumption that warehouse receipts are a guarantee of the existence of an acceptable quality of the related commodity. There have been several cases of large losses on loans secured by fraudulent warehouse receipts; moreover, even if no fraud exists, a warehouse receipt does not guarantee the quality of the goods stored under it. Specialists in the matter therefore recommend a number of detailed procedures to validate the loans, including investigation of the following: warehouse licensing requirements, insurance coverage, physical contents of containers, hedging arrangements, and spoilage exposure. The policy problem here, as with receivable commitments under dominion of funds, is whether the servicing costs resulting from the full implementation of these procedures will make such credits uneconomical except at finance company rates. Because all respondent banks except one indicated that loans against warehouse receipts are infrequent, apparently the general policy is to avoid these commitments.

**Inventory loans**

The second type of loans secured by inventories is quite different so far as credit techniques are concerned. Unlike warehouse receipts for staple commodities, the inventories of trade and manufacturing firms are not in a form convenient for collateral purposes. And, in contrast to receivables, inventories differ widely in physical form, and possession must remain with the company. As a consequence, several alternative collateral techniques have been developed for different types of situations. There are: (1) chattel mortgages, (2) field warehousing, and (3) continuous or floating liens.

*Chattel mortgages.* The chattel mortgage arrangement gives the lender a prior lien on particular items of tangible personal property. The mortgages must be related to clearly identifiable items of property; they must be recorded with the proper public authorities; and specific releases must be granted, perhaps under trust receipts, as items are sold. Because of the legal requirements, chattel mortgages are most adaptable to the financing of inventories consisting of a restricted number of items with relatively high unit values; the financing of auto dealers' new and used cars under so-called "floor plan" arrangements is a leading example. Chattel mortgages also are often used in agricultural loans against livestock. The main problems are to make sure that the legal technicalities are fulfilled and to check regularly that items held under chattel have not been sold without proper releases. Substitution of similar items voids the mortgage, and for that reason careful control of the property is required.

*Field warehousing.* In the collateral technique of field warehousing, an independent warehouse is established on the borrower's premises; warehouse receipts evidencing title are held by the bank, and releases are authorized as provided in a loan agreement. Although the device has certain complexities, it is less of a drawback than might be expected, because specialists in field warehousing arrangements are available. The field warehousing companies, whose staffs are qualified through experience to execute the numerous technical requirements, perform a very useful service. However, since servicing costs are considerable, the technique is economic only for relatively large loans. Since large borrowers usually can obtain unsecured credit, field warehouse arrangements are limited to special situations. Most common is a situation where a very large inventory must be stored on the premises of the borrower. The liquor and canning industries are examples of industries in which this technique is applicable.

*Continuous or floating liens.* Most versions of the Uniform Commercial Code provide for the use of continous (floating) liens on inventories under the same general procedures used for receivable assignments. All existing and after-acquired inventory can be brought under the assignment. It is necessary, of course, to allow the debtor to sell his finished products, and if the sale occurs in the ordinary course of business the lien does not follow the property as such. Instead, the lender automatically obtains a prior claim on the proceeds (cash or accounts receivable) of the sale. This claim, it may be noted, is senior to that obtained by the financer of accounts receivable alone. Under the legal rules imposed by the UCC, it is therefore prudent policy either to take a general and continuous lien on both inventory and receivables or to make absolutely sure that the debtor is precluded from pledging inventory elsewhere.

The problem of the combined continuous assignment is that the borrower may then expect that the total loan commitment should exceed 100 percent of receivables because of the additional collateral provided. Perhaps 70 percent of receivables and 50 percent of inventories would be a normal expectation. Several respondents indicated that commitments of these proportions were frequently considered. Therefore, if a receivable commitment alone of perhaps 70 percent to 80 percent of outstanding accounts provides adequate financing, the desirable policy may be only to obtain assurance that inventory cannot be pledged elsewhere. Combined assignments would be reserved for cases in which the total financing requirements might at times exceed the volume of receivables alone. But it should be noted that the liquidation value of inventories may vary widely. Standard raw materials or finished products with known markets (new autos) may well liquidate at book value or more, but work in process or specialized products may offer only scrap value in liquidation. For this reason, an inventory lien may possibly add substantial support to a loan, or such a loan may be de facto little more than an unsecured credit.

As indicated in Chapter 8, because of risk and servicing costs, rates on credits secured by receivable and inventory assignments carry a significant premium over the prime rate. Depending on competitive conditions, average balances and expectations, the size of the loan, and the financial condition of the borrower, the rate premium varied between 1 percent and 4 percent, with an average premium of about 2 percent indicated. If adequate policing procedures in the form of audits, legal filings, and other records are followed, it is doubtful whether modest-sized loans (less than $50,000) are profitable from an opportunity cost standpoint, even at a 4 percent premium over the prime rate. Therefore, a positive policy on small commitments must usually be justified on the basis of community service, social desirability, or future business expectations.

## Loans against Marketable Securities and Life Insurance

Loans secured by bonds, stocks, and cash values of life insurance are made both to individuals and corporations for a wide variety of purposes and for varying lengths of time. Their regular business purpose is to enable security dealers and underwriters to finance inventories of securities purchased for resale. But in addition, because most securities are readily hypothecated with a minimum of cost and inconvenience, they are often used to secure loans on terms more favorable than would otherwise be possible. For example, the rate might be lower, or financial statement requirements may be waived. Some banks even allow continuous borrowing under the assignment of adequate marketable collateral. Most, however, definitely discouraged the practice: such loans are difficult to justify under tight money conditions, they may end up in estates, and such credits violate the need to encourage sound financial planning. Some loans in this area may be highly sensitive in nature—e.g., credits extended to executives of important corporate customers to finance purchases of stock under option agreements or for personal investment. It is probable that most banks would prefer to avoid such commitments, but they may appear necessary to retain the corporate business, and realistically it is very difficult to impose stringent conditions, including repayment schedules, on such loans.

The policy issues on these loans tend to be less complex than on other types of secured loans because of the nature of the collateral, but two matters may be briefly considered: the discretionary loan values extended to various types of securities, and collateral control and supervision policies.

### Loan values of securities

The functional features relevant to the determination of appropriate loan value percentages are credit quality, marketability, and price volatility properties. These features would suggest that the maximum collateral value would be assigned to short-term government bonds, with appropriate reductions on other types of securities. In general, as Table 9–2 shows, this policy concept is followed on the standard classification of marketable securities.

Among bonds, respondent policies on loan values did not show significant variations between loans to individuals and loans to corporations per se. In view of the fairly homogeneous characteristics of these securities, this fact was not surprising. With respect to security dealers' credits, however, greater variations in policy emerged. Some would allow loans values no higher than for individuals, while others allowed security dealers significantly higher loan percentages. Traditionally security dealers have received preference, the rationale being that their loans are to

TABLE 9–2
COLLATERAL POLICIES: MARKETABLE SECURITY LOANS BY RESPONDENT BANKS

| Type of Security | Loan Percentage to Market Value (Median Response) | |
|---|---|---|
| | For Individuals and Corporations | For Security Dealers |
| Government bonds | 90 | 95 |
| Municipal bonds | 85 | 85 |
| Corporate bonds | 80 | 85 |
| Listed stocks | 60* | 75 |
| Unlisted stocks | 50* | 60 |
| Limited market stock† | | |
| Closely held shares | From "not acceptable" to 60 percent | |
| Investment letter stock | From "not acceptable" to 50 percent | |

* Described as the policy when Regulation U limits of Federal Reserve on margin requirements do not apply. Regulation U does not apply to loans made to brokers or dealers to carry inventories of securities.

† Range of acceptability.

finance securities inventories with a fairly rapid turnover and that consequently market exposure is of short duration. But the financial difficulties that a number of brokerage houses experienced in recent years has led some banks to structure these loans on a more conservative basis.

The loan value policies on marketable stocks require no special comment except to note that the percentages given in Table 9–2 are based on the assumption that the security portfolios are of average quality. Policies do provide for an evaluation of portfolio quality and volatility, and deviations from the indicated loan value percentages are allowable to reflect the conclusions of the evaluation. In this connection it is typical practice to require additional margin when the loan equals about 80 to 85 percent of the prevailing market prices. As margin "calls" involve both expense and public relations problems with customers, a suggested technique for setting loan values on stock portfolios is to examine their past price movements and to establish the original margin percentage at a point where price declines are unlikely to bring the portfolio value down to less than about 80 percent of the loan. For example, if a portfolio is currently priced at $100,000 and a decline of 20 percent appears to be a reasonable possibility, the loan value might be established at 80 percent of $80,000 (present price less 20 percent), or $64,000; the loan value of the total portfolio would thus become 64 percent.

Because of the wide divergence in reported policies, median loan values for stocks which are not traded in the public markets could not be determined in any meaningful sense. Therefore, for these securities, Table 9–2 shows the range of responses. Some banks take the view that only securities with a readily determinable and realizable value can be used to support credits because liquidation of limited market collateral might not only take an unreasonable length of time but also involve significant price concessions. Others, however, consider that even if immediate marketability is limited the ultimate values of many such securities may be considerable. In general, a policy to consider stocks with restricted marketability as only ancillary support for a loan would seem prudent. In other words, the credits should be justifiable without such collateral, but it may be taken to provide a moderate measure of ultimate protection. Undue reliance on such collateral has sometimes been shown, particularly in loans to finance personal acquisitions of companies, and some serious work-out situations have resulted from this practice.[6]

## Collateral control policies

On collateral control policies, the first issue is that of the desirability of maintaining concentration records. Such records show the total volume of credits secured by the securities of a given company. The purpose is to indicate the total credit exposure related to the securities of a given company and perhaps to discourage additional credits or require additional margin if the concentration seems excessive. According to one view, if adequate margins are required at all times, there is no need to incur the costs of maintaining concentration records; the other view holds that such records are desirable because they may show that the total collateral in some cases represents a major bloc that might be difficult to market, particularly on "thinly" traded over-the-counter issues. A pragmatic policy would be to maintain selective records on those stocks which are known to support substantial loans from time to time.

The next policy issue concerning collateral control concerns the frequency of collateral valuation. Unless computer support can be justified, frequent valuation may be a costly process, but the cost must be balanced against the desirability of assuring adequate margins at all times. Formal or informal concentration records may be of assistance in this connection by reducing the number of securities on which frequent pricing is considered necesary. A few banks had adopted the device of using a given point movement in the Dow-Jones industrial average to trigger the valuation of all common stock collateral. If the average de-

6. As an example, some banks were known to have made major loans to a series of partnerships, known as the Parsons Group, to buy controlling interests in a number of banks. The loans were secured by the bank stocks, and because of financial problems most ended up as work-out situations. One of the more common requests for loans against closely held stock is probably from officer/director shareholders of smaller correspondent banks who wish to increase their holdings of the common stocks of their banks, and the policy problems on such credits should be obvious.

clined forty points, say, from a previous valuation level, then all stock collateral had to be revalued and margin calls sent out if necessary. In the absence of such a decline, then monthly valuation might be required.

As a device for collateral supervision, some technique of this sort seems to have considerable merit. Firms in the securities industry tend to be highly levered as a consequence of needs to finance dealer inventories and customer margin positions. Reasonably close supervision of any large loan exposure in this area would therefore seem prudent.

## Endorsements and Subordinations

### Endorsements

For the purpose of policy evaluation, endorsements may be divided into two groups. First, there are guaranties obtained from parties without a direct financial interest in the affairs of the borrowers. Second are personal guaranties obtained from parent companies or individual owners of corporate entities. Because experience has indicated that difficult public relations problems can arise from enforcing guaranties of the first type, the trend has been against their use. However, there are occasions when strong sponsorship is offered to individuals or firms whose financial position would not justify bank accommodation. The sponsors may include friends, relatives, or suppliers; and if their financial position is strong, a guaranty should add considerably to the quality of the credit.

But even though such parties presumably understand their contingent liabilities, they may show considerable reluctance to fulfill the obligation, because they are not directly involved and may feel that the bank is invoking the guaranty as a substitute for a vigorous collection effort. If the outside endorser controls other business important to the bank, the difficulties may be compounded because action against the endorser may well result in the loss of the business. In general, therefore, the recommended policy is to avoid loans whenever there is a strong possibility that recourse to the endorser may be necessary. The following statement expresses this view:

> Endorsement or guaranties are not usually a good substitute for a sound credit position, except for nominal amounts. When taken, they should be supported by a financial statement of the endorser or guarantor which shows unquestioned responsibility for the amount involved; and, when appropriate, the endorser or guarantor should be made clearly aware of the fact that he ultimately may be called upon for payment.

Endorsements of the second type are often a means of eliminating the effect of the limited liability of corporations. They may be classified into two major categories. First, many large corporations have subsidiary or affiliated companies to conduct certain operations, but the major financial capacity rests in the parent. Credit commitments extended to such subsidiaries or affiliates would normally carry the guaranty of the parent, although for legal or operating reasons it could be desirable to record the subsidiary as the prime debtor.[7] Second, in closely held corporations, the general policy is to request personal endorsements of the principals and perhaps of their spouses. The following statement of one respondent bank indicates the policy orientation in these cases: "It depends on the financial strength of the particular company, but in most cases we would want the guaranty of the principals and their spouses."

The reasoning offered in support of this policy is that family corporations may be operated in such a way as to make the distinction between corporate and personal assets a legal fiction. Through changes in salary and possibly through dividend distributions, assets can be moved back and forth at the discretion of the owner-manager family; as a result, it is argued, the bank should extend its claim to the entire package of assets and income of the principals.

Brief mention might also be made of policies regarding government guaranties of certain types of credits. First, to implement

7. In the case of pure holding companies (including bank holding companies) it might appear that a guaranty of a loan to the parent company by the major profitable subsidiary might be desirable. The courts have held that such guaranties may be unenforceable unless the subsidiary clearly derives a "direct and substantial benefit" from the loan. (D. J. Yellon, "Problem Loans in the '70s; Some Legal Problems in Drafting and Collection," *Journal of Commercial Bank Lending* 57 [Apr. 1975]: 7–8.)

foreign policy and trade objectives, government guaranties are available on certain international credits, but these will be considered in a subsequent section on international operations. Second, to implement agricultural programs, government guaranties on credits to finance the storage of grains and other agricultural commodities are routine; large urban banks, however, do not have a significant volume of such loans.

Third and most important to urban banks, government guaranties are available through the Small Business Administration (SBA) and, in some cases, on inner-city development projects. Policies on SBA loans vary widely, but unless assistance to minority groups was involved, respondents tended to avoid credits requiring SBA guaranties. The reasons given were the excessive time involved in structuring the loans considering their small size, and the SBA reluctance to terminate credits that are in serious difficulty.

On the other hand, it is salutary to note that a positive approach toward inner-city development loans was evidenced by most respondent banks, even though the policy can be seriously questioned from an optimal earnings standpoint. As indicated in Chapter 1, a strong concern with the quality of life in the city may be so vital to the long-term progress of a bank that it outweighs the near-term goal of maximization of earnings.

## Subordinations

In addition to, or perhaps in lieu of, personal guaranties on credits to closely held companies, owner-managers may be required to defer payment of any debt owed by the company to themselves, associates, or family until any bank loans are completely repaid. Such a requirement is kown as a subordination agreement. As shown by Table 9–3, policies toward subordination vary, although part of the variation may arise because a few of the respondent banks seldom encounter situations in which it seems desirable. One respondent made the following observation: "Sometimes we ask for subordinations, and this depends on the financial strength of the company. The longer the term of the loan, the more likelihood there is that subordination would be requested."

TABLE 9-3
SUBORDINATION POLICIES OF RESPONDENT BANKS

| FREQUENCY OF SUBORDINATION | TYPE OF CREDIT | | | | |
|---|---|---|---|---|---|
| | TERM | REVOLVING | WORKING CAPITAL | TRANSACTION LOANS | LINES |
| Regularly | 4 | 4 | 5 | 2 | . . . |
| Sometimes | 3 | 3 | 2 | 5 | 4 |
| Rarely* | 1 | 1 | 1 | 1 | 4 |

* It is probable that the respondent stating that subordinations are only rarely required intended to suggest that loans are only infrequently made to small, closely held companies.

In a given situation, the risk will increase as maturity is extended. Moreover, term, revolving, or working capital commitments are often made to relieve financial pressures or to finance expansion programs of some magnitude. Under these conditions it seems inconsistent to allow diversions of cash flows to repay debt owed to the principals or their associates. Therefore, as indicated by the majority of respondents, it is logical policy to require subordinations on long-term credits, almost as a matter of course, with exceptions granted in particular cases on the basis of superior financial standing or a strong collateral position. In the case of transaction loans or lines, in which the relationship on any given advance is presumably short lived, it would seem logical to require subordinations only when the risk position otherwise would seem excessive.

# 3

# RETAIL LOANS

# X

# CONSUMER LOAN POLICIES

## Retail Banking vs. Wholesale Banking

As noted earlier, wholesale banking in large banks is largely conducted through individual contacts between financial specialists—loan officers on the one hand and corporate financial officers on the other. Credits are structured to accommodate the unique financial requirements of borrowers in the context of the specific customer relationship along with an appraisal of the risk factors related to each individual credit. Except where special security interests are deemed necessary, physical servicing of loans is minimal and pricing policies are competetively structured in relation to the prime rate. Floating rates in recent years have dominated this section of the asset portfolio.

In contrast, retail banking is largely concerned with offering deposit and credit services to a large number of individuals on a relatively standardized basis. Deposit instruments are designed to satisfy various needs of these customers, and each customer elects from a standardized set of deposit options the instrument or mix of instruments that seems appropriate for his/her personal circumstances. Individual negotiations on rates are not allowed except in a few instances of very wealthy individuals who may purchase CDs in denominations of $100,000 or more on a negotiated basis. In the retail markets, credit services consist of instalment loan programs to finance consumer expenditures for almost any purpose and mortgage programs to finance housing purchases.[1] A very large proportion of the loans are secured and are repaid on a monthly amortization program—over perhaps two to four years for instalment loans, and twenty to thirty years for mortgages.

1. Because there is a close similarity, credit card programs are included in the instalment loan category, although the mechanics of the operation are somewhat different.

Consequently physical servicing of loans becomes a significant activity, and costs of such servicing per loan are relatively fixed, regardless of its size.

For the most part, pricing terms are on a standardized, fixed-rate basis which is designed to cover promotional and servicing costs, anticipated loan losses, and a reasonable spread over the estimated average cost of money. In the instalment area, loan prices tend to remain constant despite variations in interest rates: indeed many rates here are subject to statutory control. Mortgage rates, however, do vary in accordance with movements in long-term interest rates. But as a significant proportion of deposit money costs reflect short-term rates which are considerably more volatile, marginal cost spreads decrease during tight money periods on both instalment loans and mortgages and increase during periods of credit ease. Finally, in the retail banking markets a large proportion of the customers have little or no personal contact with officers of the bank, although of course they may be known to certain clerical employees (tellers) if they regularly visit a certain office of the bank to conduct deposit and withdrawal transactions.[2]

Retail banking has enjoyed a significant growth over the past several decades. In fact, given the propensity of corporations to minimize deposit balances, most large banks have established active retail banking programs, although where branching is restricted or prohibited (Illinois) the development of such programs is more difficult. The significant increase of the median monetary income of family units over a period of years and the present acceptance of consumer debt as a normal event, even in affluent families, have, of course, contributed to the remarkable growth in retail banking services.

## Consumer Credit: Growth and Outlook

Table 10–1 shows the growth in consumer loans extended by commercial banks between 1950 and 1976. Until perhaps 1965,

2. Promotion of retail banking services is conducted in large part through mass media advertising programs, including the use of radio, television, and newspapers. Establishing convenient branch locations as permitted by law is also an important factor in developing penetration of retail banking markets.

TABLE 10–1

INSTALMENT CREDIT HELD BY COMMERCIAL BANKS, SELECTED YEARS

(In $ Billions)

| YEAR-END | AUTOMOBILE | | MOBILE HOME* | HOME REPAIR AND MODERNIZATION | CREDIT CARDS† | PERSONAL LOANS‡ | OTHER | TOTAL |
|---|---|---|---|---|---|---|---|---|
| | INDIRECT | DIRECT | | | | | | |
| 1950 | 1.2 | 1.3 | ... | 0.8 | ... | 1.0 | 1.4 | 5.7 |
| 1955 | 3.2 | 2.1 | ... | 1.3 | ... | 1.9 | 2.0 | 10.5 |
| 1960 | 5.3 | 2.8 | ... | 2.2 | ... | 3.6 | 2.7 | 16.6 |
| 1965 | 10.2 | 5.6 | ... | 2.6 | ... | 6.3 | 4.2 | 28.9 |
| 1969 | 13.1 | 7.8 | ... | 3.0 | ... | 9.8 | 8.7 | 42.4 |
| 1970 | 12.9 | 7.9 | ... | 3.1 | 3.8 | 10.6 | 7.1 | 45.4 |
| 1971 | 12.9 | 7.9 | 4.4 | 3.2 | 4.4 | 11.5 | 6.9 | 51.2 |
| 1972 | 16.3 | 10.8 | 5.8 | 3.5 | 3.5 | 12.9 | 5.2 | 59.8 |
| 1973 | 19.0 | 12.5 | 8.3 | 4.1 | 6.8 | 15.1 | 6.1 | 71.9 |
| 1974 | 18.7 | 12.3 | 9.0 | 4.7 | 8.2 | 16.6 | 6.3 | 75.8 |
| 1975 | 17.6 | 12.6 | 8.4 | 4.8 | 9.1 | 16.9 | 6.3 | 75.7 |
| 1976§ | 19.4 | 15.0 | 8.4 | 5.3 | 9.9 | 18.2 | 6.8 | 83.0 |

Source: Federal Reserve Bulletins.

* Mobile home credit not reported separately until 1971.

† Not reported separately until 1970.

‡ Includes check credit plans which averaged about $3.0 billions in outstandings between 1972–76.

§ As of end of August, 1976.

such credit composed a very minor proportion of the total loan portfolios of large banks, and automobile financing represented over half of the total outstandings as recently as 1969. In the past decade, however, many banks have vigorously promoted new consumer credit products, primarily credit card programs. In addition, the growth of the mobile home industry provided a significant demand for credit. As a consequence, although automobile financing still represents the largest single source of consumer credit, as a proportion of the total it has diminished. Given the probable development of electronic transfer systems wherein credit card usage is facilitated, it seems entirely possible that this form of consumer credit will enjoy an above-average growth rate in the future.

However, the financing of durable goods, primarily automobiles, may have a sluggish average growth rate in the future for three reasons. First, the relative importance of consumer expenditures for these products has been declining. Automobile markets, given the problems primarily associated with the cost and availability of petroleum, have an uncertain long-term outlook. Moreover, the cyclical fluctuations in this area have become more pronounced.

Second, in recent years rate spreads have become generally less favorable on instalment loans than in the 1950–68 period. Interest rates have shown a significant upward trend since about 1968, whereas instalment loan rates have been relatively flat, largely because of statutory controls. In fact, in 1974 rates on some types of deposits (wholesale CDs) exceeded the gross rates available on most auto loans for the first time. Although the situation changed in 1975–76, if interest rates resume their upward secular trend, returns on such financing may become nonoptimal unless statutory limits are modified. As political sentiments against higher consumer credit rates seem strong, such modifications may be difficult to obtain.

Finally, although their ultimate effects remain highly conjectural, regulations and statutes with the presumed objective of protecting consumer interests have proliferated in recent years. While their aims may be salutary, their result may be a significant increase in screening problems and litigation in some consumer credit sectors. It is possible that cost increases and administrative problems consequent to compliance may induce some banks to reexamine their retail operations. The statutes and regulations include: (1) The "Truth in Lending" Act passed in 1969, administered by the Federal Reserve under Regulation Z; (2) the "Federal Fair Credit Reporting" Act of 1970; (3) restrictions on credit card issuance in 1970; (4) the Uniform Consumer Credit Code now in effect in several states; (5) the "Equal Credit Opportunity" Act of 1974; and (6) the elimination of the "holder in due course" doctrine by a Federal Trade Commission regulation in 1976.

The possible effects of some of these statutes and regulations on consumer credit policies will be considered briefly for the related credit sectors. In general, as of late 1976, most large banks appear to have adjusted their policies to the new legal requirements; indeed it is the small banks, who often cannot afford specialists in the various consumer credit areas, that may find compliance with the maze of statutes and regulations very difficult.

## Consumer Loans: Structure and Acquisition

In order to delineate the policy issues related to consumer credit, the alternative options in acquiring and structuring loans to individuals should be indicated. First, it is possible to structure them as commercial transaction loans. In this case the individual merely signs a note for the amount loaned and agrees to repay the entire amount at the end of the prescribed period. Like commercial loans, these single-payment advances may be secured by the pledge of specific collateral or they may be extended on an unsecured basis. The only difference is that the loans are for personal expenditures rather than for financing business needs. Except, perhaps, for a few purely wholesale banks in the major money market centers, banks have always extended loans of this type to deposit customers—although these loans have never been an important outlet for bank funds. No special policy issues are involved in these loans; it might be noted that collateral policies on these credits were considered in Chapter 9.

The second structural form represents single-purpose loans to individual borowers wherein there is repayment of principal and interest in regular instalments, usually monthly. The purpose may be to acquire consumer durables or to finance some special expenditure, such as for travel, education, or medical services. Many of these loans, particularly automobile loans, are secured by chattel mortgages against the goods financed; and policy issues with respect to collateral values consequently emerge.

Besides the amortization feature, the method of computing charges on such loans differs materially from that used on single-payment loans. For consumer instalment loans, the so-called add-on method is standard practice. This term means that the stated rate is applied against the original amount of the loan for the entire period, rather than against the unpaid balance. The result is that the effective interest rate is roughly double the indicated rate on the original amount. To illustrate: If a $100 loan for one year is made at an "add-on" 4 percent rate, the effective rate will be about 8 percent, because $4 interest will be charged (4 percent of $100 for the entire year) although the average loan balance for the year, assuming complete amortization of the principal over the period of the loan, will be about $50. On instalment loans, the practice is to quote rates in terms of so much per hundred dollars of loan per year. For example, on an automobile loan the quoted rate may be "$5 per hundred."[3] The total charges on a $1,000 car loan for two years would thus be $5 times 10 times 2, or $100; the approximate average outstanding balance on this loan over the two-year period would be $500, and the effective simple interest rate about 10 percent. Because of the method of computing the charges, the gross return on instalment loans is usually higher than on other types. But, as will be shown below, servicing costs absorb a much larger portion of the gross return on these loans than on most commercial loans. Therefore the net return advantage is considerably less than a comparison of gross rates alone would suggest.

While the structure is the same, most large consumer credit operations acquire a high proportion of their instalment loans by "purchasing" loans technically made by dealers selling the prod-

3. Under the Truth in Lending Act, the borrower must be informed of the simple interest equivalent of the add-on rate, but the main promotion and comparison is still based on a percentage per hundred of various loan categories.

ucts or services to be financed. The customer makes application for a loan to the dealer, and the dealer in turn sells the loan to the bank. Dealer-originated loans are classified as "indirect credits," and in the typical instance there is no personal contact with the borrower, at any time. Many of the unique features of a consumer loan operation arise in connection with indirect loans. Policies in this area include a set of arrangements with dealers as part of the lending process.

Credit card operations have elements of both the direct and indirect formats. The card is issued to holders and each credit is separately evaluated, but the bank negotiates with individual merchants on the terms of extending credit under the card. Returns to the bank take the form of a discount applied against the original purchase and a charge against the holder on the balance outstanding after a specified period, usually 30 days. Finally, consumer credit is also extended under personal lines of credit; but, this form of credit occupies only a minor role in most banks.

## Consumer Credit: Operational Concepts

A volume consumer loan operation is conducted like an assembly line in an automobile factory. The bank must be prepared to receive several hundred loan applications a day from largely unknown individuals, to render a decision on the application within an hour or so, and to service up to a hundred thousand or more loans on a monthly payment basis. The total quantity of physical servicing is thus quite important, and cost control through efficient servicing methods plays a highly important part in the returns generated on the portfolio.

### Universe approach

On consumer loans, the statistical principles of probability applied to a large and homogeneous universe tend to control the approach to risk exposure. In a large universe of such loans there is a statistical certainty of some losses, which are regarded as part of the normal operating cost of the operation. Portfolio quality is measured by the computation of certain portfolio performance ratios; the most common are deliquency amounts stratified by time periods (30, 60, 90 days) as a percentage of outstandings, and monthly losses as a percentage of total monthly payments (liquidation) on various categories of loans. The efficiency of the credit-screening process is then judged by the degree to which the loss and delinquency ratios are maintained within tolerable limits as measured against probability expectations. Control is exercised through regular management reviews of the pertinent data. For example, excessively low delinquency and loss ratios may be evidence of unduly stringent screening in some instances; and credit authorization standards can be liberalized accordingly.

## Credit control

Table 10–2 shows the nature of a monthly report submitted to management on the status of the instalment loan portfolio. In general, it is expected that total delinquencies will average about 2 percent during prosperous periods and perhaps 3 percent during recessions. In this instance only the personal loan and collateral loan categories seemed to represent a potential problem, and because 30-day delinquencies are regarded as less serious, the problem appeared minimal. But trends should be carefully reviewed, and, if unfavorable, possible revision in screening standards considered. In the example, the trends were favorable beause the immediate past had represented a recession period. Although not shown in Table 10–2, the ratio of monthly charge-offs to total payments (liquidation) is also monitored to evaluate performance. The targets for this ratio, based on empirical experience, are that 1 percent or less is good, between 1 percent and 1.25 percent is acceptable, but a ratio of over 1.25 percent for any extended period of time suggests that a review of credit standards might be advisable.

Because credit losses are an inherent part of the operation, it is sometimes alleged that consumer loans are, by nature, of lower quality than commercial loans. In fact, however, the consumer loan portfolio considered as a universe may have less risk than the commercial loan portfolio. Each individual consumer loan may indeed entail more risk than the great majority of business credits; but a default on one or two large loans in the latter category may

TABLE 10–2
UNIVERSE DELINQUENCY ANALYSIS OF INSTALMENT LOANS
(Management Report, January 1976)

| Type | Number | Amount | Average Loan Amount* | Delinquency Percentage | | | | Total | |
|---|---|---|---|---|---|---|---|---|---|
| | | | | 30-Day | 60-Day | 90- or Over | Total | Last Month | Same Month 1975 |
| Indirect Auto | 12,369 | $26,394,000 | $2,134 | 1.18 | .21 | .19 | 1.57 | 1.91 | 2.57 |
| Direct Auto | 4,912 | 9,173,000 | 1,867 | .62 | .17 | .15 | .93 | 1.31 | 1.58 |
| F.H.A. Title I | 2,598 | 4,893,000 | 1,883 | .64 | .25 | .18 | 1.07 | 1.17 | 2.12 |
| Recreational Items | 1,663 | 5,328,000 | 3,204 | .54 | .09 | .18 | .81 | 1.67 | 2.16 |
| Furniture and Appliance | 1,555 | 556,000 | 357 | .66 | .30 | .35 | 1.31 | 2.42 | 4.18 |
| Personal Loans | 4,904 | 4,919,000 | 1,003 | 1.16 | .31 | .80 | 2.27 | 2.45 | 2.72 |
| Collateral Loans | 2,745 | 5,366,000 | 1,934 | 2.02 | .49 | .58 | 3.09 | 2.76 | 3.23 |
| Total | 30,746 | $56,629,000 | | | | | | | |

* Represents average balance currently outstanding on loans in each category and not the average original amount.

have serious results, while a hundred or so chargeoffs in the consumer area may represent a very minor proportion of the total outstandings and merely bear out probability expectations.

A consumer loan operation may be viewed as the competitive mass merchandising of a credit service package consisting of three elements: (1) the amount of financing charges; (2) efficient customer service through prompt approvals, liberal terms, and reasonable collection methods; and (3) special inducements extended to the volume dealers. These inducements usually include some combination of the following policies: to accept a fair proportion of high-risk credits, to finance inventories through floor plan loans, to limit dealer liability on the paper generated, and perhaps to grant rebates of part of the financing charges.[4]

## Consumer Credit Policies: Profitability Factors

As Table 10–1 shows, about 50 percent of the total instalment credit extended by commercial banks has consisted of loans to finance the acquisition of new and used automobiles, although in recent years the proportion has declined somewhat, largely because of the introduction of bank credit cards. The reason for the emphasis on auto loans is very persuasive: earnings tend to be greater even though the rates charged tend to be less. This paradox can be explained by the relative size of the loans in the various categories and the substantial overhead costs incurred in processing and servicing loans regardless of size. For example, it has been estimated that fixed costs amount to between $20 and $30 on every consummated loan. On a $200 credit for two years, a rate of $10 per hundred or more would therefore be required in order to break even. For this reason, instalment loans of less than about $300–500 are not attractive, despite rates ranging from $10 to $15 per hundred.[5]

4. E. B. Rdgeway, Jr., "Consumer Instalment Credit," *Robert Morris Associates Bulletin* 38 (Mar. 1956): 240–41.

5. This conclusion is supported by the fact that the majority of the respondent banks did not make any indirect appliance loans, on which average loan size tends to be less than $500. A detailed study of costs and yields on instalment loans supported this policy. W. C. Gallups, "Installment Lending by Commercial Banks: A Cost and Yield Analysis" (unpublished dissertation, University of Michigan, 1968), p. 226.

This point illustrates an important element in the composition of the total charges on a consumer loan; a large proportion can be properly considered a means of covering processing and servicing costs rather than an interest charge related to the price of money as such. As a policy matter, heavy servicing costs induce banks to discourage small loans, although there is the view that such loans may have promotional benefits, particularly if made on a direct basis, by introducing customers to the use of the instalment credit facilities of the bank.

From an earnings standpoint, there is reason to encourage the largest possible loans with maturities extended for two years or more. On the other hand, from the standpoint of risk control, the natural tendency is to reduce the size of loan requests and to provide for a rapid pay-out if possible. But because the individual risk appraisal is subordinated to a universe risk approach and because the fixed processing and servicing costs are substantial, the appropriate policy target in a consumer credit operation might be to maximize the number of loans of optimum size, perhaps between $3,000 and $5,000 with average maturities of perhaps twenty-four to thirty-six months. This means encouraging increases on requests for loans for moderate amounts and avoiding short maturities of a year or less. For example, if an application for $400 for vacation expenses shows evidence of credit extended by other institutions, then so long as the risk is within reasonable limits a consolidation of all new and existing credit into one larger loan with a maturity of about two years should probably be recommended.

### Types of loans

Table 10–3 shows the frequency of instalment loans by purpose categories for the respondent banks and also the estimated percentage of consumer credit outstanding by major programs.[6] Because they are relatively large and demand is repetitive in nature, auto and unsecured personal loans were considered frequently by all the banks. Although most reported that policies

6. Credit cards and personal lines of credit are not instalment loans as such but give multipurpose credit to consumers up to certain limits as explained later in this chapter.

TABLE 10–3

CONSUMER CREDIT POLICIES: LOAN UNIVERSE

(Respondent Banks)

| Purpose of Loans | Frequency | | | |
|---|---|---|---|---|
| | Frequently | Sometimes | Rarely | Never |
| New and used auto | 8 | . . . | . . . | . . . |
| F.H.A. Title 1 (home improvement) | 5 | . . . | 1 | 2 |
| Home improvement (non-F.H.A.) | 5 | 3 | . . . | . . . |
| Furniture and appliances | 3 | 3 | 2 | . . . |
| Unsecured personal loans | 8 | . . . | . . . | . . . |
| Boats | 5 | 2 | 1 | . . . |

PERCENTAGE OF OUTSTANDING LOANS

| | Range of Responses and (Mean) | | | |
|---|---|---|---|---|
| | 1971 | | 1975 | |
| Credit card | 0–65 | (24) | 7–84 | (33) |
| Auto loans | 12–56 | (37) | 2–44 | (33) |
| Other instalment loans | 20–55 | (36) | 14–47 | (36) |
| Personal lines of credit | 0–6 | (3) | 0–7 | (3) |

still permitted home improvement loans, which also tend to be of large amounts, difficulties with policing dealers and limits on FHA rates have led some to reduce emphasis in this area. Because of nonoptimal size, furniture and appliance loans were not promoted in most banks. Programs to finance acquisition of pleasure boats had become significant in the majority, although some still considered them exceptional.

The data clearly indicate that credit card programs have become increasingly important in consumer credit operations. In fact, one respondent indicated that over 80 percent of its outstandings represented credit card usage and two others showed 50 percent or more of outstandings in this area. However, a sharp division of promotional policy on credit cards still remained as of 1976; half of the respondents indicated that less than 13 percent of outstandings represented credit cards while the other half showed 35 percent or more in this category. Although still the single largest source of instalment loans, auto credits had declined in relative importance, and personal lines of credit remained at insignificant levels.

## Terms of Specific-Purpose Loans (Autos)

A large proportion of specific-purpose loans are made to acquire cars; discussion of these credits will be limited to direct and indirect auto loans. Table 10–4 shows the policy parameters on terms offered by the respondent banks. With the exception of maximum maturity limits, the data suggest that terms are somewhat more liberal on dealer-originated credit (indirect) than on direct loans. However, although not shown in the data, a few banks offered a range of rates to direct borrowers. Conceptually, rate differentials based on credit quality and perhaps deposit relationships would seem appropriate policy. The drawback is that in a mass processing operation, where decisions must be rapid, productivity is fostered by limiting the number of decision variables, and from this standpoint standardized rates are clearly preferable.

In general, consumer loan rates advanced only modestly between 1972 and 1976 despite the large increase in interest rates overall during this period. Statutory limits were one reason for this relative insensitivity, but in addition it is probable that

TABLE 10–4
POLICY PARAMETERS ON NEW AUTO LOANS
(Respondent Banks)

| Policy Feature | Direct | | Indirect | |
|---|---|---|---|---|
| | Range | Median | Range | Median |
| Average maturity (Original in months) | 26–36 | 34 | 28–38 | 36 |
| Maximum maturity (in months) | 36–48 | 42 | 42–48 | 48 |
| Processing time | 1 hr. to 5 days | 24 hrs. | 1 hr. to 2 days | 3 hrs. |
| Percentage rates* | | | | |
| 1972 | 9.75–12.00 | 10.2 | 8.86–12.00 | 9.3 |
| 1974 | 9.75–12.00 | 10.5 | 9.75–13.00 | 10.2 |
| 1976 | 10.64–12.83 | 11.5 | 10.20–12.83 | 12.08 |

* Based on simple interest equivalent of add-on rate where first payment occurs after 30 days.

intense competition for these loans between banks, finance companies (including the large captive finance companies of General Motors and Ford), and credit unions probably restricted rate increases.

### Maturity limits

The major change in policies over the past several years has been an extension of the maximum maturity limits from 36 months to 48 months. The major captive finance companies initiated the move during the 1975 recession, and although some banks were reluctant to follow, the majority apparently have done so. The reason for the reluctance was the fact that on 48-month loans, annual amortization of principal may be less than annual depreciation.[7] The consequence is that collateral values become (after a year or so) less than the loan obligations and exposure to higher loss rates results.

On the other hand, the major incentive for the change was probably that with the extended limits monthly payments could be held down despite a sharp escalation in auto prices, and as a consequence, consumer demand for new cars (and loans) increased. In addition, given the fact that origination and servicing costs are relatively fixed, larger loans over some extended time periods yield higher rates of return. The trade-off results on the 48-month programs have yet to be tested, but if it is recognized that credit standards on such loans must be higher than on others, then the net results may well be favorable from a profitability standpoint.

### Response time

In the retail credit markets, liberal policies are considered necessary to implement a vigorous marketing strategy. Borrowers and dealers of course desire to finance the largest possible proportion of the total price over an extended period and to obtain answers

7. On a $3,000 loan for 36 months at a 7 percent add-on rate, the principal is reduced by $1,100 the first year; on the same loan for 48 months the reduction is $900 or 18 percent less per year. The monthly payments decrease from $121 to $96.

on loan requests as soon as possible. Dealers in particular demand rapid service, because they would like to consummate transactions as soon as a customer reaches a positive decision and before he leaves the premises. Therefore, if the policy objective is to obtain a high volume and penetration of these markets, then rapid decisions on applications are imperative. From the responses on processing time shown in Table 10–4, it can be inferred that some have decided essentially to remain outside the indirect dealer market. The same respondent that reported only 2 percent of outstanding consumer credit in auto loans (as shown in Table 10–3) also indicated an average processing time of several days on applications. In contrast, those banks reporting average processing time of an hour or so indicated that indirect auto loans were a large percentage of the total portfolio.

### Dealer relations

The reason for the moderately more liberal terms on indirect than on direct credits is that volume auto dealers have been in a strong negotiating position with respect to their financing sources. Both finance companies (including captive finance companies) and banks have actively solicited their business, and as a result, volume auto dealers have been in a position to demand and obtain competitive concessions on credit terms. In fact, additional concessions on terms beyond those shown in Table 10–4 also have been frequently obtained. These include rebates of part of the charges on the loans and acceptance of a reasonable proportion of high-risk paper that would be rejected on direct applications.[8]

Indirect loans therefore give rise to additional policy problems involving dealer relations, and these issues are of recurring concern to bank managements. First, there is the basic issue of whether net returns after losses and rebates justify active continuance of dealer programs. As noted above, rates on auto loans have increased less rapidly than interest rates generally. After

8. Banks with extensive dealer programs report that they expect delinquencies on indirect loans to be almost twice as high as on direct loans. These banks also reported that between 50 and 60 percent of auto loans were obtained through dealers. All respondent banks reported that they offered dealer rebates on indirect loans.

processing and servicing costs, credit losses, and dealer rebates have been allocated to a $6 per hundred rate (shown as the average prevailing level in Table 10–4), average net returns might equal about 8 to 9 percent on the funds committed to this area. Because returns on alternative commitments, such as municipals, have sometimes exceeded this level, there has been reason to question dealer programs.

The situation has resulted in a policy dilemma. A policy to phase out indirect auto credits could be justified only on the grounds that the probabilities heavily favor a continuance of historically high interest rates. But once such credits have been phased out, a reversal in policy would be extremely difficult because dealers expect consistency in policy from their financing sources and tend to discriminate against a source with an inconsistent record. The wide difference between respondent banks with respect to terms on these loans probably represents contrasting resolutions of the issue. Some have established terms which in essence have phased out indirect loan programs while others have actually liberalized terms despite higher average levels of interest rates and consequently lower yield spreads between money costs and consumer loan rates.

Many volume auto dealers have, moreover, come to expect significant amounts of additional credit support as a consequence of competition for their paper. Such support includes floor plan loans at the prime rate (despite significant servicing costs), financing of leasing operations—again at preferred rates— and favorable terms on mortgage and term loans. While the earnings of most dealers are adequate, many auto dealers operate with a heavy debt in relation to net worth. The bank's total credit risk exposure may thus reach questionable levels, because it is difficult to enforce normal credit standards on loan requests from volume dealers and still remain in a preferred position to obtain their retail paper. This factor lends additional support for a policy of recurrently analyzing dealers' total credit packages and terminating a given package if it involves either excessive risk or inadequate returns. While evidence is fragmentary, terminations have apparently been infrequent. There is therefore some reason to question prevailing policy on dealer credit reviews.

A further development in 1976 might well lead to closer monitoring of dealer operations than in the past. The Federal Trade Commission issued a regulation that effectively eliminated the traditional "holder in due course" doctrine on consumer loan instruments. Under the holder in due course doctrine, a bank had the legal right to collect on paper purchased from dealers, even though the goods or services provided may have been subject to controversy as to quality and performance.[9] Legally, therefore, banks were not required to investigate dealers' marketing and service standards, although the established policy has been to terminate relations with clearly unethical dealers.[10] However, there historically have been certain problem areas in this connection. Home improvement credits might be singled out for special mention; there have been recurrent allegations that some financial institutions (not necessarily banks) have bought paper from transient dealers who performed poor quality work, disappeared from the scene, and left consumers responsible for payment because of the holder in due course doctrine.

Legal changes which enable the consumer to impose a defense of substandard performance should increase the incentive to monitor and eliminate problem dealers. From a public policy standpoint, such a change would seem desirable, even though it would increase the burden on banks to maintain a more continuous review of dealer standards than has been necessary in the past. The proposed Uniform Consumer Credit Code, which has been adopted by several states and is pending in others, gives

9. In certain jurisdictions, courts have denied due course status where evidence indicates that the financer participated in the transaction at the outset in some way, and the courts have liberally construed facts to support such evidence. One decision included the following statement: "In this day of demonstrated need for emphasis upon consumer protection and truth in lending, special consideration must be given to preventing the misuse of negotiable instruments to deprive instalment purchasers of legitimate defenses." Jones v. Approved Bankcredit Corp., Supreme Court of Delaware (1969), as quoted in the *Banking Law Journal*, Oct. 1970, p. 948.

10. A survey of reactions to the FTC regulation produced the following statement: "Some bank and finance company executives emphasized that their leverage over the vendor protects them from most of the possible problems the new FTC rule might cause. . . . 'We can cut them off, stop accepting their paper for further financing if customers consistently complain.' " On the other side, some evidenced concern that new dealers without a track record might find it difficult to arrange financing sources. (*Wall Street Journal*, May 5, 1976, p. 3.)

statutory relief from the holder-in-due-course doctrine. A lawyer, specializing in bank matters, commented as follows on the possible effects of this development:

> The theory of the Code appears to be that financing institutions purchasing dealer paper are in a better position to prevent the sale of shoddy goods or services than the consumer who has normally entered into only a single isolated transaction with the seller. This means, of course, that banks will have to be more careful and selective in choosing the dealers with whom they do business. They should take steps to protect themselves, by, for example, establishing higher dealer reserves or purchasing more paper on a recourse basis.[11]

But in addition, the possibility that some instalment buyers might attempt to avoid payment by spurious claims of product defects suggests that banks may be required to screen applicants more carefully for character and performance on past debt contracts.

## Credit Card Policies

Although a few banks introduced local credit card plans many years ago, the major impetus to their development came with the introduction of regional, national, and even international plans in the late sixties. Between 1969 and 1976, outstanding under credit card plans more than tripled from $2.3 billion to $9.1 billion; and while this rate of growth is not likely to be sustainable, outstandings will probably more than double during the next decade.

The attraction of widely accepted national bank credit cards lies in their convenience. Consumers can make a wide variety of purchases both in this country and abroad and receive one monthly bill covering everything purchased under the card. The advantage to merchants is that they can make credit sales without operating a credit system to investigate, bill, and follow up on collections. Some large retail units with well-established credit or card systems, including large department stores, oil companies,

11. W. E. Murane, "The Impact of the Uniform Consumer Credit Code on the Banking Industry," *Banking Law Journal* 90, No. 4, (Apr. 1973): 275.

and airlines, were reluctant to enter bank card programs. But as bank cards have now been issued on an extensive scale, even large merchants have found it increasingly necessary to accept them in order to remain competitive in their markets.[12]

Similarly, as a greater proportion of customers have found the convenience of credit cards attractive, even banks that are primarily wholesale in nature have found it expedient to enter the area. As recently as 1971 half the respondent banks did not have a credit card program, but by 1976 all had joined one of the two national programs. Moreover, if electronic transfer systems (ETS) partially replace checks as the payment mechanism in future years, the nationwide and even international computer linkages of the credit card programs may well become the major ETS implementation means.

The two major bank card programs, Mastercharge and BankAmericard, have similar features. Banks pay a flat charge plus a small fee on outstandings, usually one-fourth of 1 percent, to the national sponsors in return for their promotional activities and for usage of nationwide computer credit records and transfer facilities. Besides promotion in national media, participating banks usually conduct marketing programs on the local level. These programs are directed both at attracting prospective card holders and persuading merchants to accept the cards for credit sales.[13] The two aspects are interrelated, however, because card holders are attracted to widespread merchant acceptance and vice versa.

*Customer solicitation.* To induce merchants to accept the cards, and to cover the substantial fixed costs involved in promotion and operations, policies must be directed toward achieving a consider-

12. As of 1976, most airlines would accept the major national credit cards; some large retailing chains, Kresge for example, had terminated their own credit programs and moved entirely to making credit sales through the use of the national credit cards.

13. Some major banks under franchising agreements are also involved in licensing a program to other banks in specified geographical regions. A fee is obtained from licensees, varying in amount according to the services performed for each licensee; in addition the card becomes more attractive to both cardholders and merchants as it achieves greater penetration into contiguous regions. It is legally possible for banks to offer both Mastercharge and BankAmericard to their customers, but prevailing policy is to concentrate on one or the other.

able number of active card holders. At one time mass mailings of unsolicited cards were used to obtain the initial thrust, but fraud and credit losses were considerable in some cases, and widespread complaints from customers led to a statutory ban on this procedure. Active solicitation by direct mail and telephone, of both bank customers and noncustomers, supplemented by mass media advertising is now the prevailing means of obtaining applications for cards.

*Credit screening.* Policies on screening applicants also present problems. Because control techniques are only partially effective in limiting credit usage, a convincing case can be made that credit card applicants should be screened more closely than applicants for specific instalment loans. On the other hand, close screening may make it difficult to achieve target goals for both the number of card holders and the amount of dollar outstandings. Resolution of this policy tradeoff has been difficult. Some banks have incurred continued credit losses of 2 percent or more of liquidations. At this loss rate, the program usually produces little if any profit to the bank. Extensive promotional programs combined with a high rejection rate seem to be the only feasible means of resolving the tradeoff. The objective is to obtain maximum market penetration of good credit risks. In this connection, the market is not necessarily identical with that of instalment loans. A number of consumers find the convenience of credit cards very desirable, but at the same time these individuals may have sufficient resources to finance single purchase items even of fairly large amounts.[14]

*Credit limits.* Table 10–5 shows the credit and rate policies of the respondent banks' credit card programs. Two forms of credit limits are imposed. First, total credit outstanding under a given card at a given time is subject to restriction. The responses indicated that limits of $300–$500 may be imposed on some customers but strong customers may obtain maximum credit limits of at least $3,000 (about $4,000 was the median maximum limit),

14. The fact that finance charges are not imposed on credit cards except after a prescribed period means that there is no incentive to pay cash for purchases even though it is readily available in a deposit account. Desire to avoid add-on rates may deter these individuals from instalment loan contracts but not credit card usage.

and one respondent stated that card limits up to $10,000 had been authorized. There is, however, a real problem in enforcing the limits. If a customer makes a number of modest purchases in a short period of time, then the total credit exposure can be well over card limits before remedial action is possible.

TABLE 10–5

CREDIT CARD POLICIES

(Respondent Banks)

| POLICY AREA | PRACTICE |
|---|---|
| *Credit* | |
| Total card limits | |
| Range of minimums | $300–$500 |
| Range of maximums | $3,000–$10,000 |
| Floor limits (by number of banks) | |
| $50 | 1 |
| $25–$500 | 2 |
| $50–$500 | 5 |
| *Rates** | |
| Merchant discount percentages | |
| Range of minimums | .5–2.5 |
| *Median* | *1* |
| Range of maximums | 5–12 |
| *Median* | *5* |

* All respondent banks charged 1½ percent per month on amounts outstanding after 30 days or 18 percent per annum. This is legal maximum in many jurisdictions.

Floor limits on merchants are only a partial solution to the problem. These specify that if a cardholder makes purchases above the specified amount at a given point of sale, then the merchant must obtain authorization from the issuing bank, which can, in turn, access a national credit file in a few seconds. Floor limits necessarily must be related to the average size of purchases from a given merchant. Otherwise practically every charge would have to be specifically authorized at, say, an airline where small unit purchases are unusual. The presumption, however, is that a series of inquiries to exceed floor limits will provide early notice that card limits have been exceeded. This control is not really an effective monitor of excessive card usage, however, because it is possible to make a large number of purchases—practically all of them within the floor limits—in various places. Therefore, card and floor limit controls should not be construed as adequate substitutes for careful credit screening of applicants before cards are issued. Losses of several thousand dollars on some credit cards have been experienced despite the modest card and floor limits imposed on usage.

**Sources of returns**

Returns on credit card usage are derived from two sources: a percentage discount on the purchases, borne by the merchant, plus a monthly charge against unpaid balances outstanding beyond a specified time period.[15] Merchant discounts represent compensation for the economic benefits of immediate cash for credit sales, monthly billing services, and the transfer of credit risk to the bank. Given the fact that marginal costs are low on computerized operations such as credit cards, high volume merchants can negotiate percentage discounts that represent a real bargain for the service package. Table 10–5 shows discounts as low as .5 percent, or 6 percent annualized, which is less than the average prime rate in recent years. On the other hand, low volume operations which generate small unit purchases can expect to incur a discount of 4 percent to 6 percent on their credit card sales in order to cover the fixed costs associated with billing and administering the account.

Policies with respect to charges on unpaid balances were generally standardized except for the determination of the amount of such balances subject to charges. A charge of 1½ percent per month, or 18 percent annualized, represents statutory limits in many states, so it has become the standard rate. There are, however, three alternative methods that are used to determine the

15. Although the major card issuers regard the precise universe data as confidential, for 1975 in one respondent bank with a volume card operation, merchant discounts provided about 27 percent of total revenues, finance charges about 66 percent, and the balance was largely from interbank service fees. As the card programs appear relatively homogeneous, it is probable that these proportions are roughly the same for the banking universe.

balance subject to finance charges. These are (1) adjusted previous balance, (2) average daily balance with a "free ride" on purchases, (3) average daily balance, including new purchases.

The first method was in general use until about 1973. It involves billing a customer for new purchases at the end of a billing period, deducting payments and returns, and assessing finance charges only on any balance outstanding against "old" purchases made in prior billing periods. Customers thus had the current billing period to retire all "new" and "old" purchases without further finance charges.

The average daily balance method assesses the finance charge against the average daily amount of funds used subject to the finance charge ("old" purchases) instead of against the balance at a given point in time (method 1). The logic is that the actual amount of funds advanced, rather than a balance as of a cutoff point, should be subject to the charge. Thus a customer purchasing early in a billing cycle would pay more than one purchasing late, assuming that neither repaid within the "free ride" period .

The third method in its extreme form assesses a finance charge on all funds used on a daily basis from the day the purchases are posted to the account; in other words, finance charges are imposed on all accounts. For competitive reasons most banks waive the finance charge if a complete payment is received within 30 days, but they impose the charge for all average daily outstandings from the date of purchase if payment is delayed beyond 30 days. This method is logically the most consistent as it charges the customer for the funds actually advanced for the precise number of days the advance is outstanding, but its final form will probably depend on competitive pressures.[16] Indeed, with the feature of a waiver on finance charges for prompt payment, it is the method generally in use on large credit card operations handled through computerized billing systems.

16. Competing financial institutions entering credit card finance have offered some major promotional features. It was reported that Massachusetts Savings Bank in 1976 offered a 1 percent rebate on all monthly purchases, paid automatically into a savings account. At the same time Citibank announced that a 50¢ monthly "service fee" would be imposed to cover processing and mailing costs against accounts that pay promptly. Policies along these lines to eliminate "free rides" may well be restrained because of competition from nonbank institutions. (*Forbes Magazine*, May 15, 1976, p. 50.)

## Effects on asset management

Finally, it has been observed that if credit card outstandings continue to escalate, problems related to their effects on general asset management policies might arise. Reviewing the possible outlook, a bank executive offered the following comment:

> The use of bank credit cards is at the option of the holder and, although the banking community might accelerate the use through active promotional programs, no device has yet been developed for dampening the use in times of tight money. . . . This means that this type of credit will force its way into commercial banks' portfolios regardless of management decisions, and the expected mushrooming growth of this financial instrument could result in some serious distortion of the portfolio mix. This could not only adversely affect bank liquidity as bankers seek to meet the traditional credit demands facing them and accommodate the increased card credit growth as well, but it could also result in a denial of credit to conventional users, especially in periods of tightening conditions.[17]

Although it is true that banks cannot control usage of credit cards and, as shown in Table 10–1, outstandings under bank credit cards increased by almost $3 billion during the 1974 period of monetary restraint, the amounts involved remained small compared to total assets and liabilities. Therefore, except possibly for a few small or moderate-sized banks where credit card outstandings may represent a significant proportion of assets, it is doubtful if an asset management problem consequent to the usage of credit cards will be of any material significance for a number of years .The real problem in 1974 was that credit card operations became unattractive on an "opportunity cost" basis when market interest rates reached 12–13 percent on prime instruments, because merchant discounts and monthly charges were fixed by contractual agreements and statutory law respectively, and therefore could not be adjusted to reflect market conditions.

17. Frederick Deane, Jr., *Journal of Commercial Bank Lending* 52 (May 1970): 25.

## Organization Structure for Consumer Loans

To conclude this chapter, the nature of the organization structure required to operate a full-service consumer credit operation might be indicated. First, the structure must be geared to process several hundred applications a day and to service 100,000 or more outstanding loans. Second, while the time factor is less critical on credit card applications, on single-purpose instalment loans both dealers and direct borrowers are inclined to require an answer on each credit within a very short time. As shown in Table 10–4, it is prevailing policy to offer one- to three-hour service on purchased paper and to require only a slightly longer time to process direct loans.

The organization structure appropriate to meet these objectives calls for establishing batteries of specialists trained to perform a single task within the processing operation. To illustrate, perhaps twenty or more clerical personnel will have the sole duty of transcribing applications received from dealers over the telephone. Another group of "investigators" will verify the information on the applications and obtain the past credit record of the individuals from a central credit bureau, all within a few minutes. A third group of "credit authorizers," probably specialized according to types of loans, will review the data on the applications and make the decisions. The decisions on the applications are then called back to the prospective borrowers by the telephone operators. An operating group then handles the mechanics of the completed loans. Finally, specialists in the collection of past-due loans take over when necessary. Officers supervise the entire operation and may be called in to review sensitive cases involving dealer relations. In addition, a large part of the officers' time may also be devoted to personal calls on dealers that generate indirect instalment loans or merchants with contracts under the credit card program to discuss various elements in the credit service program. On the whole, however, clerical production activities dominate the consumer credit operation.

Analyses of universe performance, broken down by types of credits and perhaps by dealers, dominate loan administration procedures in consumer loan departments. Productivity and cost control goals are established and performance measured against these goals.[18] For example, to obtain adequate productivity, constraints are often imposed on investigators and authorizers as to the amount of data required and the time spent on the investigation of individual credits. When a few basic elements in the credit indicate an acceptable risk, policy dictates terminating the investigation at that point. Supervisory criticism, therefore, is directed at excessive as well as inadequate analysis. This approach is entirely foreign to the basic concept of credit analysis on commercial loans, where it is traditional to conduct thorough investigations and tolerate excessive analysis unless it is obviously outside the range of relevant factors.

18. As a broad-gauge measure of relative overall performance in the consumer credit operation, the number of loans per employee in this department is sometimes compared to similar data for other banks. For example, at one time a respondent reported 686 loans per employee whereas other banks in the area showed 404–585 loans per employee, indicating that its productivity was well above average.

# XI

# REAL ESTATE LOANS

## Portfolio Role of Mortgages

Because the largest source of demand for mortgage credit comes from individuals seeking to finance home ownership, mortgage operations are usually classified as part of the retail banking services. However, mortgages against real property are also possible in many situations related to wholesale operations. For example, term loans can be secured by a mortgage on the real property.[1] Other loans based on real estate operations may also be a part of the wholesale banking function. These include (1) residential construction loans to contractors, (2) financing of apartments, hotels, and motels, (3) construction and permanent mortgage loans on stores, offices, and other commercial buildings, (4) specialty mortgages extended to such borrowers as private clubs and churches, and (5) lines of credit extended to finance the activities of mortgage bankers.

To make the situation even more complex, the Federal National Mortgage Association (FNMA, or more commonly Fannie Mae) provides a secondary market in FHA- and VA-insured mortgages. In addition some banks actively deal with other financial institutions in the mortgage market. As a consequence, mortgages can now be purchased or sold in the secondary market on the same impersonal basis as investment securities. The mortgage

1. Literally, these are mortgage loans; but in the national banking statute and in most states they may be legally classified as commercial loans not subject to statutory mortgage restrictions, if made to manufacturing and industrial businesses where the expected source of repayment is operating earnings, and if the mortgage is taken only as a precaution against contingencies. (U.S. Treasury Dept., Comptroller of the Currency, *National Banking Laws and Related Statutes* [Washington, D.C.: U.S. Government Printing Office, 1960], p. 71.)

portfolio, therefore, may be obtained through all the major methods of acquiring earning assets: (1) investment acquisitions, (2) commercial loans, and (3) retail credits extended to individuals and perhaps groups in the community.

The thrust of public policy in the mortgage area has been quite different from that in the consumer loan field, where protection of consumers through the "Truth in Lending" statute and the broadly based Uniform Consumer Credit Code has marked governmental concern.[2] In real estate finance, the major goal has been to stimulate construction of housing though measures designed to increase the supply of mortgage credit. The insurance and secondary market programs are examples of such measures; in addition Regulation Q restrictions on maximum savings and time deposit rates have been justified on the grounds that savings flows into savings and loan associations must be protected. Public policy is likely to continue to be directed toward increasing the flow of funds into the mortgage markets; these policies will probably take the form of a combination of making mortgages more attractive and putting pressure on financial institutions to acquire them.

Table 11–1 shows the trends in bank holdings of the several categories of mortgages between 1965 and 1975.[3] In addition, as time deposits by law and custom are regarded as the only funding source of mortgages, the amounts of such deposits for all insured banks are also shown. The trends of the data imply some significant policy changes in the mortgage area over the past decade or so. First, bank holdings of government-insured mortgages (FHA and VA) have showed practically no increase over the decade. Probably the major reason is that governmental control over terms on these mortgages has often made them less desirable than other instruments. Second, the increase in commercial and conventional mortgages has been substantial but less than the increase in time deposits, and increases in most other loan categories, although not shown in Table 11–1, also generally exceeded the

2. Disclosure requirements for fees and settlement costs on mortgages are required under the "Truth in Lending" Act and are implemented by Regulation Z of the Federal Reserve, Section 226.4 (8) (2), as amended October 28, 1975.

3. The Federal Reserve changed its format in compiling the data as of 1971, so that to a minor extent the data may not be comparable. However, the distortions so produced should not modify the percentage changes to any significant degree.

TABLE 11–1
MORTGAGE LOANS OF COMMERCIAL BANKS
(In Billions)

| Year | Residential: FHA | Residential: VA | Residential: Conventional | Multifamily* | Commercial | Farm | Total | Time Deposits† | Mortgages as Percentage of Time Deposits |
|---|---|---|---|---|---|---|---|---|---|
| 1965 | $7.7 | $2.7 | $22.0 | . . . | $14.4 | $2.9 | $49.7 | $146.1 | 34.0 |
| 1967 | 7.7 | 2.7 | 27.2 | . . . | 17.9 | 3.4 | 58.9 | 183.1 | 32.2 |
| 1969 | 8.0 | 2.7 | 33.9 | . . . | 22.1 | 4.0 | 70.7 | 194.2 | 36.4 |
| 1971 | 8.3 | 3.0 | 36.7 | 4.0 | 26.3 | 4.2 | 82.5 | 271.8 | 30.3 |
| 1973 | 8.2 | 3.3 | 46.5 | 6.9 | 38.7 | 5.4 | 119.1 | 369.7 | 32.2 |
| 1975 | 6.4 | 3.3 | 66.9 | 6.6 | 45.5 | 6.4 | 135.1 | 440.0 | 30.7 |
| Percentage increase | | | | | | | | | |
| 1965-75 | –16.6 | 22.2 | 234.1‡ | | 216.9 | 120.7 | 171.8 | 201.2 | –10.0 |

Source: Federal Reserve bulletins.

* Multifamily included in conventional residential category until 1971.

† Total for all insured banks.

‡ Includes multifamily in 1975 data for purposes of computing percentage increase.

growth in mortgage loans over this period. Therefore, although many banks continue to be fairly active in the mortgage market, the role of mortgages in the loan portfolio appears to be moderately declining in importance.

The major problem with mortgages over the past decade is that associated with any long-term fixed-rate asset during a period where interest rates have shown a major increase. Table 11–2 shows that during the 1965–76 period residential mortgage rates advanced considerably, because of the general upward trend in interest rates on long-term debt instruments. But because residential mortgages are made for final maturities of twenty to thirty years (perhaps for average maturities of twelve to twenty years because of amortization), the annual average return on the portfolio mix of old and new mortgages necessarily lagged well behind the annual rate increases on new mortgage commitments. Thus in 1975–76 when new mortgage yields averaged almost 9 percent, the entire portfolio might have had an average yield of 7 percent or so.

TABLE 11–2
REAL ESTATE MORTGAGE
ANNUAL AVERAGE RATES AND YIELDS

| | Conventional Mortgages (New Homes) | | FHA-Insured Loans Secondary Market Yields |
|---|---|---|---|
| Year | Contract Rates* | Estimated Yields | |
| 1965 | 5.81 | NA | 5.47 |
| 1966 | 6.25 | NA | 6.38 |
| 1967 | 6.46 | NA | 6.55 |
| 1968 | 6.97 | 7.12 | 7.21 |
| 1969 | 7.81 | 7.99 | 8.26 |
| 1970 | 8.44 | 8.52 | 9.05 |
| 1971 | 7.60 | 7.74 | 7.70 |
| 1972 | 7.45 | 7.60 | 7.53 |
| 1973 | 7.78 | 7.95 | 8.19 |
| 1974 | 8.71 | 8.92 | 9.55 |
| 1975 | 8.75 | 9.01 | 9.19 |
| 1976 | 8.69† | 8.94† | 9.04† |

Source: Federal Reserve bulletins.

* Rate paid by buyer exclusive of fees and other charges. Yields include such fees and charges.

† Average for first 6 months of the year.

As a consequence, under the conditions that prevailed in the past decade, a mortgage policy sensitive to the trend and fluctuations of interest rates would have been highly desirable. Indeed, given a reasonable possibility that Regulation Q might be eliminated in five years or so, which might significantly increase the interest-rate sensitivity of savings and time deposits, then a major asset management policy issue emerges concerning the appropriate degree of rate sensitivity of the assets. To increase such sensitivity, the likely decision would be to restrain the rate-insensitive mortgage portfolio or, alternatively, to innovate policies aimed at increasing the rate sensitivity of this portfolio.

## Pricing

### Existing policies

On a large proportion of the mortgage portfolio, pricing policies have typically had the following elements: (1) fixed rates based on local market conditions are offered for full term; (2) front-end fees are often imposed to cover origination costs, but these also typically have a profit component; (3) rate differentials between customers are usually allowable and are based on a mix of considerations, including an evaluation of the direct (personal accounts) and indirect (business affiliation) customer relationships, credit risk, and size of the loan; (4) prepayment penalties are moderate or absent from the contract. The latter element has sometimes resulted in the ability of sophisticated customers to refund their loans or demand rate concessions consequent to a major decrease in interest rates, but of course if interest rates increase, the bank cannot ask for a rate improvement. This mix of pricing policies resulted in reasonable returns for many years when retail time and savings deposits showed steady growth, and interest rates in general fluctuated within a moderate range generally below mortgage rates.

But in recent years, notably in 1974–75, market rates on prime money market instruments have sometimes advanced well beyond Regulation Q limits on retail time and savings accounts. As a consequence, so-called "disintermediation" took place as some depositors withdrew their accounts to make direct investments at higher rates in the short-term financial markets. Under these conditions, many banks found it necessary to increase substantially their sale of large wholesale CDs at costs well above prevailing mortgage rates and of course substantially above average returns on the mortgage portfolio. In other words, the marginal cost of funds to make and carry mortgages significantly exceeded their returns. The inevitable consequence was that current mortgage commitments were often sharply reduced or eliminated (with exceptions for good customers) and the desirability of an active mortgage-lending operation on a long-term basis came into question.

### Proposed policies

To mitigate possible negative spreads on the carry of the mortgage portfolio, the use of variable rate pricing has been proposed. Conceptually variable rate pricing could be identical to floating rates on commercial loans. But because long-term rates are less sensitive than short-term rates on which prime rate movements are based, the typical proposal has been to adjust rates only at prescribed intervals.

For example, in 1976 Bank of America offered "Vari-Rate" mortgages at 1/4 percent below prevailing mortgage rates; on these loans rates would remain constant for one year and then change at six-month intervals on the basis of a cost-of-money index. The maximum change at any one time was limited to 1/4 percent, with the further constraint of a maximum increase of 2.5 points over the life of the loan but with no limit on reductions. The reason for the constraints on upward rate increase was not explained, but it may be conjectured that they were introduced in order to obtain consumer acceptance and mitigate political opposition to the concept.[4] The mechanics of adjustment are to retain a fixed monthly payment, but the term of the mortgage

4. The political opposition is based on the view that borrowers are entitled to stable mortgage costs and also that they would not understand the pricing formula. The following quotation is illustrative of the opposition: "Retreating a third time under Congressional fire, the Federal Home Loan Bank Board withdrew proposals to allow variable-rate mortgages for one-to-four family homes. . . . But it adopted amendments authorizing such variable mortgages on multifamily and commercial properties." (*Wall Street Journal*, Nov. 5, 1975, p. 31.)

would change as the proportion of the monthly payment devoted to interest charges increased or decreased.

As an alternative, it has been suggested that the Canadian policy on mortgage lending be adopted. This policy has been described as follows:

> Typical Canadian mortgage loans have a five-year maturity and a fixed-interest rate, with amortization based on a 20-to-30 year term. These mortgage rates "reflect the competitive market" and are closely related to rates paid on five-year term deposits, enabling a lender to match asset and liability maturities. . . . At the end of the five-year term, the mortgage borrower can either pay off the unamortized principal or refinance the loan with another five-year mortgage loan at whatever interest rate is then prevailing.[5]

The advantages of this approach are that it is consistent with existing statutory and regulatory law and it is probably easier for customers to understand. However, unless there were contractual assurance that the mortgage would be refinanced if not in default, customers might well be uneasy as to their status at the end of each five-year period. Moreover, from the standpoint of the lender, a major cyclical saving in interest rates could be consummated within a five-year period. Therefore, unless five-year deposit funds are available in volume to fund mortgage commitments, a disintermediation scenario similar to that of 1974–75 could still produce negative spreads. In general, five-year time deposits have represented only a small fraction of total deposits in the banking system so the availability of such funds on a major scale is open to question.[6] However, the elimination or liberalization of Regulation Q limits might well enable banks to solicit retail deposits of these maturities more effectively.

The five-year rate adjustment policy would probably provide a more effective remedy against inadequate spreads between

5. Bank of America, *Policy Statement on Mortgage Lending,* as quoted in *Wall Street Journal,* Apr. 6, 1976, p. 8.

6. As of October 1975, for example, for all insured commercial banks retail time deposits with maturities beyond four years amounted to about $38.5 billion or about 10 percent of the $383.5 billions in total time and savings deposits. Wholesale CDs of such maturities were not reported, although, because of the nature of that market, it is assumed they are trivial in amount. Data from Table 1, *Federal Reserve Bulletin,* Apr. 1976, p. 313.

money costs and returns on a mortgage portfolio due to a secular increase in interest rates than would the first method, where there was a 2.5 point "cap" on rate adjustments. In the past twenty to thirty years (the term of most residential mortgages) money costs have shown a secular increase of considerably more than 2.5 points. While extrapolation of past trends is always highly conjectural, historical evidence at least suggests that a 2.5 point adjustment over a long-term period may fall well short of matching an increase in money costs. It is probable that pricing modifications on mortgage loans will be difficult to achieve on a basis completely satisfactory to banks and consumers, but some changes along the lines suggested above would seem probable, in view of the trends in the financial markets over the past decade or so.

## Mortgage Portfolio: Legal and Policy Constraints

Statutory and administrative regulations are more detailed in mortgage lending than in any other general loan classification. The probable reason for the singular legal attention to mortgages is that historically such loans were considered unsuitable for commercial bank portfolios and the National Banking Act originally prohibited them altogether. As often seems to happen in such circumstances, modifications in the law could only be obtained by legislation that included a number of specific limitations.

One restriction in the national banking law, and in the laws of many states, is that conventional mortgages are limited to 70 percent of time deposits or to the amount of capital and surplus, whichever is greater. However, because time and savings deposits have increased at a much more rapid rate than mortgage commitments, this constraint has not inhibited policy in the vast majority of banks. In fact, the general policy is to impose much more rigorous voluntary constraints on the mortgage portfolio than the law requires.[7] In some banks the portfolio is of such minor

7. As shown in Table 11–1, at the end of 1975 mortgages amounted to 30.7 percent of total savings and time deposits at insured commercial banks. At large weekly reporting commercial banks as of March 31, 1976, real estate loans were $60.4 billions and savings and time $225.9 billion or a percentage of 26.7, but excluding large wholesale CDs, the percentage was 39.4 percent. *Federal Reserve Bulletin*, Apr. 1976, p. A18–A22.

proportions that the issue has never arisen, but the following statement of one respondent is an example of such a policy decision, when the matter has been considered: "Under present policy, real estate mortgage loans are not allowed to exceed 45 percent of the total of *individual* time and passbook savings accounts."

One reason for the limitation is that the mortgage portfolio is long-term in nature and thus less flexible as money market conditions change; another is that time deposits derived from corporations in the form of large CDs are subject to wide fluctuations based on rate considerations and are not considered suitable to support long-term mortgage commitments.

The opinion was also expressed that under certain conditions restrictions might be imposed on the mortgage portfolio well before any general policy limits were reached:

> In addition to the amount of capital and savings deposits we also consider other factors and ratios, such as our liquidity and our overall loan demand, prior to determining our mortgage loan program for the ensuing period.

The significant inference is that the mortgage program is determined *after* the prospective loan demand from other sources has been evaluated. It would appear, therefore, that most mortgage commitments have a lower priority than other types of loans and are likely to be restricted if loan demand from other sources is heavy. A similar priority is suggested by several respondents' policy to limit mortgage commitments under tight money conditions solely to deserving deposit customers. In other words, the purely retail mortgage operation has been a prime candidate for restriction when problems of fund allocation arise.

Until the 1975–76 period, when loan demand from other sources decreased and deposit inflows increased (characteristics of recession and easy money), commercial banks tended to expand their mortgage programs. As late as 1971–72, this policy was evident; between 1971 and 1973, it is notable that, on the basis of the data in Table 11–1, mortgage loans of banks increased by 44.4 percent. But in 1975, a year of recession and monetary ease, commercial bank holdings of mortgages increased by only $3 billion or by about 2 percent.[8] And at late as November of 1975 a sample of banks surveyed by the Federal Reserve indicated that 21.6 percent were less willing to make mortgage loans than earlier in that year, compared to 15.8 percent which stated they were more willing to extend such loans.[9]

Apparently the adverse yield spreads shown on the mortgage portfolio during the highly restrictive period of 1974 made many banks highly cautious with respect to mortgage policies. Moreover, loan losses in certain sectors of the mortgage portfolio had greatly increased, which also probably induced a cautious policy on the mortgage account. Therefore, the future role of mortgages in loan portfolios seemed rather uncertain as of late 1976. If variable rates become more prevalent and monetary conditions become less volatile, then banks may again enter the mortgage market on a significant scale. But otherwise, this sector of the loan account may remain relatively stagnant or at the least show a rate of growth well below that of other loan categories.

## Mortgage Policies

### Nonresidential properties

While loans against residential properties dominate mortgage portfolios, as shown by Table 11–1, substantial amounts of mortgage credit have also been advanced against other types of properties. Policy decisions, therefore, are required as to the properties that will be considered eligible for mortgage commitments. The respondent banks indicated a distinct bias against permanent mortgage commitments on transient rental properties, such as apartments, motels, and hotels. Only a few would even consider such loans, and then only if they were for 10-year maturities at about 60 percent of cost or appraisal value. The substantial risk that most of these loans seem to involve and the fact that they must be made for relatively large amounts were the reasons usually given for the negative attitude. Another dis-

8. At the end of 1974, commercial bank holdings of mortgages were $132.1 billion and at the end of 1975 they were $135.1 billions. (*Federal Reserve Bulletin*, Apr. 1976, p. A42.)

9. "Changes in Bank Lending Practices, 1975," *Ibid.*, p. 311.

advantage is that large loans of this type do not as a rule result in deposit balances of proportionate dimensions.

In sharp contrast, however, was the positive policy toward extending permanent mortgages against commercial structures, such as manufacturing facilities, stores, and office buildings. In cases where the properties are directly owned and occupied by regular commercial customers, the policy was particularly positive. For example, if a department store which is a customer of the bank desired mortgage financing on branch locations, it would obviously be imprudent to have a policy of refusing such loans. In short, these commercial mortgages are accepted as an integral part of the wholesale banking operation, and seem in essence to be considered as extended maturity term loans. Maturities were generally limited to about 15 years, fully amortized, with maximum commitments limited to about 70 percent of cost or appraisal values. Rates are often on a floating basis about 1 to 2 percent above the prime, but fixed rates of perhaps 2 points over prime might be offered in some instances.

Life insurance companies and to some extent pension funds have been active in the commercial mortgage market for many years. These institutions, however, acquire the mortgages on an investment basis with maturities up to 20 or 30 years, and they often include an equity participation in the return. About half of the respondent banks indicated in 1971 that their policy would probably move in this direction, as the following statement shows: "We intend to take equity participations on a percentage of the base gross income. This will vary according to the type of property involved." The other half, however, indicated a definite bias against such participations on commercial mortgages. Questions of legality under banking law and regulations were raised, as well as the possibility that participations might encourage excessive risk positions. But as of late 1976, the concept of equity participations had yet to be implemented in most respondent banks.

Policy with respect to mortgages against nonprofit specialty properties, such as churches and clubs, is generally to consider them only if there is a direct or indirect customer relationship. Because the properties usually have limited alternative use value, the security for such loans, measured by prospective market value, is often less than the amount of mortgage credit needed. Moreover, some question may exist as to the reliability of the source of repayment under adverse circumstances, since repayment usually depends on voluntary pledges or dues levied on the members. However, important individuals in the community often sponsor the loans, and sometimes the deposit relationship is reasonably satisfactory. The general policy, therefore, is to provide mortgage financing of reasonable proportions to local church or club properties if the loan has strong sponsorship, if it seems to meet a vital community need, or if there is an established customer relationship.

### Residentials

As shown in Table 11–1, banks have become inactive in extending mortgage loans under government-insured programs. Moreover, in this area Congress and the Department of Housing and Urban Development establish the specific terms in some detail, so that discretionary policies of banks are minimal. Therefore, government-insured mortgages will not be specifically considered except to note that, as of 1976, the general policy of respondent banks was to extend them only by exception. The yield spreads in this area have generally been unattractive as alternatives. And since these loans were largely acquired through a investment type of operation, banks have not been obliged to continue active programs in FHA and VA loans.

The data in Table 11–1 indicated that as of the end of 1975 conventional residential mortgages represented about half of the total mortgage portfolios. Although as indicated above, the fixed-rate characteristic of mortgage loans has resulted in a sharply reduced rate of growth, continued commitments will be required to offset the automatic amortization process and hold the portfolio at a constant size. Data on average terms extended by all mortgage lenders, of which banks are well less than half the total universe, are shown in Table 11–3. For comparative purposes, the range and modal policies of respondent banks with respect to terms are also shown.

The time series data suggest that not only do contractual rates vary with monetary conditions but other terms are also sub-

TABLE 11–3
RESIDENTIAL MORTGAGES: CONVENTIONALS
(Average Terms on New Homes Financing, All Lenders)

| | CONTRACT RATE (In Percentage) | FEES AND CHARGES (In Percentage) | MATURITY (Years) | LOAN/PRICE RATIO | LOAN AMOUNT (Thousands) |
|---|---|---|---|---|---|
| 1970 | 8.27 | 1.03 | 25.1 | 71.7 | 25.2 |
| 1971 | 7.60 | .87 | 26.2 | 74.3 | 26.5 |
| 1972 | 7.45 | .88 | 27.2 | 76.8 | 28.1 |
| 1973 | 7.78 | 1.11 | 26.3 | 77.3 | 28.1 |
| 1974 | 8.71 | 1.30 | 26.3 | 75.8 | 29.8 |
| 1975 | 8.75 | 1.54 | 26.8 | 76.1 | 33.3 |
| 1976* | 8.69 | 1.50 | 27.4 | 76.9 | 33.5 |

Source: Federal Reserve Bulletins.
* As of first quarter.

| *Respondent Banks (Terms)* | *Range* | *Mode* |
|---|---|---|
| Maximum loan appraised value | 66% to 80% | 75% |
| Maximum maturity | 20 to 30 years | 25 years |
| Deposit requirements | Sometimes to always | Sometimes† |

† Stated as during tight money periods or alternatively when constraints on growth of mortgage portfolio considered desirable.

ject to some variation as financial market conditions change. It is notable, for example, that fees and charges tend to increase, and maturities and the loan/price ratio tend to decrease in periods of tight money. The exact timing of the changes in terms is difficult to assess, because mortgage commitments antedate closings by several months. As policies on terms relate to commitments whereas the data are based on closings, the effect of restrictive policies in one period may well show up in the data for a subsequent period. Thus rates and fees in 1975 increased from 1974 and this probably reflects the fact that in 1974 monetary policy was highly restrictive. Moreover, unlike earlier periods of monetary ease, 1976 did not bring significant declines in long-term interest rates, and, as a result, conventional mortgage rates remained well above their average levels of previous years.[10]

10. Monthly data on government security yields show that in August of 1974, three-month treasury bills registered a peak yield of 8.74 percent at a time when long-term governments gave a yield of 7.33 percent; by April of 1976 bill yields had

Although some respondents were clearly not competitive in the residential mortgage market in 1976, on average the policy constraints on maximum maturities and the ratio of loan amount to appraised value were more or less in line with the market data. However, in recent years mortgage policies have shown a definite trend toward requiring a deposit relationship from borrowers; in contrast to consumer credit policies where deposit relationships are not a factor in the decision.

Some rather subtle policy problems were reported on both rates and the maximum size of loans. While the preferred policy is to avoid mortgages on very expensive properties, large banks have a number of close personal contacts with important executives of customer firms. A possible conflict thus arises between the commercial loan and mortgage loan departments; that is, the commercial lending officers sometimes request policy exceptions both as to rates and loan amounts on mortgages for these individuals because such customers control very profitable wholesale business and therefore require special consideration. Despite understandable reluctance to admit it, preferential treatment seems to be an accepted fact in most banks. In this connection, the one bank which had always confined mortgage accommodation to deposit customers offered the best terms on rates and would accept larger loans. In this case, the mortgage operation seemed clearly a service activity for the commercial loan department.

Finally, there is a policy option to obtain private mortgage insurance on conventional mortgages. These plans typically offer insurance for a specified "top" part of a loan, or alternatively allow the insurer to pay out the loan and foreclose on the property. For example, if the amount of a mortgage is $10,000, then the first 20 percent of $2,000 might be insured, thus reducing the bank risk to $8,000. As the loan is amortized, however, the percentage is applied to the outstanding balance. The charge for the insurance service amounts to about 2 percent of the amount of the mortgage paid over a 10-year period. While the result is a

---

declined to 5.0 percent but long-term governments still sold on a 7.0 percent basis. The fact that inflation expectations are an important factor in determining long-term rates but not in short-term rates was a major reason advanced for this unusual behavior of the term structure of interest rates.

moderately lower return on the conventional portfolio, the plans offer a risk protection feature that may be attractive to some banks with a large credit exposure in this area.

### Financing of Interim Construction

Certain unique features of the construction industry control lending policies with respect to that industry. First, a considerable period usually elapses between the first planning of a building or tract and the final occupancy by a permanent owner. Second, many lenders interested in permanent financing, such as life insurance companies, are not equipped to handle the interim financing required for the construction process. Third, because the land development and construction process is lengthy, substantial capital is required to carry work in process; as a result, contractors usually require large borrowings in relation to their equity. Construction mortgages may be obtained, but they require considerable servicing in the form of inspections of progress, assurance of lien discharges to subcontractors, and so forth. The ability of the contractor to perform quality work in full accord with required specifications is of crucial importance. Fourth, in residential operations each property is of modest value and requires decentralized local servicing, whereas many institutional lenders desire large blocs in one package with no servicing responsibility. As a result of these features, various options have been developed to finance construction projects.

One option is to make straight commercial loans to contractors who specialize in custom rather than tract building and to specialty subcontractors. The policy issues here are essentially similar to those governing all seasonal and working capital loans. However, they are often classified in a high-risk category, since adequate collateral is difficult to obtain, because the performance bonding company usually has a prior line on the receivables and often the equipment is not entirely free of debt incurred on purchase. Therefore unsecured loans may be the only practical expedient. Because the credit experience with many contractors has been unfavorable, screening and servicing policies are usually rigorous.

A second approach is to extend construction mortgage commitments directly to developers of properties and then extend progress loans as work proceeds. Although these loans are secured by mortgage liens during the progress stage, the expected sources of repayment are permanent mortgages executed upon completion. Therefore, the preferable arrangement is to finance construction on properties already sold to final buyers who have obtained firm end mortgage commitments from long-term lenders (perhaps the mortgage department of the bank itself). However, as the final mortgages will be closed only if the physical specifications are fulfilled and all applicable mechanics liens of labor and subcontractors discharged, adequate servicing of these loans requires frequent audits and inspection. As a consequence, risk control involves substantial costs. Rates therefore, tend to be above permanent mortgage rates, and servicing fees are often added.

Moreover, in view of the severe problems that emerged in the real estate area in 1974–75, particularly in residential tract projects and the multifamily area (apartments and condominiums), policies on construction loans became definitely negative in many banks. The loans to many Real Estate Investment Trusts represented a particular problem. While many were under lines of credit and thus not strictly classified as real estate loans, a number of banks were forced to take over the construction mortgages on the properties financed by the trusts in partial liquidation of ther claims. Many large banks that had financed Real Estate Investment Trusts in 1971–73 thus acquired an involuntary set of construction loans. The effect on discretionary policy in this area was of course of a negative nature.

## Mortgage Bankers: Financing Policies

As explained above, a significant part of the funds available for end mortgages is generated from large national institutions, such as life insurance companies, although each loan is of moderate size and must be serviced locally. Because of these circumstances, intermediaries known as mortgage bankers have emerged to provide bridge financing and local servicing. Some banks or their parent holding companies have entered the field, either directly or through subsidiaries, but most confine their activities to credit commitments to independent mortgage bankers. The main activities of mortgage bankers may be summarized as follows: (1) They originate (close and disburse) final mortgages and sell them in bloc packages to pre-committed institutional investors, primarily life insurance companies, while continuing to service them for a set fee. (2) To obtain mortgages, they may offer or arrange for builders' construction financing, especially on tract developments. (3) Less frequently they originate and close mortgages when a commitment for ultimate sale has not been received. Charges for servicing, fees for the origination and closing of mortgages, and a mark-up on their sale provide the main sources of income. Mortgage bankers usually generate favorable deposit balances through escrow payments received from borrowers to prepay taxes and insurance.

The normal arrangements with long-term investor clients provide that the mortgage bankers must fully complete the end mortgages, including the payment of the entire purchase price to the contractor, and also that they must accumulate sizable mortgage "inventories" until blocs of an appropriate size are obtained. The result is that capital needs are quite large, both in absolute amount and in relation to earnings. Therefore, mortgage bankers may seek credit commitments along one or more of the folowing lines: (1) loans against fully completed mortgages, either FHA or conventional, that have a take-out commitment by a long-term lender; (2) loans against closed mortgages not yet sold; (3) unsecured lines to finance construction of contractors.

Two types of policy constraints are typically imposed against these demands. First, limits, based on the net worth and performance record of the mortgage banker, are placed on the total commitment. In strong situations, the limit may be five times net worth for lines to finance closed mortgages with firm take-out commitments, scaled down to perhaps 50 percent of net worth on funds advanced to finance contractors. These constraints prevent open-ended claims for credit in the case of advances against closed mortgages, and they limit risk exposure in the case of funds to be used to finance contractors. Second, limits are placed on specific drawings under the line; these are based on collateral values assigned to the end mortgages and percentages of construction cost, if contractor financing lines are permitted.

Table 11–4 shows respondent banks' policies on the second type of limits. Although a few banks required a margin of 10 percent on insured mortgages subject to a take-out commitment, most would advance 95–100 percent of the committed amounts. Since risk here is limited to the voiding of the commitment on the part of the long-term lender, which is very unusual, nominal margins would certainly seem justified.

TABLE 11–4
POLICIES ON COMMITMENTS TO MORTGAGE BANKERS BY RESPONDENT BANKS

| TYPE OF LOAN | LOAN TO COLLATERAL VALUE* | |
|---|---|---|
| | MORTGAGES SOLD (Percentage) | MORTGAGES UNSOLD (Percentage) |
| Loans against closed mortgages | | |
| *Government insured:* | | |
| Single-family | 90–100 | None to 90 |
| Multifamily | 90–100 | None to 90 |
| *Conventional:* | | |
| Single-family | 75–100 | None to 90 |
| Multifamily | 75–100 | None to 90 |
| Commercial | 70–100 | None to 90 |
| Construction loans | None to 70 percent of construction cost† | |

* Collateral value is defined as commitment value on sold mortgages. On unsold mortgages, loan percentage is based on current market value in secondary market.

† Most banks reported no loans in this category.

Policies with respect to advances against completed but unsold mortgages showed much greater variation. Some banks refused to consider such loans either against insured or conventional mortgages on the grounds that long-term lenders have sometimes withdrawn from the mortgage market. If that occurs and advances against unsold mortgages are outstanding, the result may be a stagnant loan which can be liquidated only through a distress sale of the collateral. However, if margins allow for a shrinkage in value because of rising rates, then ultimate risks can be satisfactorily controlled even if continuous borrowings under the lines might have to be tolerated for perhaps a year or more. Therefore, a selective policy to finance the stronger mortgage bankers on this basis would seem more appropriate.

There was a definite aversion to a policy of extending unsecured lines to mortgage bankers for financing construction. Only a few banks would even consider such lines, and they showed a cautious approach. For example, one offered the following statement:

> Loans may be made up to 70 percent of construction costs, with a 10 percent holdback and with loans in this category on a highly selected basis. Terms could vary depending upon strength of contractor or mortgage banker.

Because contractor loans have shown a high risk potential and because direct policing of contractors is relinquished, the highly selective policy toward mortgage banker lines for this purpose would seem justified.[11]

Finally, from time to time mortgage bankers have requested banks to grant intermediate-term credit to carry completed mortgages for periods of a year or more because long-term lenders desire to delay the execution of their take-out commitments. The arrangement, known as mortgage warehousing, involves some difficult policy issues.[12] It is needed because the flow of funds of large institutional investors, particularly life insurance companies, is fairly regular and does not fluctuate cyclically to any great extent. In contrast, the supply of new construction, and of mortgages, may show substantial cyclical fluctuations.

The policy problem on these requests arises from the fact that during boom periods in the construction industry, when the

11. The rapid inflation of 1974–75, accompanied by interest rates of between 13 percent and 15 percent on floating rate construction loans, caused considerable financial difficulties for many contractors and their financing sources. In June of 1975, for example, a large and respected mortgage bank in Florida, Commonwealth Corporation, went into bankruptcy because of defaults on contractor loans. Lines of credit from banks to finance contractor advances amounted to $63.1 million. The work-out of these loans under Chapter 11 bankrutpcy proceedings was still in progress as of late 1976.

12. The label "mortgage warehouse" is often applied to any loan to finance an inventory of completed mortgages. However, it would seem desirable to differentiate between short-term financing for accumulation purposes, where turnover is fairly rapid, and intermediate loans, where the mortgages are really "warehoused" in blocs for periods up to a year or more.

supply of new mortgages tends to outrun the flow of institutional funds, many banks may experience or anticipate difficulty in accommodating loan demand from other sources. A policy dilemma results. On the one hand is the fact that mortgage warehouse loans tie up bank funds for a considerable period. Moreover, banks are reluctant to act as the safety valve to relieve the strain on other financial institutions and in the process increase the strain on their own resources. On the other hand, the highly satisfactory deposit relations with mortgage bankers and institutional investors may be at stake. In consequence, policy seems to be equivocal. The following statements suggest the prevailing attitude:

> We do not encourage warehousing of loans over extended periods but may be forced to do so on a selective basis.
>
> We warehouse for extended periods only for topnotch companies where balances are involved.

Since escrow balances of established mortgage bankers are often substantial, the pragmatic approach will probably continue to prevail on loans of this type.

# 4

# LOAN REVIEW AND ADMINISTRATION

# XII

## LOAN ADMINISTRATION AND REVIEW POLICIES

### Alternative Concepts of Loan Administration

The role of loan administration in a commercial bank can be viewed in several ways. It can be viewed as a staff or support function to the line lending programs. In this role, it may be assigned some or all of the following tasks: (1) loan accounting, (2) maintaining loan documentation files, (3) physical handling of collateral assigned to and in possession of the bank, (4) credit analysis and processing of loan applications, (5) loan audits and review.[1] While these activities are highly necessary and should be performed efficiently, if loan administration is limited to operational services of this type, its policy role becomes minimal. Some banks, on the other hand, have the policy of assigning major problem loans, including "work-out" situations, to a separate group or department, and also charge this group with the responsibilty for reviewing and evaluating credit exposures in various sectors of the loan portfolio. The title of "Loan Administration and Review" has sometimes been assigned to this group.[2] These functions are also essentially staff in nature and have no policy responsibilities.

1. See J. R. Grandstaff, "Loan Administration—A New Direction," *Journal of Commercial Bank Lending* 56 (Sept. 1974): 56–59. In this article, the author indicated that in his bank a central department had been established to perform these functions—most of which represent operational support and do not include policy decisions—for all the loan activities.

2. The First National Bank of Chicago, for example, shows a "Worldwide Administration and Review" division as one of the activities in the Executive Department. Other divisions in this department include law, control, audit, business and economic research, corporate affairs, and government relations. These are all clearly staff operations and while they report to top management, on policy decisions they are advisory only.

However, it is also possible to view the administration function as including the active management of the loan portfolio in the context of changing economic, social, and political conditions. At this level, it involves the monitoring of existing policies and introducing modifications as they appear appropriate. The executive officers plus the major loan department heads presumably are charged with these major policy reviews, and of course staff reviews and reports are essential inputs to the process.

For our purposes, therefore, loan administration will be defined to include the following responsibilities: (1) to establish, monitor, and revise policies designed to restrict expansion of the loan portfolio during periods of active monetary restraint; (2) to appraise the contribution of appropriately defined lending units to the profits and growth of the bank and to institute changes in their operational policies as seem appropriate; (3) to establish policies and procedures to ensure the integrity of the loan operation (the conflict of interest problem); (4) to review and evaluate periodically the major components of the loan portfolio from the standpoint of risk exposure.

## Policy Guidelines: Total Loan Portfolio

Traditional approaches to asset management policies have usually suggested that various liquidity and capital adequacy constraints may cause some banks to establish policy guidelines governing the maximum allocation of funds to the loan portfolio. The liquidity constraint was usually developed from establishing a set of asset priorities, in turn related to potential fluctuations in deposits. Primary and secondary asset reserves against deposits were given first priority, and the balance of the deposit-generated assets could be used for loans. While it was recognized that individual banks might vary in their liquidity needs, rough benchmarks for the loan-to-deposit ratio of about 65 percent to 70 percent usually emerged.[3]

The capital adequacy constraint was based on the concept that both total assets and assets subject to risk should have an appropriate relationship to total capital in order to assure the solvency

3. See Roland I. Robinson, *The Management of Bank Funds* (New York: McGraw-Hill Book Co., 1962), pp. 134–35.

of the bank. In addition, the need to inspire confidence on the part of the large depositors and the regulatory authorities in the basic soundness of the bank has also received emphasis.[4] Although some rather complex models for the evaluation of capital adequacy have been suggested and used by some regulatory authorities, the typical result was a risk asset constraint of about 8 to 10 times capital.

However, changed conditions in the nature of banking markets modified significantly the constraints that the traditional approach to liquidity placed on the total loan portfolio. In the first place, large banks have instituted sophisticated liability management programs which include Fed Funds and other short-term borrowings plus the active purchase of wholesale CDs in the open market to meet liquidity needs caused by increased loan demand or deposit runoffs. Moreover, the suspension of Regulation Q ceilings on the rates of large purchased deposits eliminated their exposure to serious declines during periods of very high interest rates. As a result, the need to maintain a significant reservoir of liquid assets cannot be viewed as an absolute requirement for large banks with nationally recognized names.[5]

During periods of extreme credit stringency, some large money center banks have tolerated loan-to-deposit ratios in excess of 100 percent (Fed Funds and other short-time borrowings are excluded from deposit totals). While this position may have been uncomfortable and not regarded as a desirable normal position, it indicates that maximum constraints on the loan portfolio based on liquidity considerations have not been applied in practice. Because such banks' access to purchased money was unquestioned, the policy can be defended as a temporary expedient, but only

4. Howard D. Crosse and George Hempel, *Management Policies for Commercial Banks* (Englewood Cliffs, N.J.: Prentice-Hall, 1973), pp. 70–72.

5. Moderate-sized and small banks cannot be assured of access to the open-money markets, particularly under conditions of credit stringency, so adequate asset liquidity can still be considered desirable in their cases. Moreover, a liability-management approach to liquidity may result in higher average yield spreads, but during periods of severe monetary restraint, such as in 1974, the marginal cost of funds has exceeded the marginal return on the retail sector of the loan portfolio, which for legal or competitive reasons has less flexible rates. As a result, the aggressive liability management approach to liquidity may produce more volatile earnings and some banks are reputed to have pulled back from this approach.

if the quality of the loan portfolio was high and the capital position strong.

Although active liability-management policies have enabled large banks to reduce, if not eliminate, the liquidity constraint on the management of the loan portfolio, regulatory attitudes toward capital adequacy have clearly become more restrictive in recent years. Two possible reasons might be cited. First, a few large banks and/or holding companies failed in the 1974–76 period, and others were known to have experienced significant problems in their loan portfolios.[6] Media publicity of these events triggered a predictable reaction on the part of the regulatory bodies: impose more stringent regulatory standards.

Second, it has been alleged, probably with some reason, that the development of sophisticated sources of funds, both domestically and internationally, has made the control of total bank credit less responsive to changes in the volume of legal reserves. Promoting the view that credit expansion should be supported by adequate capital has apparently represented a partial and selective supplement to the management of the supply of legal reserves. Up until recent years, the problem was one of enforcement, for under the Federal Reserve Act per se, the Fed does not have the specific power to constrain risk assets in some proportion to capital. Its examining staff could make recommendations to management, but as there are no definitive guidelines on capital adequacy, the subject banks might and often did argue that in their opinion the recommendation was not well founded.

But the provisions of the 1970 amendments to the Bank Holding Company Act gave the Federal Reserve some new leverage over most major banks. Under this statute the Fed has the exclusive power to approve or deny permission for all proposed acquisitions and de novo subsidiaries of bank holding companies. In other words, the Fed may exercise "permission control" over holding company growth. As practically every large bank is now

6. The Franklin National Bank of New York and Hamilton Bancshares of Memphis, Tenn., were two highly visible failures during this period. National news media also obtained a "problem list" maintained by the regulatory agencies; it included several major money center banks. The problems of the banking industry then received considerable publicity in subsequent Congressional hearings that criticized regulatory laxity.

part of a holding company complex, the Fed found that it could exercise considerable leverage over asset policies deemed excessively expansive through a published opinion which flatly denies all requests to acquire or organize subsidiaries on the grounds that the capital support for the entire complex is "inadequate." One publication that investigated this development offered the following comment:

> So the Federal Reserve will continue trying to contain the expansion of credit by having Brenton Leavitt press on the capital levers. Let a bank extend itself too much in ways that the Fed cannot control, and the Fed will say "no" to it in ways that the Fed *can* control.[7]

As a result of this development, it is entirely possible that capital considerations might constrain a major expansion of the loan portfolio at certain times. Indeed, a major avowed purpose of the "permission control" program under the Bank Holding Company Act is to make banks more sensitive to both the need to ration credit during periods of monetary restraint and the need to maintain adequate quality controls on the loan portfolio.[8]

The above comments, however, relate to regulatory constraints applied on a very selective basis against a presumed minority that have engaged in highly aggressive loan programs which either appear to involve excessive portfolio risks or are inconsistent with the prevailing monetary posture of the Fed. While the decisions represent a "warning" to the entire universe, presumably many banks would find little need to constrain loans because of capital adequacy problems. Moreover, from a secular standpoint, if the loan portfolio has become subject to long-term growth constraints because the rate of loan growth has regularly exceeded the rate

7. *Forbes*, July 1, 1974, p. 50. Brenton Leavitt was then the head of the Banking Structure section of the Federal Reserve and apparently had the authority to pass on capital requirements considered necessary to justify acquisitions and subsidiary company formations. The new control mechanism was appropriately termed "Leavittation." Developments since the date of the quoted article suggest the process has continued as a number of major holding company operations, including the largest in the United States (BankAmerica Corp.), have had acquisitions denied. It is interesting to note that the Bank of America subsequently publicly stated that a more conservative posture toward future growth had been adopted.

8. *Ibid.*, p. 50.

of capital growth through retained earnings, then the appropriate policy would be to seek additional capital either through subordinated debentures or common stock offerings. In other words, the long-term growth of the loan portfolio through existing and contemplated loan programs should be projected; and if capital appears inadequate on the basis of these projections, then plans to obtain additional capital should be formulated and implemented.

## Loan Administration: Credit Restraint

Given the political problems of restraining inflationary expansions through restrictive fiscal policies, monetary policy has often been forced to bear the burden of seeking to contain inflation within tolerable limits. The result has been recurrent periods of severe monetary restraint, wherein the Federal Reserve has reduced the growth rate in bank reserves to levels well below that necessary to support the prevailing demand for bank credit.

### Alternative options

Perhaps the most difficult and important task of loan administration emerges during such periods. It is to seek a means of reducing or completely eliminating expansion in the loan portfolio while at the same time maintaining intact the long-term competitive position of the institution with its commercial customers and in the retail loan markets. This is no easy matter, because policies instituted to achieve temporary restraint may have adverse long-term results. For example, reducing or eliminating auto dealer rebates and more rigorous credit screening of dealer-submitted paper may well appear desirable from the point of view of short-term profitability, because rates are relatively insensitive in this area. But such action may encourage important dealers to seek alternative sources of financing. Then when the period of restraint ends, a resumption of the prior relationship (which now appears very desirable) may be impossible to obtain, since, from the dealers' standpoint, the other sources have proven to be more reliable.

Therefore, it is logical to assume that banks will continue to meet the reasonable credit needs of established customers and probably will not consider it feasible to eliminate those retail loan programs in which a substantial investment in personnel, promotion, and facilities have been made. Under these assumptions, the options open are fairly limited, and it is generally conceded that they include some combination of the following:

1. Restrict or eliminate solicitation or acceptance of new customers.
2. For existing customers, place constraints on the purposes for which loans will be extended and enforce pricing policies more rigorously.
3. Attempt to increase turnover of the loan account through reducing maturity limits or eliminating some types of long-term credit.
4. Screen credit standards more rigorously with the objective of upgrading portfolio quality at the cost of losing some marginal customers.
5. Place restrictions on "investment type" loans, defined as those where there is an absence of close customer relationships.

Of course, it is also possible to attempt to "end-run" the restraint through aggressive liability management, but for two reasons this option may not be completely feasible. First, the marginal cost of funds may increase well above the marginal return in some loan programs, which may seriously impact profitability. Second, large banks often have active expansion programs in progress and thus tend to be more sensitive to regulatory persuasion through "permission control."

**Policy implementation**

Given the probable set of options, Table 12–1 shows the preference patterns of respondent banks during the 1974–75 period of monetary restraint. The data indicate that the preferences varied to a considerable extent. One bank in fact reported that it placed only minimal constraints on its wholesale loan policies with the exception of lines to finance companies, which in large degree represent "investment" type credits. At the same time this bank

TABLE 12-1

LOAN ADMINISTRATION: MONETARY RESTRAINT RESPONSES
(Respondent Banks, 1974–75 Period)

| TYPE | DEGREE OF RESTRAINT IMPOSED | | | |
|---|---|---|---|---|
| | GREAT | SOME | MINOR | NONE |
| *Commercial Loans* | | | | |
| New customers (local) | ... | 2 | 3 | 3 |
| New customers (national) | 4 | 3 | ... | 1 |
| Term loans (existing customers): | | | | |
| Reduce maturity limits | 1 | 5 | 1 | 1 |
| Reduce acquisition loans | 5 | 2 | ... | 1 |
| Reduce equity buyout loans | 5 | 2 | ... | 1 |
| Raise credit standards | 3 | 2 | 3 | ... |
| Increase balance requirements | 3 | 4 | 1 | ... |
| Lines (finance companies) | 3 | 5 | ... | ... |
| Lines (non–finance companies): | | | | |
| Impose commitment fees | ... | 2 | 3 | 3 |
| Limit increases | 4 | 4 | ... | ... |
| *Retail Loans* | | | | |
| Mortgages: | | | | |
| Residential | 1 | 4 | 3 | ... |
| Commercial | 4 | 3 | 1 | ... |
| Construction loans | 4 | 3 | 1 | ... |
| Consumer credit: | | | | |
| Indirect | 2 | 3 | 4 | ... |
| Direct | ... | 1 | 6 | 1 |

took the extreme step of practically eliminating its dealer programs in indirect loans. But despite the considerable variation, the data suggest that there were clear preferences for certain constraint policies as follows:

1. There seemed to be a fairly pervasive policy to reduce the solicitation of non-local wholesale customers to a greater degree than local customers. The rationale is that relationships with national customers are subject to more uncertainties and also that there is some obligation of a bank to give priority to its community.
2. There was a consensus that bank loans for certain purposes should be constrained. Acquisition and equity buyout loans are often construed to be "nonproductive" in nature, and a majority of respondents indicated great restraint in those areas.

3. In the term loan area, all respondents enforced supporting balance policies more rigorously although to varying degrees, and there was a general inclination to raise credit standards in this area. Term loans, perhaps more than other credits, may be based on future balance expectations following completion of expansion programs, and as a result normal requirements may be waived. But apparently waivers become less available in tight money periods.

4. Finance company lines generally were subject to restraint because of the impersonal nature of the relationships.

5. Increases in line commitments to all customers were subject to considerable scrutiny. Basically the view was that a good customer had a "call" on the bank for a line of about five times average balances, but increases beyond that level should be on an exception-only basis.

6. Since mortgages represent long-term fixed-rate loans, intuitively one would expect major restrictions here during a period of monetary restraint. It was somewhat surprising, therefore, to find that residential mortgages were subject to only moderate constraint. For the most part, such mortgages were limited to depositing customers only and this policy was construed as moderate in nature. On the other hand, commercial and construction mortgages generally were severely limited. The risks on construction credits often appear to be above average and unless the end mortgages seem attractive, there is little incentive to seek such loans. On commercial mortgages, risk experience also has sometimes been negative in recent years, and in addition some have been "investment" in nature.

7. The general consensus was that only moderate restraint should be imposed on the consumer credit sector. As economies of scale are very important here, especially on the credit card operation, the logical tendency is to take a long-run view of its profitability. Once lost to a competitor, the business of both dealers and consumers cannot be easily regained, and, therefore, volume targets may be forgone for several years if such programs are subject to major constraint on even a temporary basis. Moreover, in the credit card area, customer usage determines outstandings and any significant reduction here would be difficult to achieve on a short-term basis. Some banks eliminated or cut back marketing programs aimed at soliciting new cardholders, but it is doubtful if

this constraint had any immediate significant effects on outstandings. As there is a normal attrition in cardholders, reduced solicitation might affect outstandings with a lag of a year or so. But given the fact that monetary restraint periods have usually lasted less than a year, the adjustment mechanism for controlling credit card volume is not sensitive enough to be effective during such periods.

Finally, although not listed above under the normative options, some large bankers apparently used the bankers acceptance instrument to relieve pressure on the loan portfolio by transfering customer accommodations from direct loans to the open money market. Traditionally used as a financing instrument in international trade transactions, only a moderate amount of bankers acceptances have been related to domestic transactions. But in 1974, the volume of "other" acceptances (not related to international trade) increased during the year from $3.1 billions to $10.4 billions.[9] Essentially instead of lending funds to a customer, the bank would "accept" a time draft on it, which in effect guaranteed payment at maturity and the draft could then be sold in the open market based on the credit standing of the accepting bank rather than the borrower.

*Forecasts of commitment usage.* In large banks a large proportion of the total loan portfolio typically consists of draws under firm commitments, such as revolving credits, and open lines of credit. Under ordinary circumstances, the usage under these commitments will probably show random and perhaps some seasonal fluctuations. However, these variations are usually moderate, empirical experience provides a reasonable guide as to their extent, and thus routine asset or liability management techniques can accommodate the obligation to meet the fluctuation in usage.

But usage also tends to fluctuate significantly in accordance with changes in monetary policy imposed by the Federal Reserve.[10]

9. *Federal Reserve Bulletin,* May 1976, p. A25. Monthly figures show that most of the increase took place between April and October of 1974, when monetary policy was highly restrictive.

10. In this connection the President of the Mellon Bank in Pittsburgh made the following comment: "Suffice it to say that borrowings under firm commitments and lines of credit constitute a significant portion of our total domestic loans and represent an even larger portion of the swing in total loans over the business

As might be expected, usage has shown significant increases when monetary policy is restrictive, conditions are strained in the financial markets, and liquidity pressures on banks are severe. The loan administration issue that emerges is, therefore, to estimate what the exposure to draws under existing lending commitments would be under conditions of severe monetary restraint, and presumably then to establish some maximum level of such commitments which the bank can prudently tolerate.[11] In fact, in 1973 the Chairman of the Board of Governors of the Federal Reserve specifically indicated that all except small banks should establish some policy along these lines:

> The apparent large volume of bank commitments currently outstanding and sharply increased takedowns thereunder are indicative of the need for special attention to this matter at this time. (1) Each bank should maintain a record of the aggregate volume of its commitments to lend. (2) Furthermore, it should periodically make a careful judgment as to the potential volume of takedowns of these commitments under reasonably foreseeable loan demand. . . .[12]

The problem with implementing policy in this connection has been that past empirical experience on usage rates has not been an effective forecasting device. For example, one major bank reported that its maximum usage under firm commitments was 51 percent in 1959–60, 57 percent in 1965–66, and 60 percent in 1970, and maximum draws under line reached 36 percent in 1970 as compared with a previous high of 32 percent.[13] Some banks

---

cycle." J. H. Higgins, "Loan Commitments," *Journal of Commercial Bank Lending* 54 (July 1972): 4.

11. In the 1969–70 period, there was some regulatory criticism to the effect that some banks had failed to exercise proper control over total line commitments. The following comment was made by a member of the Federal Reserve Board: ". . . it would seem reasonable from the banks' point of view to increase reliance upon changes in lending terms and conditions particularly with respect to policies concerning new commitments. This would avoid a situation such as the current one, where liquidity is cut to the bone, nondeposit sources of funds have been all but cut off, and yet banks face a large overhang of unused commitments." George W. Mitchell, "Bank Lending Practices and Changes in the Monetary Environment." *Journal of Commercial Bank Lending* 52 (Dec. 1969): 27.

12. Dr. Arthur Burns, letter of April 6, 1973, to all chief executive officers of State member banks with deposits over $100 millions.

13. J. H. Higgins, "Loan Commitments," pp. 5–7. The record during the subsequent tight money period of 1974–75 was not available.

have turned to developing sophisticated time series forecasting models. However, a detailed study of the problem using sophisticated statistical techniques (such as Box-Jenkins time series analysis) came to the following conclusion:

> It was found that the level of line borrowings was positively related through a partial adjustment model, at statistically significant levels, to the level of line commitments and to two interest rates posited to reflect the cost and availability of intermediate and long-term corporate financing. . . . [But] in the preferred specification the model parameters did not appear to be stable through time.[14]

In other words, each period of monetary restraint has had unique features which make forecasting of commitment usages on the basis of features and relationships that prevailed in previous periods open to significant error. But experimenting with and improving such models as forecasting devices might well be useful to a partial solution of the administrative problem. The maximum percentage usage during *any* past period plus arbitrary safety margin might be a basis for policy here until forecasting models are improved.

## Performance Evaluation

With the possible exception of consumer credit, commercial banks have been slow to apply rigorous profit center analysis to lending units. This is probably because of the considerable problems involved in developing meaningful data, particularly in the commercial loan area, and the considerable expense of implementing comprehensive cost programs. For example, a commercial loan officer in the course of his activities might be responsible for the development of some profitable trust business. Under a profit center evaluation system, it would be necessary to make a quantitative estimate of the value of this contribution. In short, the activities of loan officers often extend beyond departmental lines and may include intangibles that are difficult to measure.

14. R. R. Simonds, "Bank Line—Commitment Practices and Models for Forecasting Line Borrowing" (unpublished doctoral dissertation), University of Michigan, 1975, pp. 218–19.

The following response of one bank illustrates the problem: "We are developing a profit center approach to evaluate loan operations and using it as it develops, but it's pretty rough and as of now our evaluation is mainly by the seat of our pants."

Despite the difficulties, however, a number of large banks, following the lead of industrial companies, have instituted a formal profit center approach to assist in the evaluation and administration of the various lending operations. The availability of computer programs to process and evaluate the data has probably encouraged the development. Although the general concept of profit centers has been accepted, views as to appropriate implementation seemed to vary widely. Some banks have defined the relevant profit center rather narrowly; in the commercial loan area each group is considered a separate center, or in the case of retail credits, each major loan type. The credit card operation, for example, would be a separate profit center.

Assuming a reasonable degree of independence in group decision making, this approach has the advantage of informing management precisely where there has been a strong or weak performance. In retail credit, it may also suggest which types of loans should be promoted and which downgraded or even eliminated. Its disadvantages are that it increases the cost allocation problems and may adversely affect cooperation between groups or components of the loan operation. Knowledge that performance comparisons are likely to be used as important determinants of promotions and salary increases could lead to considerable internal competition with consequent tensions and conflict. Moreover, in the commercial loan department, assignment of customers to the loan groups may be along industry or other specialty lines, and consequently differences in performance may be very hard to evaluate. For example, it may be difficult to compare results from finance company lines with results obtained by the group assigned to handle mortgage bankers. If carefully used, however, the analysis may help to indicate which loan areas should be encouraged and which should be discouraged. Since the retail credit operation is less personal and has fewer interfaces between the several markets—auto loans and credit cards, for example—these disadvantages may be of less significance there.

A second approach to evaluating performance has been to break down the commercial loan profit centers along geographical or major divisional lines. For example, the Metropolitan, U.S., and International divisions are considered the major profit center units in one bank. Again the results might not be strictly comparable and the need for cooperation must be considered, particularly on credits extended to large multinational firms. But relatively senior management administer these major units, and operational integration can be made the responsibility of these few individuals, who are more likely than group heads to identify with the basic goals of the entire bank.

Finally, there was the view that the total commercial loan operation should be considered a single profit center, because in this way the maximum team effort could be obtained, and in addition there would be fewer revenue and cost allocation problems. However, when profit centers are very broadly defined, it naturally becomes difficult to identify the specific points of strength and weakness within the bank, which of course is highly desirable for administrative and planning purposes.

It is probable that banks will continue to experiment with performance evaluation systems. Computer technology has made it possible to manipulate large quantities of data with a minimum of effort once suitable software programs have been designed. It would seem highly appropriate that banks use this technology to improve administrative decision making. At the same time, care must be used in interpreting profit center data and in communicating to the personnel involved the purposes of the evaluations, so that competition between units does not adversely affect total results.

## Conflict of Interest Policy

It is reasonable for society to expect that both a high level of competence and personal integrity will govern policy formulation and its implementation in commercial banks. A clear fiduciary responsibility is associated with the powers to hold demand deposits, the major component of the money supply, and also to hold the liquid savings of the public. Although the special statutory and administrative regulations imposed on banks are designed to assure that this responsibility is discharged, the regulatory process cannot be expected to cover all possible instances of dubious conduct. Decision making must be decentralized and fragmented, particularly in the loan areas where a large number of heterogeneous credit decisions must be made on a recurrent basis. Therefore, banks are confronted with the problem of establishing policy standards for personal conduct, communicating these policies to a considerable number of individuals, and monitoring compliance through effective information and review procedures.

The principal potential problem in the area of personal conduct arises out of possible conflicts of interest. Because these may take so many different forms and do not directly involve illegal diversions of funds to personal use, the legal regulations governing banks do not cover the problem to any significant extent. As a result, whether policies will be stringent or tolerant with respect to possible conflicts of interest is largely a matter for internal management to decide. And indeed there did not seem to be any consensus among respondent banks as to the appropriate policy and its implementation in this area.

For example, on the stringent side, most respondent banks required all officers to complete an annual questionnaire on their personal financial affairs designed to reveal any potential conflicts of interest. One such questionnaire required detailed information on the following matters:

1. Financial interests, held personally or by near relatives, in any activities of customers of the bank or in association with such customers.[15]

2. Financial interests in any competitive or correspondent bank.

3. Any outside business interest, including directorships, consulting relationships, and real estate holdings.

4. Indebtedness to financial institutions and individuals.

15. An example: a mortgage loan officer invests personal or family funds in an apartment project being constructed by a land developer who is a borrowing customer of the mortgage department. The bank may not finance the project involved, but other deals are so financed. The issue is whether the lending officer may not be influenced in his decisions by the relationship described.

5. Near relatives holding positions with any borrowing customer or in a firm supplying goods or services to the bank.

It should be emphasized that these activities or relationships were not summarily prohibited. But if the information submitted on the questionnaire disclosed any conflicts of interest, then the officers concerned were disqualified from participating in credit decisions with respect to borrowers in which they or their families had "significant financial interest." There were, however, differences of opinion as to the appropriate definition of a "significant financial interest." The extreme view was expressed as follows: "If a loan officer holds securities of a company, policy forbids his participation in loan decisions." More typically, the financial interest was considered significant only if it amounted to about 5 percent or more of total assets of the officer or more than 1 percent of the total common stock of the company. Definitions along these lines were based on the view that moderate holdings of securities of large publicly owned companies, say General Motors, are unlikely to result in any practical conflict of interest problem. On the other hand, if the holdings represent either a fairly substantial proportion of an officer's assets or more than a nominal amount of the total shares outstanding, then it should be construed as a proprietary interest with a consequent conflict of interest problem.

For three reasons a highly sensitive policy toward actual or potential conflicts of interest can be recommended. First, in the aftermath of Watergate, governmental bodies, prodded by the media, have become increasingly critical of corporate ethical standards. Therefore, companies, including banks, can expect recurrent investigations of their policies and practices along these lines. And it may further be expected that the communications media will "sensationalize" even minor revelations of alleged misbehavior. Second, exposure of corporate payments for questionable activities has led the SEC to require increasingly detailed disclosures of corporate activities, and it would seem entirely possible that ultimately all potential conflict of interests might have to be disclosed. Finally, stockholder and consumer litigation against corporations has escalated rapidly in recent years, and there is some legal opinion to the effect that management and directors might be held personally liable for any loss if it can be shown that there was a demonstrable conflict of interest in the transaction.[16] If a bank can show clear evidence of positive and vigorously implemented policies to eliminate conflicts of interest, it is on much firmer ground to defend against charges that asset acquisitions were not made on an entirely objective basis. Therefore, active policies to reveal, monitor, and eliminate conflicts of interest in the decision-making process would seem highly desirable.

Although the matter was not specifically covered in inquiries made to the respondent banks, conflict of interest policies should also be applied to bank directors. It is traditional and probably desirable practice to invite executives of important customer companies to sit on the board. Besides controlling business of considerable importance to the bank, these executives provide valuable inputs on a number of policy issues. Although the companies involved are usually of above-average quality and the credit judgments are usually routine, it is good practice to have a director leave the room when the board is reviewing a credit commitment to his company. The minutes should show that the director was physically absent when the final decision was made, and it is further recommended that board policies preclude preferential terms or rates for bank officers or directors or for companies they are associated with.[17]

16. In an article related to the cost and difficulty of obtaining insurance for officers and directors against "wrongful acts," the following comments were made: "Because awards to plaintiffs and legal fees are soaring, such coverage is becoming more expensive and harder to get. . . . Action by the Securities and Exchange Commission and related shareholder suits strengthened federal disclosure laws and broadened the grounds on which shareholders could sue directors and officers. Indeed, directors and officers have since been held personally responsible by courts for such vaguely defined acts as improvident investment of corporate funds. . . . and even failure to exercise 'reasonable care' in the selection of a depository bank that failed." *Wall Street Journal,* July 12, 1976, p. 1.

17. The importance of a rigorous policy in this connection is suggested by the alleged cause of the failure of U.S. National Bank of San Diego in 1973. It has been alleged that the forced merger of this billion-dollar bank into the Crocker National was primarily due to large insider loans placed by C. Arnholdt Smith, President, to affiliates he controlled. Largely because of these loans, which were in partial or total default, classified loans at one time reached 337 percent of the capital of the bank. (M. Mayer, *The Bankers* [New York: Ballantine Books, 1974], p. 394.)

Finally, as a consequence of certain court decisions, administrative policies must be structured to avoid any possible conflicts of interest between the trust and the commercial loan departments. In a major case, a court held that any person who, because of a special relationship with a company, has access to nonpublic information pertinent to an appraisal of its securities must either disclose the information or refrain from all trading in or recommendations concerning its securities.[18] Most credit files of the commercial loan department contain confidential data on all customer companies. The purpose of the data is to assist in future credit decisions, and there is a clear obligation to prevent unauthorized use. The trust department, on the other hand, is concerned only with the purchase and sale of a company's securities on an impersonal basis because it rightly considers that its main goal is to maximize the investment performance of the funds entrusted to it. Information contained in the credit files on certain companies could be of considerable value to the trust department in reaching investment decisions. However, a reasonable interpretation of the Texas Gulf Sulphur doctrine would suggest that such information could not be used without public disclosure,[19] and its disclosure would clearly violate understandings with commercial customers as to the treatment of confidential information in the credit files.

As a consequence, internal policies have been increasingly structured to ensure a complete insulation between the trust and commercial loan activities. Successful defense against alleged use of insider information may depend upon the introduction of clear evidence that there were effective policies and procedures to deny the trust department access to the credit files. In fact, a strict interpretation of the court and SEC decisions could justify a policy of denying an officer access to the credit files on any company in which that officer held an investment. Otherwise, any

18. SEC v. Texas Gulf Sulphur Co., 401 F. 2d 833 (2d Cir. 1968).

19. In another case Merrill, Lynch used information obtained in connection with an underwriting operation on McDonnell-Douglas to advise certain institutional clients to dispose of the stock. The SEC found this action violated the insider information rules. Merrill, Lynch, Pierce, Fenner and Smith, Inc., CCH Fed Sec. L. Rep. 77, 629 (SEC 1968).

transactions by the officer in the company's securities would seem exposed to the challenge that insider information could have been used as the basis for the decisions. From the tenor of the court cases, it would appear that circumstantial evidence or reasonable inferences can be used in a determination that insider information has been illegally used.

## Portfolio Analysis

The discussion of the environmental context of banking in Chapter 3 noted that in general economic conditions had been favorable for almost thirty years after World War II. Few large banks had shown any significant loan losses. In addition, rather substantial loan loss reserves had been established; under a statutory formula, provisions for possible future loan loses were deductible from taxable income, and it was presumed that any unusual loss experience in the loan portfolio could be charged against the reserve with no impact on earnings or capital. Therefore, careful and regular reviews of the loan portfolio to appraise potential loss exposure hardly seemed necessary. In fact, some respondent banks reported that their organizations did not include a separate loan review and analysis section.

But when the economy experienced only a moderate recession in late 1974 and early 1975, problem loans in some large banks reached alarming proportions and most had defaults and loan losses well in excess of previous experience.[20] Also in late 1975 SEC acounting regulations were amended to require a stratified classification of the loan loss reserve, wherein part is to be considered a deferred tax liability, part included in retained earnings, and only the remainder, about 40 percent of the previous total set up under the statutory formula, available as a valuation por-

20. The Robert Morris Associates, an association of bank lending officers, annually publishes loan loss experience of banks that voluntarily offer the data. In 1975, banks with assets of more than $1 billion reported gross charge-offs as a percent of the commercial loan portfolio of .83 percent, or about double the .42 percent in 1974. The universe might well have even more adverse results as "problem" banks might well be reluctant to supply data. (Robert Morris Associates, *Domestic and International Commercial Loan Charge-Offs* [for year ending December 31, 1975], [Philadelphia, Pa: By the Associates, 1976], Table 2, p. 9.)

tion to absorb charge-offs automatically.[21] The change in effect increases the potential impact on reported earnings of exceptional loan losses, because additional charges against earnings are now required when the valuation portion alone reaches a level that seems questionable in terms of future loan loss possibilities.

In view of these developments, it is not surprising that every respondent bank had a formal loan review process and portfolio evaluations were made on a regular basis. In most cases a separate group or division, reporting to executive management and/or the board of directors, was assigned full-time to carry out the function. Their duties, in addition to review and evaluation, might include assistance on (or takeover of) workout arrangements for problem loans. In some instances, one or more officers were assigned temporarily to workout loans in a particular industry; the Real Estate Trust industry represented a conspicuous instance where such assignments were not unusual.

The appropriate procedure for analysis and evaluation of the retail loan portfolio is quite different from that of the commercial loan account. As the retail credit portfolio is structured on the universe principle, it is properly evaluated on a universe basis, usually by major loan classifications. Table 12–2 shows a condensed form of such an analysis for a hypothetical portfolio. In addition, the amounts of outstandings in each category and comparisons of the data with appropriate prior periods might also be shown in order to reveal any adverse trends. From the data in the table, the universe performance would seem adequate, in the absence of any adverse trends, with the possible exception of home improvement loans. Here management (or the board) might request a critical review of the screening policy, since losses to liquidation are running significantly higher than for banks generally in that Federal Reserve district. Otherwise, it would seem that a vote of confidence could be extended to the consumer loan department, although market penetration data might also be requested to make sure that undue conservatism in loan policy was not causing an undesirable trend in relative outstandings.

21. This observation assumes that variations in past average loan loss experience were not significant as between banks. A larger portion of the total loan loss reserve would be allocated to the valuation portion if past loan loss experience on average had been at a high level.

TABLE 12–2

PORTFOLIO ANALYSIS: CONSUMER LOANS

| Type of Loan | Delinquent Loans: (Percentage of Total) | | | Loss/Liquidation (In Percentage) | |
|---|---|---|---|---|---|
| | 60 Days | 90 Days | Over 90 Days | Portfolio | Federal Reserve District |
| Auto—direct | 2.8 | 2.1 | 0.7 | 0.67 | 0.89 |
| Auto—indirect | 4.1 | 3.0 | 1.2 | 1.12 | 1.25 |
| Home improvement | 5.3 | 4.5 | 2.1 | 1.83 | 1.34 |
| Personal loans | 3.0 | 2.6 | 0.6 | 0.58 | 0.75 |
| Credit cards | 6.1 | 5.0 | 2.7 | 1.94 | 2.15 |

Review and evaluation of the commercial loan portfolio represents a more difficult problem because the credits vary widely as to amount, type, and risk. A comprehensive review of each credit would require an intolerable amount of time. Therefore, a reasonable compromise is to require periodic analyses of large credit exposures and frequent reviews, perhaps monthly, of past-due loans above a specified amount. Individual reports might be requested on large past-due loans, including contemplated action and the reasons for it. Past-due loans below a certain amount could be reported merely as a percentage of the entire universe of that size.

In the periodic reports on large credits, a credit rating schema would seem desirable. In that way, a more precise insight into the quality of the portfolio can be obtained. One respondent bank used the format shown in Figure 12–1 to appraise all large credit exposures in the commercial loan portfolio. Only a summary listing of Rating I and II loans was given in the report, but for loans of lower ratings all executive officers and directors were provided with the kind of detail shown for the hypothetical Jones Chevrolet (Figure 12–2).

Assuming that policy allows a reasonable risk exposure on commitments to commercial customers, then a reasonable proportion of rating III and IV loans would be a normal expectation, perhaps 10–15 percent in III and 5 percent in IV of the total commercial loan portfolio.[22] The objective in rating V is of course zero, but until it exceeds perhaps .5 percent of the total account, it would not be out of line with normative probability expectations based on past charge-off experience.[23] The reasons for the lower ratings might be queried on a case by case basis, and if credit policies or their implementation are responsible, then remedial actions might be instituted, including personnel changes under some circumstances.

22. In fact, unless a bank deals almost exclusively with large prime customers, a very low proportion of rating III and IV credits may suggest an unduly conservative credit policy. Large and profitable customers have emerged from commitments that would be classified at the origin as III and some, if ancillary business is significant, might be made at origin on a IV rating, although this would be very exceptional.

23. Robert Morris Associates, . . . *Commercial Loan Charge-offs,* p. 9.

## COMMERCIAL LOAN PORTFOLIO QUARTERLY REVIEW AND EVALUATION

Report of all secured and unsecured loans in excess of (appropriate amount) as of (given date). The dollar total outstanding of these loans is ......% of our total Commercial Loan Portfolio. The ratings assigned to each credit, with I representing the highest and V the lowest, are categorized as follows:

Rating I: ......% of Commercial Loan Portfolio

Prime loans based upon liquid collateral with adequate margin or supported by a strong financial statement of recent date.

Rating II: ......% of Commercial Loan Portfolio

Loans with a satisfactory repayment program, supported by generally acceptable collateral or current satisfactory statement figures, together with adequate secondary source of repayment.

Rating III: ......% of Commercial Loan Portfolio

Loans supported by adequate collateral or financial figures, but lack one of more of the following:

a. Established liquidation program to retire loan within a reasonable length of time.
b. A working capital commitment where repayment is contingent upon the financial progress of the company over a period of years.
c. Land development loans on residential projects where construction appears slow in relation to the established repayment program required.

Rating IV: ......% of Commercial Loan Portfolio

Loans having characteristics which involve more than normal risk, such as, but not limited to:

a. Loans lacking sufficient supporting strength.
b. Loans not meeting our customary standards, but made because of other considerations.
c. Loans lacking sufficient current supporting credit information.
d. Loans where the obligor is not complying with the terms of the indebtedness.

Rating V: ......% of Commercial Loan Portfolio

Work-out loans on a liquidation basis, loans where the background of the obligor has been determined as questionable, and loans where the collateral or financial condition of the obligor has shown a substantial deterioration.

Submitted by:
F. D. Hardnose
Senior Vice-President

**Fig. 12–1. Analysis forms for hypothetical commercial loan portfolio.**

| | |
|---|---|
| NAME: | Jones Chevrolet, Inc. |
| RATING: | IV |
| BALANCE: | $356,925 |
| HIGH CREDIT: | $650,000 |
| COLLATERAL: | Term loan for 7 years secured by accounts receivable, machinery, equipment, and parts inventory supported by the personal guaranty of Amos Jones. To pick up a $125,000 term loan balance, and to provide additional working capital. |
| RATE: | 120% of the prime rate of interest. |
| REMARKS: | The loan was approved by the Board of Directors on April 7, 1973. The June 30, 1976 financial statement shows current assets of $1,186,000, total liabilities of $984,000, net worth of $289,000, with a debt to worth of 3.3 to 1. Sales for the year ended June 30 were $10,002,000 compared to $9,292,000 for 1975. Net profit after taxes was $56,000 with depreciation of $29,000 and executive salaries and bonuses of $112,000. The Company's commercial checking account has averaged $55,122 for the last twelve months. Retail paper submitted to the bank totaled $2,586,000 for the year ended June 30, 1976, as compared to $2,019,000 for the similar period of 1975. |

**Fig. 12–2. Details on two hypothetical loans rated below II.**

| | |
|---|---|
| NAME: | Jones Leasing, Inc. |
| RATING: | III |
| BALANCE: | $986,535 |
| COMMITMENT: | $1,500,000 |
| COLLATERAL: | Assignment of leased rental income, a security interest in inventory, and the cross guaranty of Jones Chevrolet, Inc. |
| PURPOSE: | To finance leased vehicles. |
| RATE: | All new loans are written at one-half of 1% over the prime rate of interest for the term of the lease. |
| REMARKS: | This commitment was approved by the Board of Directors on July 15, 1975. For the fiscal year ending April 30, 1976, Jones Leasing showed total income of $268,000 and an after-tax net profit of $22,000. Checking account balances have averaged $19,225 over the past eleven months. On September 14, 1975, the following aging of lease payments was taken from the Company's accounts receivable ledger: |

| | |
|---|---|
| 0/30 days | $20,212.04 |
| 31/60 days | 10,508.79 |
| 61/90 days | 6,230.30 |
| Over 90 days | 4,752.99 |
| Prepaid | (2,151.99) |
| Total | $39,372.13 |

**Fig. 12–2** ***Continued***

# 5

# INTERNATIONAL POLICIES

# XIII

## INTERNATIONAL BANKING: NATURE AND SCOPE

### Special Features

The basic objectives guiding policy formulation for the international activities of a commercial bank are the same as for the domestic operation. These are (1) to increase or retain profitable deposit or other relationships with customers, (2) to provide the appropriate services in a competitive context at a reasonable cost to the bank, (3) to obtain the maximum gross returns on the services rendered, again in a competitive context, and (4) to hold the risk exposure of the bank within tolerable limits. The overall purpose of these several objectives is to promote the maximum rate of earnings return and growth consistent with a prudent risk exposure.

Moreover, in performing its major function, that of a financial intermediary to acquire funds (deposits) and to loan these funds to others, the basic principles are the same in the international markets as in the domestic markets. They are to acquire the deposits on a reasonably assured basis at a minimum cost and to lend such funds at tolerable risk levels, where reasonable spreads between money costs and loan yields are obtained. As to commitments to major domestic corporate customers, the policies and decisions involved on both domestic and international needs are usually made in the bank's home office and the international department may serve only as a funding source for foreign currency requirements. However, in the case of international loans, terms and pricing of the loan commitments may be more closely related to the funding sources than is typically true of domestic commitments.

But the international department also conducts several operations which have no parallel on the domestic side. First, there is the foreign exchange trading operation. Through an international network of dealers and banks, foreign currencies are constantly purchased and sold. Some banks seem to regard this activity primarily as a customer-service requirement in which risk exposure is to be minimized and break-even results expected. Others seem to have a more aggressive policy in this area in the form of tolerating greater risk exposures on currency positions with a view to obtaining positive trading profits. The present international system of floating exchange rates has increased both risks and profit potentials, and policies have been reassessed in some banks as a result—usually toward a more defensive posture.[1] In any case, as foreign exchange trading policies are largely separate and independent of lending policies, they will be not be specifically considered in this section.

A second operation unique to international banking is the financing of specific shipments of goods through bankers acceptances drawn under letters of credit. In domestic trade, most goods are shipped on an open account basis, giving rise to accounts receivable, which of course may be financed in total by a bank loan. However, because open account shipments are not customary in many countries and also because credit checkings across international boundaries are more difficult, the bankers acceptance mechanism is used instead. Under this arrangement the credit standing of the bank is substituted for that of the customer; the bank accepts a time draft covering the cost of the goods which guarantees payment at maturity. While the transaction resembles a short-term loan in the sense that the bank relies on the customer to pay the draft at maturity, no funds are actually advanced. The revenues are obtained through imposition of fees for the use of the bank's credit standing rather than through interest changes.

Third, for customers' international activities banks provide more extensive services than is customary on the domestic scene.

1. The following policy statement is illustrative: "A keystone of our foreign exchange policy has been always to budget low for trading profits. At no time is pressure applied to induce our traders to take unnecessary risks or excessive positions to maximize profits. (G. R. Baker and A. F. Miossi, *International Services*, Continental Illinois Report, Oct. 30, 1975, p. 23.)

These might include local currency loans, economic and political analysis of countries, and introductions to indigenous financial institutions, commercial firms, and governmental agencies. An international department designed to provide these services on a world-wide basis will probably have a fairly complete library of information on the financial markets and economy of each country in which any significant volume of business is conducted. In addition, the home office organization structure may develop along specialty lines, analogous to the specialized industry groups that are found in the domestic commercial loan operation. The usual pattern is geographical specialization, possibly supplemented by certain functional specialties.[2] The world is divided into areas or zones and a separate officer group is established for each zone.

The policy issue confronting major banks in the development stage of their international operation is whether the expected volume of business can justify an organization based on zone specialities. A breakdown along these lines should of course improve the quality of international services, but it also represents a significant commitment to staff and facilities that would be difficult to reverse once the operation was fully established.

Fourth, in many foreign countries, the private sector often tends to occupy a subordinate role to government. Therefore, a substantial proportion of the business of both the bank and its customers will probably either be done directly with government agencies or subject to close government supervision and approval. In these countries, therefore, it is usually essential to establish close and continuing political contacts and relationships.

Fifth, in most European countries, with the exception of England, banks are permitted a much wider scope of activity than in the United States. Bank activities on the continent may include stock brokerage, direct equity investments, commodity trading, underwriting of security issues, and insurance operations through subsidiaries. As a consequence, if a U.S. bank acquires

2. The multinational banking directory of the Chase Manhattan Bank, which lists their foreign branches, officers, affiliates, and home office zone groups, consists of 92 pages. Besides zone breakdowns, specialties are noted in Eurocurrencies, International Trade Services, Commodity Financing, Portfolio and Investment Banking, and International Economic Forecasting.

a subsidiary or affiliated bank in these countries, the scope of its indigenous operations may be expanded well beyond the limits allowed the home office.[3] Home office supervision of activities outside the normal framework of domestic banking, therefore, may be required.

Sixth, specialized financial institutions, such as the savings and loan associations and consumer finance companies, which are part of the institutional pattern in the United States, seem to be even more prevalent abroad. Factoring, leasing, investment banking (merchant banking), and medium-term financing are among the activities that may be conducted through specialized companies. Because their access to resources may be limited, they may welcome an affiliation with a major American bank. They have the advantage of being established indigenous operations, and U.S. banks have been active in acquiring either a controlling or substantial minority interest in these specialty operations. Control of these companies' policies has sometimes been difficult; indeed a few have caused significant problems to the related U.S. banks. Therefore, the aggressive development of ancillary financial interests abroad has seemed to abate in recent years; in fact some complete or partial liquidation of positions was notable in the 1974–76 period. However, it is probable that U.S. banks will continue to acquire equity positions in existing banks and other financial institutions abroad on a selective basis; alternatively, de novo institutions may be organized often in association with other banks, both foreign and domestic. In brief, investment type activities tend to be more significant on an ongoing basis in international than in domestic banking.

## The Eurocurrency Markets

A major feature of substantive international programs is active participation in the Eurocurrency markets. As applied to U.S. banks, this market essentially consists of the purchase of deposits denominated in currencies other than that of the host country and either redepositing the funds in other banks or lending them

3. It may also involve a risk. In 1970, the Swiss subsidiary of the United California Bank failed because of losses, estimated to range up to $40 million, incurred in the trading of cocoa futures. The parent bank in order to maintain its reputation in Europe reportedly paid all creditors' claims.

on a variety of terms to borrowers in the public or private sector anywhere in the world. Technically, for example, a Eurocurrency deposit would arise if a bank in New York purchased a deposit denominated in German marks or English pounds. But by and large the market is dominated by Eurodollars, which consist of dollar deposits in banks outside the United States, including Canadian banks and overseas branches of U.S. banks.[4] Since World War II the U.S. dollar has been the official reserve currency for most countries outside the Soviet bloc, and consequently it has replaced the English pound sterling as the major international medium of exchange. Despite the devaluations in recent years, it remains the principal trading currency and, therefore, loans denominated in dollars have become standard in many areas of the world. Although the superior stability of the German mark and Swiss franc has increased the role of these currencies over the years, primarily as an international hedge against a decline in the value of the dollar, they are not in sufficient supply to support international liquidity requirements and also to finance trade and capital movements on a world-wide basis.

### Reasons for growth

The diversion of dollar liquid assets to Eurodollar deposits is superficially easy to explain. Rates and maturities have regularly been more attractive than on domestic money market instruments, such as CDs, Treasury bills, and acceptances. Table 13–1 shows the prevailing rates for quarterly intervals on one-month to six-month CDs as compared to similar-maturity Eurodollar rates between 1971 and 1976. The positive yield spread shows considerable variance, but in general Eurodollar deposits have offered at least a .5 percent premium over domestic CD deposits.[5] And Euro-

4. It is estimated that about 70–75 percent of all Eurocurrency deposits are represented by Eurodollars; German marks constitute 14–17 percent, Swiss francs about 7-9 percent, and English sterling the balance. Data for computations contained in Bank for International Settlements, *Annual Reports*.

5. Some domestic banks that have no international operations as such have placed funds in the Eurodollar market (since 1974, when the restraints on the use of domestic dollars abroad were eliminated) through time deposit placements in foreign banks (usually Canadian) payable in U.S. dollars. Such deposits represent a temporary layoff of excess liquidity on which rates have been more attractive than on alternative domestic money market instruments. The operation is essentially that of interest arbitrage and if used generally should reduce the spread between the Eurodollar markets and domestic market rates.

TABLE 13–1
SHORT TERM YIELDS
$ EURO vs. CDs

| Year | | 1-Month | | | 3-Month | | | 6-Month | | |
|---|---|---|---|---|---|---|---|---|---|---|
| | | $ Euro | CDs | Basis Pts. Spread | $ Euro | CDs | Basis Pts. Spread | $ Euro | CDs | Basis Pts. Spread |
| 1971 | March | 5.19 | 3.90 | 129 | 5.31 | 4.00 | 131 | 5.81 | 4.15 | 166 |
| | June | 7.75 | 5.10 | 265 | 7.50 | 5.30 | 220 | 7.50 | 5.55 | 195 |
| | Sept. | 9.63 | 5.40 | 423 | 9.00 | 5.60 | 340 | 8.88 | 5.80 | 308 |
| | Dec. | 6.13 | 4.50 | 163 | 6.13 | 4.85 | 128 | 6.13 | 5.10 | 103 |
| 1972 | March | 4.63 | 3.50 | 113 | 4.94 | 3.80 | 114 | 5.44 | 4.25 | 119 |
| | June | 4.25 | 4.15 | 10 | 4.56 | 4.40 | 16 | 5.25 | 4.70 | 55 |
| | Sept. | 5.06 | 4.80 | 26 | 5.44 | 5.15 | 29 | 6.13 | 5.50 | 63 |
| | Dec. | 6.00 | 4.95 | 105 | 5.94 | 5.25 | 69 | 6.18 | 5.50 | 68 |
| 1973 | March | 8.50 | 6.25 | 225 | 8.31 | 6.55 | 176 | 8.19 | 6.75 | 144 |
| | June | 8.50 | 7.50 | 100 | 8.56 | 7.80 | 76 | 8.69 | 7.85 | 84 |
| | Sept. | 11.44 | 10.55 | 89 | 11.50 | 10.90 | 60 | 11.50 | 9.50 | 200 |
| | Dec. | 10.81 | 9.70 | 111 | 10.38 | 9.30 | 108 | 9.81 | 9.00 | 81 |

*Continued*

Table 13–1, *Continued*

| Year | | 1-Month | | | 3-Month | | | 6-Month | | |
|---|---|---|---|---|---|---|---|---|---|---|
| | | $ Euro | CDs | Basis Pts. Spread | $ Euro | CDs | Basis Pts. Spread | $ Euro | CDs | Basis Pts. Spread |
| 1974 | March | 8.94 | 8.45 | 49 | 8.56 | 8.30 | 26 | 8.56 | 8.00 | 56 |
| | June | 12.06 | 10.80 | 126 | 11.88 | 11.10 | 78 | 11.88 | 10.85 | 103 |
| | Sept. | 12.75 | 11.90 | 85 | 13.88 | 12.15 | 173 | 14.06 | 12.00 | 206 |
| | Dec. | 11.00 | 9.60 | 140 | 10.63 | 9.50 | 113 | 10.63 | 9.30 | 133 |
| 1975 | March | 6.75 | 6.30 | 45 | 7.25 | 6.35 | 90 | 7.56 | 6.40 | 116 |
| | June | 6.00 | 5.35 | 65 | 6.00 | 5.65 | 35 | 7.00 | 6.15 | 85 |
| | Sept. | 6.63 | 6.40 | 23 | 7.25 | 6.80 | 45 | 8.31 | 7.70 | 61 |
| | Dec. | 6.63 | 5.55 | 108 | 6.94 | 6.25 | 69 | 7.69 | 6.90 | 79 |
| 1976 | March | 5.38 | 5.15 | 23 | 5.56 | 5.40 | 16 | 6.31 | 5.90 | 41 |
| | June | 6.25 | 5.50 | 75 | 6.56 | 6.00 | 56 | 7.25 | 6.55 | 70 |

Source: Salomon Brothers, *An Analytical Record of Yields and Yields Spreads*, New York, 1976 edition.

dollar placements can also be made on an overnight or weekly basis, whereas CDs can only be offered with a minimum of one month. While T-bills and acceptances can be purchased for maturities of less than a month, their supply is limited and their rates are relatively unattractive.

But the fundamental explanation for the growth in these deposits rests in the reasons *why* rates are more attractive in the Eurodollar market. Several reasons have been advanced. First, Eurodollars deposits do not have a reserve requirement if employed overseas, and second, regulations and customs that inhibit deposit and loan rates and loan maturities in many domestic markets do not apply to Eurodollar transactions.[6] Third, U.S. controls instituted to ameliorate balance-of-payment problems, while now largely eliminated, greatly reduced the ability to fund international loans with domestic dollars when they were in effect. As a consequence, Eurodollar deposits became the major source of international loan funding. Finally, large unit-size deposits and loans dominate the Eurocurrency market; many loans are structured through syndication groups of a number of banks. The consequence has been that somewhat narrower spreads tend to prevail in these markets than is customary or acceptable in most domestic markets.[7] In fact, narrow spreads mean that deposit rates can be higher and effective loan rates lower than in the domestic markets, and, given interest sensitivity on the part of both depositors and borrowers, this should lead to a continued growth in the Eurodollar market so long as the spread pattern continues.[8]

6. These noted in G. Bell, *The Eurodollar Market and the International Financial System* (New York: John Wiley & Sons, 1973), pp. 9–11.

7. In the 1968–73 period considerable criticism of Eurocurrency banking was based on the view that spreads had become too narrow to justify the risks involved. For example: "While interest rate differentials clearly permit Eurobanks to offer cost advantages to depositors and borrowers, it may seem that the banks themselves must get pinched between converging deposit and loan rates. And, indeed, steamy competition has driven the Eurobanks to operate on very narrow margins of as little as .13 to .25 percent for prime name banks and .5 percent for prime industrial or commercial firms." (H. V. Prochnow and H. V. Prochnow, Jr., eds., *The Changing World of Banking*, [New York: Harper & Row, 1974], p. 105.)

8. A specific analysis of the factors controlling the size of the market concluded: "Thus the paramount determinant of the size of the Eurodollar market is the width of the margins on which Eurobanks are prepared to operate." (G. Dufey

**Eurodollar intermediation process**

As foreign branches are the primary medium by which U.S. banks participate in the Eurocurrency markets, the data on the assets and liabilities of such branches, shown in Table 13–2, suggest the nature and growth of the intermediation process conducted in these markets. As to growth, the data show that asset and liability totals increased by a factor of about 3.487 between 1970 and 1975 inclusive, which represents an average annual compound percentage growth rate of roughly 30 percent. Clearly this growth rate was remarkable, but almost half of the totals represented interbank transactions, most of which are described as overnight or at most weekly funds. Eurocurrency traders (not loan officers) conduct these operations on the basis of fractional spreads, often in close association with foreign exchange traders; indeed they often share communication facilities. Therefore, in a technical sense the purchase and redeposit of Eurocurrencies between banks may be construed as a dealer trading process with position limits imposed by credit officers responsible for interbank relations.

Because the purchase of Eurocurrency deposits and their redeposit in other Eurobanks is largely a short-term trading operation to obtain fractional turnover spreads—and indeed it may be conducted on a breakeven basis to maintain visibility in the market—it is difficult to consider this activity as part of lending policies per se. However, the Eurocurrency traders are often responsible for funding loans, and in some instances interbank transactions may represent advances of several months or more, or essentially unsecured loans. Therefore, policies with respect to interbank transactions will be briefly considered as part of the framework of credit and pricing policies.

Official institutions, presumably mostly central banks, both borrow from and offer funds to the market, but on balance Table 13–12 shows that offerings are considerably larger than the borrowings. These institutions hold foreign currencies both for exchange stabilization purposes and also for official reserves against

---

and I. Giddy, "Credit Creation and the Growth of the Eurodollar Market," Research Paper No. 127, Graduate School of Business, Columbia University, July 1976, p. 46.)

TABLE 13–2
U.S. BANKS
ASSETS AND LIABILITIES OF FOREIGN BRANCHES
(In Billion of Dollars)

| | 1970 | 1971 | 1972 | 1973 | 1974 | 1975 | 1976* |
|---|---|---|---|---|---|---|---|
| *Assets* | | | | | | | |
| Claims on U.S.: | | | | | | | |
| Parent bank | 7.2 | 2.3 | 2.1 | 1.9 | 4.5 | 3.7 | 3.3 |
| Other | 2.5 | 2.5 | 2.6 | 3.2 | 2.4 | 3.1 | 3.4 |
| Claims on Foreigners: | | | | | | | |
| Other banks | 17.0 | 24.6 | 36.7 | 56.4 | 60.3 | 68.4 | 74.2 |
| Official institutions | .7 | 1.7 | 1.7 | 2.7 | 4.1 | 5.9 | 7.9 |
| Nonbanks | 11.6 | 17.8 | 22.9 | 33.7 | 46.8 | 54.5 | 57.6 |
| Total | 39.0 | 48.9 | 66.0 | 97.9 | 118.1 | 135.6 | 146.4 |
| *Liabilities* | | | | | | | |
| To U.S.: | | | | | | | |
| Parent bank | 0.7 | 0.7 | 1.0 | 1.6 | 5.8 | 12.1 | 16.5 |
| Other | 1.9 | 2.4 | 2.6 | 4.0 | 6.2 | 8.1 | 11.5 |
| To Foreigners: | | | | | | | |
| Other banks | 24.8 | 31.1 | 42.5 | 65.4 | 65.7 | 72.2 | 75.4 |
| Official institutions | 4.2 | 5.5 | 8.5 | 10.3 | 20.2 | 22.8 | 21.5 |
| Nonbanks | 7.4 | 8.8 | 11.5 | 17.7 | 20.2 | 20.8 | 22.8 |
| Total | 39.0 | 48.5 | 66.1 | 99.0 | 118.1 | 136.0 | 147.7 |

Source: *Federal Reserve Bulletin,* Table 21a, Apr. 1973, and Table 19a, Sept. 1976.
Note: Excludes interbranch assets and liabilities and minor amounts not separately classified; because of exclusions assets and liabilities do not necessarily balance.
* Preliminary data as of June 30, 1976.

domestic currencies, and returns on such funds can be obtained through placement in the Eurocurrency markets.

Nonbank foreign sources of funds (liabilities of branches) are substantial in amount but their borrowings (assets of branches) significantly exceed their deposits and the gap increasingly widened between 1970 and 1976 inclusive; in the latter year, about 40 percent of branch assets were in this category and about 15 percent of liabilities. This category represents the private sector for the most part and on the asset side constitutes the loan portfolio analogous to domestic commercial loans. Finally, it is notable that with the January 1974 removal of limits on the use of domestic funds overseas, parent banks and others in the United States have greatly increased their placements in the Eurocurrency markets. Indeed in 1970, during a domestic credit crunch, significant amounts of Eurrodollar funds were repatriated to the United States, whereas in 1976 domestic placements (branch liabilities) in the market were almost three times the takings from the market (branch assets). If the interest rate disparity shown in Table 13–1 continues, the gap between placements and takings may grow even larger in the future.

The phenomenal growth of the Eurocurrency market has raised the issue of the need for an international regulatory structure to (1) assure its soundness as an international finance mechanism, and (2) prevent its operation from neutralizing internal monetary policies. As to the first need, it has been alleged that the widespread practice of extending term credits from Eurocurrency time deposits with three-or six-month maturities could precipitate a liquidity crisis in the event of some unsettling development that might dry up even temporarily the placement of such time deposits. However, the fact that the major financial institutions throughout the world, including several central banks, have heavy stakes in the viability of this market suggests that massive efforts would be taken to prevent a major crisis in the Eurocurrency markets.[9]

The second need may arise from a more serious problem, but it is difficult to conceive of an appropriate regulatory structure to meet it. In essence, the ability of financial institutions and corporations to tap or place large amounts of funds in the Euro-

9. In 1974–75 the failure of a few banks and rumors about problems of others caused severe strains in the Eurocurrency markets as some found it difficult to obtain funds at all or were required to pay premium "risk" rates. The reported response: ". . . the major central banks of Europe, Japan, and the U.S. have publicly reassured banks or foreign branches of banks under each jurisdiction that they will stand ready as 'lender of last resort' in case of trouble; . . . if a bank is behaving itself but gets into trouble through no fault of its own, the central bank will stand behind them. If a bank is misbehaving, through making risky loans or engaging in other questionable practices, it might still be rescued for the sake of preserving other banks it might be linked to. But in such a case . . . the rescue would be conditioned on removal of the management of the bank." (René Larre, general manager of the Bank for International Settlements, as quoted in the *Wall Street Journal,* June 13, 1975, p. 4.)

currency market means that it becomes more difficult for national monetary policies to obtain the desired degree of tightness or ease in the domestic money markets. One opinion holds that central banks could attempt to insulate domestic interest rates by restricting the ability of national institutions to direct funds to, or repatriate them from, the Eurocurrency markets .Therefore, although the phenomenal growth of the free international markets in Eurocurrencies has been a major development affecting international banking strategies, some uncertainties seem to exist concerning the markets' future freedom from intervention, either individual or collective, by the central banks.[10]

## Growth of International Operations

Until the early sixties, large commercial banks, except for a few coastal banks, confined their international activities primarily to foreign exchange trading and to financing specific export and import transactions through the bankers acceptance mechanism. They maintained correspondent relations with banks in a number of countries to assist in the documentation and collection process related to foreign trade. On occasion they might call on these correspondents to provide technical assistance and local currency loans to bank customers. By and large, however, they did not provide a comprehensive package of international banking services. As manufacturing and commercial operations of U.S. companies abroad were mainly confined to a few giant corporations that found it relatively easy to arrange suitable banking connections, the rather minimal scope of most international operations could be justified.

However, for a number of reasons, international activities have come to occupy a considerably more important role in the business strategies of major banking institutions. Perhaps the most important direct cause of this reorientation was the expansion of corporate customers into foreign markets through direct investments in subsidiaries and affiliates abroad. As an increasing number of their

10. The imposition of reserve requirements on Eurocurrency deposits through international agreements of central banks and/or open market operations by a few international official institutions to promote ease or tighten the market have been proposed. However, as of 1976, these ideas were still in the discussion stage. (*Wall Street Journal*, June 13, 1975, p. 4.)

important customers became multinational in scope, the large regional banks became increasingly vulnerable to competitive pressures exerted by the few coastal banks that had long had a fully developed network of international operations.

In reviewing the international program of one respondent bank a senior officer offered the following comment: "In order to retain the major portion of certain customers' domestic business, we decided that it was necessary for us to expand and improve the scope of our activities abroad." In short, much of the original impetus towards the expansion of international programs was primarily defensive in character, in the sense that important domestic business was exposed to competitive inroads unless the quantity and quality of foreign banking services could be substantially upgraded. However, as costs of establishing facilities abroad are usually considerable, it is doubtful if the volume of business available in many areas can provide an adequate earnings return on the required investment. Therefore, although regional banks are gradually increasing the number of their foreign branches in certain strategic locations, branching on a large scale abroad will probably be restricted to a few banks.

Several developments provided the impetus for establishing at least one offshore banking facility, preferably a London branch, during the late sixties and early seventies. The first was the explosive growth of the Eurocurrency loan markets during this period. Because the market is centered in London, active participation in it is greatly facilitated by a London operation. Table 13–3 shows the parallel growth of the Eurocurrency markets and the establishment of London branches by major U.S. banks since 1965.[11] Since 1965, the number of such banks represented in London has almost tripled, and during the same period total bank loans in the Eurocurrency markets increased more than tenfold. Of course many large banks from throughout the world also established London facilities to participate in the market, so the growth pattern for Eurocurrency loans cannot be assumed as accruing primarily to U.S. banks.

11. As of 1975 only one respondent bank out of seven with assets in excess of $2 billions had not established a London branch. Most had established their branches since 1965. The holdout bank indicated that entry into the London market was under serious consideration as of 1976.

The data show that a definite surge in London branch openings occurred in 1968–69. Two special reasons can be cited for this fact, neither of which is operative as of 1976. The first was that Regulation Q limits on CD rates were sometimes below open market rates during the 1966–70 period, which caused considerable liquidity pressures as CDs ran off and could not be renewed. Banks with London branches obtained partial liquidity relief through the purchase of Eurodollars in the London market (where rates were uncontrolled) and then relending these funds to the home office. Both in 1966 and again in 1969–70, home office borrowings from foreign branches increased at a rapid rate. While the removal of Regulation Q on wholesale CDs has eliminated the need for this source of liquidity relief, this action of the Fed could not be assumed in advance. Therefore, the liquidity safety valve offered by the Eurodollar market probably triggered a number of decisions to open London branches in the 1968–70 period.

The so-called Voluntary Foreign Credit Restraint program in

TABLE 13–3
U.S. LONDON BRANCHES AND EUROCURRENCY BANK LOANS

| DATE OF ORIGIN | BRANCHES ESTABLISHED* | EUROCURRENCY LOANS OF BANKS† (In $ Billions) |
|---|---|---|
| Prior to 1965 | 9 | . . . |
| 1965 | 4 | NA |
| 1966 | 0 | 15 |
| 1967 | 1 | 19 |
| 1968 | 9 | 30 |
| 1969 | 7 | 44 |
| 1970 | 3 | 57 |
| 1971 | 2 | 71 |
| 1972 | 1 | 92 |
| 1973 | 3 | 132 |
| 1974 | 5 | 177 |
| 1975 | 0 | 197 |
| Total | 44 | |

Sources: *Bank of England Statistical Abstract,* No. 1, 1970, pp. 66–7, and No. 2, 1975, p. 65 (branches); and Bank of International Settlements (loans).

* Five U.S. banks have two branches in London area. Therefore, 39 different American banks were represented in London as of 1975.

† Excludes transactions between banks, but all foreign Eurobanks included.

effect between 1965 and early 1974 also provided a reason to establish an offshore facility. This program, designed to prevent deterioration in the U.S. balance of payments position, rigorously limited to essentially a rollover basis bank loans funded from domestic deposits to finance the overseas requirements of American firms and other customers (except for import and export transactions) in countries defined as "developed" by the Treasury and Federal Reserve. Canada was excepted, but all of Continental Europe, Britain, most of the Middle-East, and most communist countries were included in the "developed" category. Therefore, to fund customer financial requirements in these areas, access to the Eurocurrency markets was essential and many large banks responded accordingly by establishing an offshore branch in either London or Nassau; either location could be used to book Eurocurrency deposit purchases and loans outside the credit restraint program.[12]

## Outlook

As foreign credits can now be funded with domestic deposits and home office borrowings of Eurodollars for liquidity purposes are no longer necessary, it is doubtful if many additional U.S. banks will establish overseas facilities. During 1975 and the first half of 1976, not a single U.S. bank opened in London. In fact, three U.S. banks closed representative offices in London, and maintaining such offices is often a prelude to establishing a full branch. The reason given:

> Since the unnerving banking collapses in London in 1974, London-based branches often have had to pay premiums to attract funds. Currently funds are available but what would they do with them? . . . Local loan demand is down, credit-worthy governments and corporations abroad are getting scarcer, and foreign-exchange

12. An officer of the Federal Reserve made the following comment concerning the growth of U.S. banking facilities overseas: "The internationalization of United States banking was closely associated with the rise to prominence in the world economy of multinational corporations which require broadly diversified financial facilities in a large number of countries. Another important factor was the program of capital controls . . . which put pressure on United States banks to establish banking facilities abroad in order to serve the borrowing needs of their customers operating overseas." (R. A. Debs, "International Banking," *Monthly Review,* Federal Reserve Bank of New York, June 1975, pp. 123–24.)

volume limps along at 60 percent of the year-earlier page. Until there's a much stronger world economy, the City's population of alien bankers is apt, at best, to remain flat.[13]

The major change in the balance of payments of the OPEC countries relative to other countries of the world has also posed a serious problem to international banking, and its resolution was not clear as of 1976. A significant proportion of the huge surpluses of the oil producing countries, mainly in the Middle East, have been "recycled" through the Eurocurrency markets, but on a basis that has apparently increased operational risks in these markets. According to one source, the so-called "petro-dollars" have been concentrated in overnight deposits and some banks have used such deposits to fund credits of longer maturities.[14] Thus a limited number of depositors have come to control a large volume of short-term funds, and, while it would be impossible for these funds to withdraw from the market as a whole, one or more banks could suffer a large erosion of funds if for any reason the "approved list" of eligible banks was revised to exclude their names. The predictable result was described as follows:

> The response of Euro-banks . . . was to cut their credit lines rather ruthlessly for all but the very best names. Quality became the watchword . . . and rate structures in virtually all money and loan markets reflected this preference for quality. *In the Euro-market even banks with good names, but less well-known than the prime banks, were forced to pay a premium over the rates offered to the bigger institutions.* [italics mine]. . . . One consequence of this tiered rate pattern was that many banks at rollover dates for syndicated term loans were forced to refinance their commitments at rates close to or above the rates payable by the borrowers. Fears were then widespread in the London financial community that some of the smaller banks participating in the Eurocurrency market would be unable to secure sufficient funds to refinance their medium-term loans. Some of these banks, including branches and affiliates of regional banks in the United States, began last year to pull in their horns and to scale down their Eurocurrency activities. . . .[15]

13. *Wall Street Journal*, Jan. 12, 1976, p. 6.

14. R. A. Debs, "International Banking," p. 124.

15. *Ibid.*, p. 125. Another reason why regional banks reduced their Eurocurrency activities at least temporarily was that some serious loan problems emerged in

It is possible, therefore, that a few moderate-sized regional banks may reduce the scope of their international programs, and some that have contemplated entry into the international arena may decide to postpone the decision indefinitely. But on the other side, although the explosive geometric growth rate of the Eurocurrency markets may be receding, for reasons indicated above, rapid growth in absolute terms may continue for some time. Therefore, it is probable that most U.S. banks with existing facilities abroad will continue to expand their operations in this market.

The data on the growth in assets and deposits of the London branches of U.S. banks, shown in Table 13–4, provide some evidence in support of this proposition. Data on the London subset of overseas branches are useful, because London is the center of the overseas activities of most regional U.S. banks, whereas the data on world-wide branches shown in Table 13–2 may be dominated by the few very large banks with extensive branch networks. The London branch data show that even during the two troubled years of 1974–75 deposits and loans of U.S. banks operating there increased by the second largest amount on record. Indeed, Eurocurrency deposits and loans (other currency data in Table 13–14) increased by the largest amount on record during this two-year period.

It is less clear whether the growth in international loans made both here and abroad will take place within a framework of tolerable risk exposure. The following comment is indicative of a disturbing trend in this respect:

> In 1975, however, the market for the first time was dominated by developing country loans. If one includes the non–oil-producing OPEC countries, then loans to developing countries accounted for

---

1975. It was estimated, for example, that banks extended credits of about $10 billion to finance large tankers and that a significant proportion were in de facto default as of 1976, because many large tankers were out of operation because of surplus tanker capacity. Losses of a significant amount might become visible in about 1977–78, given the time lag between default and ultimate write-off. (N. Faith, "How the World Tanker Slump May Affect Banks' Balance Sheet," *Euromoney*, June 1976, pp. 14–16.)

TABLE 13–4
MAJOR LOANS AND DEPOSITS
U.S. BANKS IN LONDON
(In £ Millions)

| | SELECTED YEARS (December Dates) | | | | | |
|---|---|---|---|---|---|---|
| | 1965 | 1967 | 1969 | 1971 | 1973 | 1975 |
| Assets: | | | | | | |
| Deposit placements (London banks only) | 199 | 489 | 1,703 | 3,182 | 6,693 | 8,390 |
| Sterling loans | 260 | 477 | 696 | 1,252 | 2,847 | 3,401 |
| Other currency loans | 879 | 2,808 | 7,533 | 8,912 | 15,475 | 24,825 |
| Total | 1,338 | 3,774 | 9,932 | 13,346 | 25,015 | 36,616 |
| Deposits: | | | | | | |
| Sterling | 351 | 477 | 696 | 1,519 | 3,945 | 3,997 |
| Other currencies | 1,081 | 2,806 | 9,059 | 11,908 | 21,676 | 32,770 |
| Total | 1,432 | 3,283 | 9,755 | 13,427 | 25,621 | 36,767 |

Sources: Bank of England, *Statistical Abstracts* for 1970 and 1975 and *Quarterly Bulletin,* Mar. 1976.

more than half the total volume raised in the medium term Eurocurrency market.[16]

Moreover, this trend apparently continued in 1976 when for several months loans to developing countries dominated the medium term credits reported in the Eurocurrency market.[17] The ability of these countries to generate sufficient foreign exchange to cover their rapidly growing external debt is of course open to serious question. The means used to control exposure here will be covered in the chapter on credit policies, but at least some large international banks domiciled throughout the world have apparently concluded that the debt burdens of developing countries can be expanded on an open-end basis. The dangers inherent in this expansion should be evident, and policies to restrict or even eliminate credit exposures in many of these countries may be prudent.

16. S. M. Yussukovich, "The Growing Political Threat to International Lending," *Euromoney,* Apr. 1976, p. 12.

17. "Medium-term Eurocredits," *Euromoney,* July 1976, pp. 108–10.

# XIV

## FOREIGN OPERATIONS: IMPLEMENTATION OPTIONS

A home office international department plus an offshore branch in order to participate in the Eurocurrency market would be the minimal facilities for implementing international operations on any significant scale. In addition, the following options are available to implement the international business of a commercial bank:

1. Conduct operations through a system of correspondent bank affiliations.
2. Establish foreign branches on a selective basis.
3. Establish representative offices in selected countries.
4. Acquire foreign banks or related financial institutions either as subsidiaries or as affiliates (with less than majority interest).
5. Participate in the equity ownership of specialized overseas financial consortia with domestic and foreign banks.
6. Establish an office or offices in the major U.S. cities where international business is conducted, principally New York or on the West Coast.

### Regulatory Structure

#### U.S. regulation

There are no unique regulatory features associated with home office international operations, which may consist of some combination of the following: foreign exchange trading, financing exports and imports through the bankers acceptance mechanism, extending credits to foreign firms or governmental units, and advances to U.S. firms to finance overseas activities. Indeed, it is theoretically possible to structure home office loans in any currency, although policies with respect to currency risks may prohibit foreign currency credits funded from dollar deposits unless properly hedged. These several operations are, of course, subject to appropriate review and criticism in the course of the examinations conducted by the Comptroller of the Currency, Federal Reserve, or State Banking Department as appropriate.[1]

Moreover, banks can establish relations with correspondent banks in foreign countries or open representative offices without obtaining special authorization of the regulatory authorities. Indeed, as Table 14–1 shows, there are sixty-four U.S. banks that state they are engaged in international banking solely through the use of foreign correspondent banking relationships. But because effective participation in the Eurocurrency markets requires an offshore banking facility, the scope of an international operation conducted only through foreign correspondents is necessarily very limited. However, it should be noted that all U.S. banks actively engaged in the international sector maintain a number of correspondent relations abroad, especially in areas where the volume of busines available does not justify the establishment of additional facilities.

The data in Table 14–1 show that as of 1976 one hundred and twenty-three U.S. banks had at least one offshore branch. Some seventy-nine of these were represented only in the Bahamas area; they may be classified as those that want a "cheap" participation in the Eurocurrency market.[2] A few years ago a number of banks had London branches for this purpose, but as of 1976 only two had not expanded their branch facilities to other areas. In all cases, specific prior permission of the Federal Reserve is required to open a foreign branch or, with certain exceptions, to acquire foreign subsidiaries or interests in foreign affiliates. At this point the regulatory structure becomes further complicated by the fact that branches, subsidiaries, and affiliates may be directly under the parent bank or, alternatively, a special U.S. international sub-

1. The failure of the Franklin National Bank in 1974 was in part attributed to large losses in foreign exchange trading operations which took speculative positions in foreign currencies that subsequently declined in value against the dollar. Special regulatory constraints on foreign exchange trading have been recommended as a result, but as of 1976 no action had yet been taken, although examination procedures may now give special attention to this activity.
2. Some banks that had only a Bahamas branch also had representative offices in London or in other areas. The Bank of England has suggested in some cases that a rep office in London would be "appropriate" before a formal branch is opened.

TABLE 14–1
USE OF ALTERNATIVE IMPLEMENTATION OPTIONS IN THE INTERNATIONAL OPERATIONS OF U.S. BANKS

| OPTION | NUMBER OF BANKS USING |
|---|---|
| *Nonbank* | |
| Foreign correspondents (only) | 64 |
| Representative offices | 69 |
| *Branches* | |
| Bahamas (or related location only) | 79 |
| London (only) | 2 |
| Multi-branches overseas (London plus others) | 42 |
| *Subsidiaries* | |
| Foreign banks | 21 |
| Foreign financial companies* | 29 |
| *Affiliates* | |
| Consortium participations† | 31 |
| Minority interests in foreign banks | 20 |
| Minority interests in foreign financial companies* | 30 |

Source: *American Banker*, Feb. 27, 1976, pp. 1B–26B.

Note: A given bank may use a number of options and, therefore, be listed under a number of categories shown in the table.

* Includes consumer finance, leasing, merchant bank, insurance, and trust companies.

† Several banks may participate in a single consortium bank.

sidiary, known as an Edge Act corporation, may represent the vehicle that holds some (or all) of the interests overseas.

A sequence of historical developments represents the major explanation of this strange regulatory system. About the time of World War I, an amendment to Section 25 of the Federal Reserve Act was passed, permitting national banks to engage in international banking either directly through branches or through subsidiary corporations empowered to acquire interests in foreign companies and banks. The subsidiaries were chartered by the relevant state or federal banking authorities, and were known as "agreement corporations" because, while chartered by the regular banking authorities, they had to agree to conform to restrictions on their activities prescribed by the Federal Reserve.

Subsequently Section 25a was added to the Federal Reserve Act, which allowed the formation of these subsidiary corporations directly upon application to the Federal Reserve Board. These corporations have come to be known as "Edge Act" corporations.[3] They are required to have a minimum capital of $2 million, and a bank is limited to an investment in one or more such corporations of 10 percent of its capital surplus.[4] As a consequence the parent bank must have capital and surplus of at least $20 million to form a wholly owned international banking subsidiary. However, it can participate with other banks in the formation of these corporations under certain prescribed conditions.

While a few so-called "agreement" corporations remain in existence, they have generally become obsolete as Edge Act subsidiaries have come to be considered the more practical alternative. Table 14–2 shows that the number of Edge Act corporations has increased substantially, as a number of large banks, acting alone or in conjunction with partner banks, have found this vehicle a flexible and convenient means of facilitating their foreign banking operations. The language of the regulation covering the scope and authority of Edge Act corporations is indicative of the flexible alternatives allowed such corporations in conducting international operations:

> Corporations should be able in their activities abroad to operate, as best meets their corporate policies, through branches, agencies, and correspondents, or through direct and indirect ownerships in foreign-chartered companies engaged in banking or other international or foreign operations, so long as their credit and other activities are in the interest of the United States.[5]

The regulatory rationale for the spinoff of overseas investments into a separate corporation may have been twofold. First the corporate solvency of the domestic bank would not be affected by

3. The international banking subsidiaries are known as "Edge Act" corporations when chartered upon direct application to the Federal Reserve Board under Section 25a, because this new section of the Federal Reserve Act was sponsored by Senator Walter Edge of New Jersey. The original Section 25 of the Federal Reserve Act, passed in 1913, also authorized national banks to establish foreign branches with the permission of the Federal Reserve Board.

4. Sections 25 and 25a, Federal Reserve Act, 12 U.S.C., secs. 601 and 618. Administrative regulations pursuant to "Edge Act" corporations are contained in Regulation K of the Board of Governors.

5. Board of Governors of the Federal Reserve System, Regulation K, sec. 211.1, as amended effective Jan. 7, 1969.

TABLE 14–2

NUMBER OF EDGE ACT AGREEMENT CORPORATIONS
(Selected Years: 1950–76)

| YEAR | EDGE ACT CORPORATIONS | AGREEMENT CORPORATIONS | TOTAL |
|---|---|---|---|
| 1950 | 2 | 4 | 6 |
| 1959 | 5 | 3 | 8 |
| 1962 | 23 | 4 | 27 |
| 1966 | 42 | 4 | 46 |
| 1969 | 64 | 5 | 69 |
| 1976 | 107* | 5 | 112 |

Sources: Federal Reserve Bank of Richmond, *Monthly Review,* June 1967, p. 3, and private correspondence with Board of Governors of the Federal Reserve System.

* As of 1976, 36 banks had one Edge Act subsidiary, 24 banks had two or more, and one subsidiary was jointly owned by 18 different banks.

international problems; second, banking law had long specifically prohibited any equity acquisitions, and it was clear that these were desirable to implement an active international program.

A number of specific authorizations and restrictions have been placed on these corporations by the Federal Reserve; some of the most significant are as follows:

1. Board approval is required for the assumption of any long-term debt.
2. Activities in the United States must be related to international activities.
3. Aggregate direct liabilities are limited to ten times capital and surplus.
4. Direct or indirect investment of less than $500,000 and also less than 25 percent of the voting shares of a foreign corporation can be made without Board approval (the "general consent" provision).
5. Investments in amounts above these limits must receive prior consent of the Board. These might include subsidiary banks or other financial institutions established on a de novo basis or the acquisition of existing banks or institutions either in whole or in part.[6]

6. *Ibid.,* secs. 211.4, 211.6, 211.7, 211.8, 211.9.

In 1966, however, there was a partial reversal of the view that equity holdings of foreign financial institutions should be in a separate corporation. Congress amended Section 25 to allow direct purchases of common stock of foreign commercial banks, but the Edge Act corporation is still required for equity interests in non-bank corporations. Pursuant to this amendment the Board has authorized national banks to acquire, subject to the prior consent of the Board, the common stocks of foreign banks up to a maximum of 25 percent of capital and surplus of the parent bank, with the proviso that the total investment in subsidiary Edge Act corporations must also be included within the 25 percent limitation.[7]

## Foreign regulation

Other countries impose restrictions on the expansion of American and other exogeneous banks into their banking markets for several reasons. First, there may be concern that large U.S. banks may come to dominate the market. Our contiguous neighbors, Canada and Mexico, seem particularly sensitive on this score and as a result completely prohibit U.S. branches or ownership interests in indigenous banks.[8] Other important countries that prohibit both foreign branches and banking subsidiaries include Sweden, Chile, Venezuela, the Philippines, and several Mid-East OPEC countries, with the notable exception of Saudi Arabia.

Second, regulation and control of entry may be imposed in order to obtain assurances that the applicants have the resources and reputation required to operate successfully in the domestic and international banking markets. In Britain, for example, permission of the Bank of England is required to open a London

7. Board of Governors of the Federal Reserve System, Regulation M, sec. 213.4, Jan. 7, 1971. Regulation M is concerned with direct activities of banks in the foreign markets and Regulation K relates to Edge Act corporations only.

8. In late 1976, it was reported that Canada was considering modifying its restrictive statute to allow charters on a selective basis for subsidiary banks of foreign banking corporations. At the same time closer control over near-bank subsidiaries would be instituted. The announced objectives of the proposal were to maximize competition and yet insure that "the control of Canada's financial system remains predominantly in Canadian hands." The objectives were recognized to be in conflict, and the compromise in part was to be strict limits imposed on the size of a foreigin intruder. (*Wall Street Journal,* Aug. 24, 1976, p. 7.)

branch. (As noted in Chapter 13, because the Eurocurrency markets are centered there, a London branch has become almost essential for a U.S. bank that desires to be recognized as international in scope.) There are no formal or published requirements comparable to our banking statutes and Federal Reserve regulatons; the procedure is for a foreign bank to make inquiry to the Bank of England and the decision is made on an ad hoc basis. The general guidelines as of 1976 for entry into the London market were set forth as follows:

1. Parent bank total assets of at least two billion dollars.
2. A favorable report on the bank from the London clearing banks and the regulatory officials of the parent bank, the Federal Reserve in the case of U.S. banks.
3. Evidence that a capable staff would be assigned to a branch, including a foreign exchange trader experienced and known to the London market.
4. To obtain insight and knowledge of the overseas institution, the Bank of England encourages the establishment of a representative office preceding an opening of a full branch operation.[9]

Subsequent regulation is on a highly informal basis except that reserves in the form of interest-bearing deposits in the Bank of England must be held against sterling deposits for domestic monetary control purposes and sterling foreign exchange operations are subject to certain limits. Other than these constraints, the regulatory process was described as follows:

> We drop in at the Overseas Bankers Club and inquire if any bank is paying a bit high in the market. If so, we make inquiries at that bank and ask for an explanation. We then encourage the bank to put its house in order and report to us its progress along these lines.[10]

9. These guidelines were obtained in a personal interview with Mr. Rodney Galpin, Head of the Banks and Money Market section, Bank of England in May of 1976. This section acts for the Bank of England in the regulation and control of banks in Britain; the decisions of the Bank of England are entirely discretionary and no appeals from their decisions are possible.

10. Rodney Galpin, Banks and Money Markets Section, Bank of England, in a personal interview. "Paying a bit high" was translated as unexplained premiums paid on Eurocurrency deposits over the London interbank offering rate (LIBOR); the implication is that the market has some reason to believe something has

Although this rather casual and informal approach to bank supervision may startle some accustomed to the formal examination procedures that mark U.S. regulatory procedures, in the context of the London market it is probably quite effective. The market is concentrated among a hundred or so international banks in London; everyone is in close daily contact with one another and as a consequence, the interbank intelligence network is highly sophisticated. Therefore, the ability to maintain a prime position in the market is probably a good indication that management policies have been reasonably prudent. However, while the Bank of England informally monitors the activities of exogenous banks operating in London, it was emphasized that primary responsibility for their solvency rests with the officials of the country of domicile and that the central bank of each country was expected to support its institutions in case of difficulty.[11]

A third reason for other countries' imposing regulation may be to ensure that foreign domiciled institutions conform to national economic policies. For example, in some countries the purpose of bank loans may be regulated so that resource allocations conform to governmental planning objectives. Malaysia, Nigeria, and Kenya all have controls of this sort. Other countries regulate interest rates on loans and deposits (Costa Rica and Greece), and others consider that the banks should support government fiscal policies through the purchase of government securities (Norway and Nigeria). And "work permits" for U.S. nationals are required in Switzerland and in a few other countries; the objective apparently is to require that a major portion of the staff be hired locally in order to reduce unemployment to minimum levels.[12]

---

occurred which should constrain the market in its placement of funds with that bank. Because Eurocurrency placements are made for periods up to six months or more on an unsecured basis, the risk position of each bank is constantly under scrutiny by other participants in the market.

11. The so-called consortium banks, owned jointly by several parent banks in various countries, represent a problem in this connection. As they have no single parent country of domicile, there is no clear source of support from a central bank. For this reason, the consortium banks during the difficult period of 1974–75 often had to pay a premium for funds. (*Wall Street Journal,* June 13, 1975, p. 4.)

12. These several illustrations of foreign regulation obtained from G. Freeman, *Regulatory and Political Environment of International Banking,* Speech at meeting of Reserve City Bankers, Boca Raton, Fla., Apr. 8, 1975, pp. 13–14.

Finally, although only inferential evidence is available, some countries apparently desire to protect indigenous banks against competition from foreign banks and/or to obtain reciprocity for entry of their own banks into the markets of the applicants. Japan represents the major case in point. Several years of negotiation have been required to obtain branching privileges there, and the following comment on the Japanese decision-making process is notable:

> One major consideration in determining who should get a branch is the willingness of the foreign bank's domicile to extend banking privileges to Japanese banks. For example, California banks have been successful in getting branches here, largely because many Japanese banks have had an easy time establishing branches there.[13]

## Implementation Options

### Correspondent banks

Table 14–1 showed that as of 1976 some 64 U.S. banks engaged in international activities solely through correspondents abroad. For the most part, however, correspondents provide minimal assistance to U.S. banks in structuring credits abroad, mainly because in most countries the resources of the indigenous banks have typically been strained to provide adequate credit accommodation to local borrowers. In fact, respondents reported that so far as loans are concerned, correspondent banks are essentially takers of funds, or in essence funds are transferred from the U.S. banking markets to support credit needs abroad. In periods of easy money, such credits may be quite attractive to U.S. banks.

The financing of imports and exports of merchandise and commodities through the bankers acceptance mechanism relies to a considerable extent on the correspondent network where the credit stature of the accepting bank substitutes for the unknown credit stature of the importer or exporter. But loans per se are not involved in these transactions, for in the ordinary case the acceptance is sold in the money market. Other than expediting acceptance financing, correspondents may offer the following services to U.S. banks, usually on a reciprocal basis:

13. *Wall Street Journal*, May 11, 1973, p. 28.

1. Collections and remittances and handling of other documents incident to transactions in that country
2. Execution of the purchase and sale of investment instruments for the account of a U.S. bank or its customers
3. Economic and political intelligence on conditions within the country
4. Assistance to customers in their relations with government agencies
5. Credit evaluations of local companies to be used either by the bank or customers of the bank
6. Introductions to local business firms for customers of a U.S. bank

There are two major advantages of using correspondents to implement foreign operations. First, the cost is minimal and can be adjusted to the scale of services required in any given locale; no investment in facilities or in staff is required. Second, the local knowledge and contacts of correspondent banks may be extensive and highly useful to a U.S. bank in rendering services to its international customers. However, given the fact that correspondents cannot serve the overseas credit requirements of domestic customers, other facilities abroad are required for a viable international lending operation.

## London (Bahamas) branch

The next step beyond foreign correspondents is to obtain a "window" to the Eurocurrency market. For this purpose, as Table 14–1 shows, some 79 U.S. banks consider a "branch" in the Bahamas area sufficient. The nature of these branches has been described as follows:

> The branch is just a tiny room—no bigger than a walk-in closet—in an office building in downtown Nassau. The midget branch contains a desk, file cabinet and telephone. There are no tellers' windows. And you never see any customers.[14]

14. *Wall Street Journal,* July 5, 1972, p. 24.

In most cases its only purpose is to "book" Eurocurrency purchased deposits generated in the home office which, if construed as held offshore, are not subject to reserve requirements and FDIC assessment.[15] The original impetus to their formation was the now-abandoned limits placed on foreign loans funded from domestic deposits in effect between 1965 and 1974; over 60 Bahamas branches were established in that period.

However, because the Eurocurrency markets are centered in London, active dealer participation in these markets requires a branch in that city. Moreover, personal contacts with domestic companies or their subsidiaries operating in the major European markets are made possible by a presence in London. But a London branch is expensive; the Bank of England insists that branches be prepared to handle most types of banking services and physical facility costs are extremely high by U.S. standards because of space limitations in the confined area of the London financial district centered around the Bank of England. Therefore, the volume of business and the revenue potential therefrom must be substantial to cover the operating costs and in addition provide an adequate return on the original investment required.

Some London operations are primarily confined to customer relations with the international divisions of U.S. companies and to providing Eurocurrency funding of foreign loans originated in the home office. Others have expanded the scope of their activities to offer an almost complete package of wholesale banking services. One respondent operation in London provided the following description of its activities:

1. Conducts an active foreign exchange and interbank Eurocurrency trading operation in five to six different currencies (about a $2.5 billion gross book at any given time).
2. Makes Eurocurrency term loans directly to customers and participates on a selective basis in syndicated credits. May lead syndicate, if appropriate on the basis of relations with borrower (about two-thirds of loans with loan authority of $10,000,000 in London, subject to country constraints).

15. Also earnings on the operation are construed as "foreign" in source, and certain U.S. tax benefits can accrue as a result.

3. Solicits sterling time deposits, largely corporate, and offers overdraft lines and term loans to both public and private sector in England (about one-sixth to loan assets).[16]
4. Offers lines and short-term transaction loans funded from Eurocurrency deposit purchases in five to six different currencies (one-sixth of loan assets).
5. Makes investments in public sector instruments similar to domestic municipal bond operations.
6. Conducts a sterling leasing operation similar to leasing program in the United States as a tax shelter against corporate tax of 52 percent in England.
7. On a very limited basis, participates in underwriting and trading of Eurobond issues.
8. Through a separate corporation operates a full line trust department.

Operations on this scale require major commitments to staff and facilities and the significant consequent costs are largely fixed in nature. Because the entire business is essentially based on yield spreads, which are volatile and sometimes narrow because of competitive pressures, considerable volume (leverage) is required to cover costs and obtain reasonable profitability. Therefore, unless a bank is prepared to assume a reasonably aggressive risk posture, it is probably well advised to operate its London facility on a minimal scale.

## Representative offices

As noted above, many countries either limit (Japan) or prohibit (Mexico) branches of foreign banks. As a substitute to obtain some presence in the area, a representative office may be opened. Table 14–1 shows that American banks had some sixty-nine such offices as of 1976, the majority in Latin American countries and the Far East, notably Hong Kong and Mexico. The offices are not permitted to book deposits or loans directly, but presumably they act as agent for the head office, although the distinction may be

16. U.S. banks are at a severe disadvantage with respect to attracting sterling demand deposits. The major British clearing banks have a nationwide collection and remittance network that cannot be duplicated by foreign-domiciled banks. Time deposits, however, are placed on a competitive rate basis similar to CDs in the United States.

vague and sometimes, according to the respondents, delicate in nature. A typical arrangement is probably a small office staffed by one or two individuals. The representative(s) will usually be nationals of the host country, often selected because of good contacts in the government and in the financial and business community. In order to acquaint them with bank personnel and policies, many are offered an orientation program in the United States. According to those respondent banks which had them, the major functions of representative offices were to provide: (1) credit evaluations of local companies, (2) financial contacts with local institutions, (3) commercial contacts for bank customers, (4) assistance to customers in obtaining governmental approvals or instructing customers on governmental regulations, (5) economic and political intelligence on the country.

The main policy issue related to the establishment of representative offices is cost justification. While the services are undoubtedly useful, there is a legitimate question as to whether they attract sufficient additional business or, alternatively, prevent the loss of enough existing business to justify the substantial recurring costs of maintaining the offices. While not as expensive as a full branch operation, representative offices constitute a substantial cost item. The annual cost of an office has been estimated at between $75,000 and $150,000 per year, depending on the location. Therefore, a clear need for a more concentrated effort in a location beyond that offered by correspondents is required to justify a decision to open a representative office. Personnel problems can also arise in a representative office; if a representative who is well connected locally is not sufficiently productive, an effort to replace him may cause some difficult problems in public relations. However, this fact may merely suggest that representatives should be carefully selected at the outset.

### Multiple branch operations

As of 1976, some forty-two U.S. banks maintained two or more overseas branches. But perhaps only ten or so had as many as five or more, and only three (Citibank, Chase Manhattan, and Bank of America) had extensive branch networks abroad. In general, representation in continental Europe, the Mid-East, and

Far East has followed the opening of a "window" to the Eurocurrency market in the form of a London or Bahamas branch.[17]

To obtain maximum penetration of international banking markets, the use of strategically located branches would clearly be preferable.[18] Because they represent direct extensions of the home office, their operating and credit policies can be closely integrated with those of the institution as a whole. Branch services rendered to a customer may be based on the world-wide value of the relationship rather than on the nature of the relationship in the particular area. In addition, if there are several foreign branches, there are increased opportunities for junior officers in the international department to obtain valuable experience overseas. Such experience would seem highly desirable for any officer who expects to make a career in international operations, as even regular transient visits cannot offer the training and insights obtained by a year or so of operating responsibilities in one or more foreign countries. The operational advantages of branch representation in the major areas of the world would include the capacity to: (1) offer direct and integrated services in these regions on a consistent policy basis, (2) provide collection and remittance facilities entirely within the bank on a world-wide basis, and (3) generate large foreign currency sources within the system through local time deposit purchases and interbranch fund transfers.

Table 14–3 shows and compares the nature of the loan functions conducted in overseas branches of the respondent banks. One had a Bahamas branch only, and its only function was to book Eurocurrency deposits and loans generated in the home office. The majority used their London branches for this purpose, but in addition the London branches all had some authority to grant Eurocurrency loans, although loan limits varied; such loans were

17. Beirut, Lebanon, had long been the preferred location of Mid-East branches, but because of the civil war in that country in 1975–76 these branches had been completely closed and moved either to Athens or in some cases to other areas of the Mid-East. The incident suggests that the probable political stability of a country should be assessed before a branch is located there.

18. Approval of the Federal Reserve must be obtained for the first branch in each country. Subsequent branches in a given country require only that 30 days' notice be given the Federal Reserve, who retain veto power. (Board of Governors of the Federal Reserve, Regulation M, sec. 213.3, as amended, Jan. 7, 1971.)

TABLE 14–3

FREQUENCY OF LOAN FUNCTIONS OF OVERSEAS BRANCHES (N = 7)

| Function | Frequency* | | | | | | | |
|---|---|---|---|---|---|---|---|---|
| | London or Bahamas | | | | Other Branches† | | | |
| | F | S | R | N | F | S | R | N |
| Eurocurrency loans | 6 | ... | ... | 1 | ... | 2 | 1 | ... |
| Book Eurocurrency transactions‡ | 5 | 2 | ... | ... | 1 | 1 | 1 | ... |
| Local currency loans: | | | | | | | | |
| To foreign customers | 4 | 1 | 1 | 1 | 3 | ... | ... | ... |
| To U.S. subsidiaries | 4 | 2 | ... | 1 | 3 | ... | ... | ... |

* F = frequently; S = sometimes; R = rarely; N = never.

† Only 3 respondents had branches outside London or Bahamas; 4 had London and/or Bahamas branch only.

‡ Defined as deposit purchases for loans generated in the home office wherein branch conducts funding or recording function only.

far less typical in other branch locations. However, the three respondents with "other" branches indicated that local currency loans to both foreign and U.S. customers occurred frequently, and most London operations included at least some sterling loans to both U.S. and foreign customers.

However, despite its definite advantages, an overseas branch system has some drawbacks. First, there is the important matter of cost. Studies have indicated that fully adequate facilities and staff require an annual outlay of several hundred thousand dollars for each branch in Europe, plus a considerable nonrecurring amount for remodeling of any rented or purchased physical quarters. Therefore, while a London branch with immediate access to the Eurocurrency market is likely to be profitable within a reasonable time, the ability of most branches to make a direct contribution to earnings for several years may be doubtful.

Second, developing and retaining the managerial talent required for a network of foreign branches may be a problem. The usual strategy is to team one or more nationals of the country with one or more Americans. So far as the latter are concerned, the combination of competence in one or more foreign languages, good analytical and managerial abilities, and willingness to serve abroad for a number of years is not easy to find. Moreover, there is keen competition for such personnel from all multinational corporations that are continuing to expand their foreign operations.

### Subsidiaries and affiliates

As vehicles to implement an international banking program, direct or Edge Act corporation investments in foreign banks or related type institutions and/or formation of de novo companies seem to have several major purposes: (1) to obtain an entry into important foreign banking markets which incidently will provide a local currency deposit base and a controlled source of other international services, (2) to acquire some visibility in the financial markets in countries where bank ownership or branching is prohibited, (3) to provide a more extensive range of financial services than is customary or allowable for foreign-domiciled banks, (4) to have a vehicle for financing larger projects than the bank alone would consider prudent.

Table 14–4 gives examples of subsidiaries and affiliates of two major U.S. banks that can be reasonably related to each purpose

TABLE 14–4
EXAMPLES OF FOREIGN SUBSIDIARIES AND AFFILIATES BY FUNCTION

| PURPOSE | COUNTRY | INSTITUTION | PARENT |
|---|---|---|---|
| Penetrate local banking markets | Austria | Conill Bank, A. G. | Continental Illinois |
| Financial market visibility | Canada | Continental Ill. Leasing & Financial, Ltd. | Continental Illinois |
| Expanded services (Merchant banking) | Britain | Continental Ill., Ltd. | Continental Illinois |
| Large project financing | Britain | Orion Banking Group | Chase Manhattan* |

Sources: Continental Illinois Corporation, *International Financial Directory* and *Wall Street Journal,* May 25, 1973, p. 26.

* Participation with five other bank shareholders in England, Italy, Germany, Canada, and Japan.

cited above. However, unlike the domestic corporate organization, the international system of subsidiaries and affiliates in many banks has shown considerable variation through time in response to changes in world economic and political conditions and in the results of the diverse units in the corporate system. Continental Illinois, for example, has made the following comment in a discussion of its international policies:

> As we consolidate our market position and increase the profitability of each of our major units, Continental plans to divest some minority holdings in foreign financial institutions that have proven marginally profitable.[19]

Although the published information lacks specificity, the experience with merchant bank subsidiaries and consortia banks has not lived up to expectations in a number of instances. The following revelation is illustrative:

> Our London merchant bank, Continental Illinois, Limited, like similar institutions in that market, encountered problems last year, primarily with real estate lending in Britain. Consequently the merchant bank provided for possible future loan losses of about $12 million in the fourth quarter of last year. That loan provision . . . was offset by an additional capital investment of $15 million from Continental Illinois Corporation in December 1974. This investment fully restored the merchant bank's capital base and demonstrated the holding company's solid support of the merchant bank.[20]

In theory a strong case can be made for participation in a banking consortium. The concept is that major banks from various countries may jointly own a bank to specialize in large international loans (primarily term loans) with purchased deposits in the Eurocurrency market representing the major visible funding source. The conceptual merits of a consortium are held to be:

19. G. R. Baker and A. F. Miossi, "International Services," *Continental Illinois Report* (Chicago, Oct. 30, 1975), p. 22.

20. *Ibid.* p. 24. Other revelations of serious loan problem in subsidiary merchant banks included Marine Midland and Western American Bank, jointly owned by several U.S. banks. In the latter case, significant amounts of problem loans, tanker and REIT credits primarily, were taken into the portfolios of the parent banks to alleviate the situation.

1. It provides a vehicle for financing large projects that may be beyond appropriate limits for any one member; the consortium and each of the participating banks can hold pieces of such loans.
2. The "instant syndicates" represented by the several participating banks can arrange large loans without the publicity connected with most syndicated financing.
3. The consortium has access to the special expertise of each participant; one may be expert in, say, shipping credits and another in petroleum.
4. The participating banks offer contacts and resources for structuring complicated financing, such as a mixed-currency financing combining a Eurocurrency and a domestic currency.[21]

In practice, however, it appears that consortia have not been an unqualified success. First, some experienced funding difficulties during the turbulent period of 1974–75 in the international financial markets. The reason was that consortia had no clear lines of support in case of difficulties from either central banks or the parent institutions, since no one country or institution could be clearly identified as responsible for back-up support. Therefore, when the markets became highly defensive on even short-term deposit placements, consortia became a logical target for restriction or elimination from "approved" lists for deposit placements.[22]

Second, the relationships with and the responsibilities of the several parent institutions in a consortium may present problems. The following observation is illustrative:

> The shareholders may compete with one another, . . . but we maintain that we don't compete with the shareholders. We work around the periphery of what they cannot do themselves. . . . How-

21. *Wall Street Journal,* May 25, 1973, p. 26.

22. Even if funds were available at a "risk" premium rate, serious earnings problems might emerge. Interest rates on term loans, the principal type made by consortia, are typically reset at specific intervals at a specific spread over the prime London Interbank Offering Rate (LIBOR). The spread in some instances became negative when the risk premium required to attract funds exceeded the contractual spread in the loan agreement. An article on consortium banks included the following comment: "You must realize that there are so many good names about, and in particular so many many *familiar* names, that anything out of the ordinary, such as a consortium bank, has to pay about an eighth of a point over the best rate." (*Euromoney,* May 1976, p. 56.)

> ever, a corporate loan officer inside a parent isn't likely to throw a good deal [our] way if he can manage it himself. . . . We must be independent, we must have our own style, but we must work in concert.[23]

The above comment implies that a consortium might be requested to finance deals of a type or with a risk exposure that the parent banks individually might not find appropriate. Underwriting of long-term issues in the Eurobond market is a probable area where commercial banks may not be entirely comfortable, particularly U.S. banks, which are by law prohibited from corporate underwriting activities. In addition, participation in large syndicated term loans to developing countries might be referred to the consortium as a substitute for direct participation. Therefore, strong and effective managerial leadership and active support and cooperation from the participants would seem highly important to obtaining a reasonable probability of adequate long-term returns.[24] But given their uneven record and the problems of maintaining prime stature in the financial markets, the long-term outlook for consortium affiliates and subsidiary merchant banks seems questionable.

### Domestic international offices

An Edge Act subsidiary is permitted to domicile its home office in a city other than that of the parent bank for the purpose of conducting or facilitating its international operations. Such an office cannot conduct any business in that city except as is "incidental to its foreign business." The Federal Reserve has construed this statutory language to mean that all the subsidiary's business must be related to international transactions. The reason for the highly restrictive interpretation is the long-standing national policy against the interstate branching of commercial banks.

23. J. Haley, Chairman, Orion Banking Group, as quoted in the *Wall Street Journal,* May 25, 1973, p. 26.

24. In the case of Orion Banking Group, after repeated changes in chief executives and significant losses in the bond trading operation, effective leadership has apparently restored profitability and reasonable credibility in the international financial markets, according to an analysis of its operations as of 1976. (P. Fallon, "How David Montagu Gave a Lead to Orion Bank," *Euromoney,* May 1976, pp. 52–57.)

However, as noted in the footnote to Table 14–2, some twenty-four U.S. banks had multiple Edge Act corporations operative in various domestic locations in 1976. Typically a regional bank may have a corporate office on both the East Coast (New York, Miami) and West Coast (Los Angeles, San Francisco). Foreign banks and trading corporations tend to be concentrated in these areas; indeed New York has become a major center for Eurocurrency syndicated loans and Eurobond underwritings. Therefore, a number of larger interior banks have concluded that to be fully competitive in the international area they should have an office in one or more of these cities.

The services offered include: (1) assistance on the physical movement of goods, including arrangements on shipping, insurance, and warehousing; (2) receiving and making payments on international transactions on behalf of customers; (3) providing contacts with trade and financial representatives of foreign countries, either governmental or private; (4) obtaining information for customers in foreign economic conditions, regulations, and taxes; (5) representing the bank in international loan syndicates.

While correspondents in these cities can provide most of these services, some interior banks have come to regard complete reliance on correspondents as undesirable for two reasons. First and probably foremost, important customers might come to identify their international banking requirements with the correspondent and might decide to transfer a significant portion of their business to the correspondent. Second, more effective control and management of these services can be obtained with an independent office directly and completely responsible to the parent bank. As in other matters, correspondents naturally tend to give first priority to their own customers. Therefore, if important customers require a considerable volume of international services that must be handled in another domestic location, an office can probably be justified through an Edge Act corporation domiciled in that city.

# XV

## INTERNATIONAL CREDIT AND FUNDING POLICIES

The international credit program of commercial banks may technically be defined as the extension of loans or credit support for loans of others wherein the proceeds are to be used to finance the international movement of goods or investment in assets domiciled outside the continental limits of the United States. This definition is, however, very broad, and in some cases a loan might be technically construed as international but, so far as the lending operation is concerned, it is essentially a domestic credit. Such would be the case, for example, with a loan made to a domestic corporation to be used to acquire assets from abroad but where the probable source of repayment is to be cash flows from domestic operations.[1]

Because the purpose of the following discussion is to appraise the policy issues and practices singular to international credits, a more restricted definition is necessary. The context of credit decisions often involves additional considerations when the borrower is a foreign government, foreign company, a foreign subsidiary of a domestic company, or when the loan is to be granted and repaid in a foreign currency. Therefore, only credits granted under one or more of these circumstances will be considered as "international." In these cases the decision framework involves special problems and policy resolutions that are not ordinarily encountered on domestic credits, which might be listed as follows:

1. Problems of risk exposure and policies of risk control
2. Policies covering credits generated in foreign branches, subsidiaries, or affiliates

1. A typical transaction would be a loan or credit support extended to a domestic customer to finance imports of inventories shipped on open account or under the letter of credit and bankers acceptance mechanism. The loan or credit guaranty is in U.S. dollars and repayment is expected through sale of the inventory in the United States.

3. Policies on participating in and structuring of Eurocurrency credits
4. Policies on an appropriate decision and review structure

## Risk Exposure Policies

The risk exposure on international credits conceptually may have four dimensions: (1) credit risk, (2) country risk, (3) currency risk, (4) "rate-gap" risk. The first of these may be defined as the risk of default due to financial or operational problems of the borrower. The second is concerned with problems that might arise because of political or economic disturbances within given countries, particularly in the so-called undeveloped countries or in those that have a history of political instability. The third relates to possible losses that might occur because of fluctuations in currency values of loans denominated in foreign currencies. The fourth arises from the fact that, whereas a large proportion of international loans are funded from short-term purchased deposits in the Eurocurrency markets, maturities of the loans may run for several years or more; the risk arises when the maturities of the purchased deposits differ from the maturities of the loans or, in the case of term loans, from the rate-reset intervals.

### Credit risk

In order to obtain some general impression of the nature and extent of credit risk exposure in the international portfolio, Table 15–1 has been prepared to show the respondent banks' estimates of the frequency of credits extended to various categories of borrowers and the terms of the borrowings. For several reasons the data suggest that credit risk per se is less in the international than in the domestic commercial loan portfolio. First, most respondents indicated that direct loans to governments and government agencies are important in the international sector and that government guarantees on loans to foreign companies are often obtained primarily in the term loan area.[2] While gov-

2. The one respondent indicating few loans to foreign governments and companies on any basis merely had the policy of not seeking such loans in their international operations; its sole objective was service to international operations of domestic customers.

TABLE 15–1
FREQUENCY OF INTERNATIONAL LOANS ESTIMATED BY RESPONDENT BANKS
(By Type of Loan and Borrower)

| Type of Borrower | Lines of Credit | | | | Term Loans | | | |
|---|---|---|---|---|---|---|---|---|
| | Frequent | Sometimes | Rarely | Never | Frequent | Sometimes | Rarely | Never |
| *Foreign Gov'ts.* | | | | | | | | |
| Direct | ... | 1 | 2 | 4 | 5 | 1 | 1 | ... |
| Agencies* | 5 | 2 | ... | ... | 5 | 2 | ... | ... |
| *Foreign Companies* | | | | | | | | |
| Gov't. guaranty | 1 | 2 | 3 | 1 | 4 | 2 | ... | 1 |
| No guaranty | 2 | 4 | ... | 1 | 1 | 4 | 1 | ... |
| *Foreign Financial Inst.* | | | | | | | | |
| Banks† | 7 | ... | ... | ... | ... | 3 | 3 | 1 |
| Others | 1 | 4 | 2 | ... | ... | 1 | 4 | 2 |
| *Foreign Subsidiaries of U.S. Companies* | | | | | | | | |
| Parent guaranty | 6 | 1 | ... | ... | 4 | 2 | 1 | ... |
| "Comfort" letter‡ | 3 | 1 | 1 | 2 | 3 | ... | 1 | 3 |
| No guaranty | 2 | 4 | 1 | ... | 2 | 1 | 3 | 1 |

* Government agencies and official institutions (central banks).
† Excludes interbank deposit placements in Eurocurrency markets.
‡ Written indication by parent of intention to support subsidiary in case of difficulty, not legally binding.

ernments may fail to meet their external debt obligations, this is defined as a country risk (considered below) rather than a credit risk, although the distinction of course is somewhat semantic in nature. The distinction is based on the fact that governments do not formally declare bankruptcy in the same sense that a private sector company may be obliged to do.

Second, lines to major foreign banks are a major source of foreign credits. While these banks are not immune to failure, by and large their record has been favorable. For example, lines to Japanese banks are common, and there has been no bank failure in Japan since World War II. The fact that any large bank failure receives considerable visibility in the financial media indicates that the event is relatively rare. Moreover, the banks in many countries are semi-governmental agencies or have usually received government support in case of difficulty. Reference here is to the major commercial banks of developed countries and not to consortia, merchant banks, and so-called "fringe" banks specializing in a particular function, such as real estate operations. The fringe banks have had a less satisfactory credit record, and in fact probably should not be included in the bank category.

In the case of foreign banks the credit risk is controlled by establishing a list of "approved" banks eligible to receive lines and deposit placements and then setting specific limits on the total credit exposure. The determination of the credit exposure is not entirely without problems as it might include acceptance credits, loan guarantees for other companies, deposit placements, and direct lines or other loans. The general policy is to include all contingent as well as direct obligations in the credit limits, which then may vary from a few million up to the legal limit of the bank.

Third, in the case of loans made to foreign subsidiaries of U.S. companies, parent guarantees are often obtained. As most U.S. companies with subsidiary operations abroad are seasoned and substantial in size, they tend to be in the higher echelon of credit risk. When a guaranty is obtained, however, it must be considered as part of the legal limit constraint on the total credit extended to the parent. Credit needs of the corporate complex in excess of the legal limits may, therefore, result in waivers of parent guaranty. Nevertheless, although two respondents indicated both lines and term loans without parent support were frequent, the majority seemed very hesitant on this score, particularly in the case of term loans. Policy disagreement on the acceptability of a "comfort" letter as a substitute for a firm guaranty was notable.[3] About half indicated they were accepted frequently while the remainder indicated such letters were never or rarely accepted; as might be expected the negative policy was more prevalent on term loans than in the case of lines. In general, it would seem that reliance on a "comfort" letter to substitute for a clearly inadequate credit position of a subsidiary is a questionably policy. Either a guaranty should be obtained or alternatively the credit may stand on the strength of the subsidiary with appropriate negative pledges to protect against a "milking" operation by the parent.

In support of this position, an experienced international banker offered the following comment:

> A strong parent is undoubtedly of great value to any company. However, creditors cannot look beyond the separate corporate identity with more than a mild hope of assistance, should trouble develop. When Castro nationalized various Cuban industries, several American parents ignored the losses of the bank lenders to their subsidiaries. There are other similar examples of more recent origin on the international scene involving various countries.[4]

A fourth factor which suggests that credit risk is relatively low on international loans is that credits extended to the undeveloped areas—parts of Africa and Asia, for example—are often protected by guaranties of U.S. international agencies, such as the Export-Import bank or the Foreign Credit Insurance Association. In most of these countries political instability is endemic and close governmental controls over all phases of economic activity are pervasive. In addition, U.S. agencies that implement foreign economic aid programs work closely with the governments con-

3. A "comfort" letter is a written communication from the parent acknowledging the debt of the subsidiary and then indicating an "intention" to support the foreign operation in case of difficulty. It is of course not legally binding and may be framed in vague language.

4. D. R. Mandich, "Fallacies in International Banking," *Bankers Magazine*, Spring 1974, p. 39.

cerned. The result is that major credits, even in the nominally private sector, are likely to carry the approval and guaranty of one or more public authorities. And in many cases, particularly in intermediate term credits, the loans may be made directly to a government agency or to a corporation established for a particular purpose with credit insurance provided by a U.S. agency.

It should be emphasized, however, that the above comments on the differences between credit risk on the international portfolio and the domestic portfolio apply only to loans structured in the international department of U.S. banks. If the scope of such credits is extended to those generated in subsidiary and affiliate operations, such as in merchant bank subsidiaries, then a somewhat greater credit risk exposure may be indicated. The evidence in support of this view is that several such subsidiaries, as noted in the previous chapter, required parent support to absorb extensive loan losses in the 1974–76 period. Loans to Real Estate Investment Trusts, direct real estate development loans, and tanker credits based on cash flow projections that failed to materialize when charter rates collapsed were among the major credit problems encountered.[5] Also a few U.S. banks that came late to the international scene attempted to expand their international program rapidly in the early seventies and are known to have bought participation in some of the problem credits, primarily syndicated term loans on tankers.[6]

## Country risk

One dimension of country risk is the possibility of a successful political revolution which might result in a disavowal of the direct debts or guaranties assumed by the overthrown government. Similarly, expropriation of or restrictive decrees on private

5. The problems suggest that home office control policies applied to certain subsidiaries and affiliates may have been seriously deficient. It might be conjectured that part of the problem was due to unfamiliarity of home office personnel with the activities of these subsidiaries that extended well beyond commercial banking as practiced in the United States.

6. In late 1976, seven regional banks instituted suit against European-American Banking Corporation to recover losses on their participations in loans to E.M.J. Colocatronics, a Greek shipping group, to finance supertankers. The allegations were the "European-American concealed the true financial position . . . from the participating bank lenders and misrepresented the arrangements for securing repayment." (*Wall Street Journal*, Sept. 14, 1976, p. 1.)

sector companies could make it impossible for these debtors to meet their obligations. The Castro takeover in Cuba was a classic example of events that resulted in practically complete losses on outstanding loans in that country. The exposure here was essentially the ability of a government to invoke its sovereign powers to default on debt incurred by a preceding regime. Thus it is termed soverign risk.[7]

To offset soverign risk, several loan techniques may be considered. One is to link syndicated loans on a cross-default provision with loans made by the World Bank. The presumption is that discrediting its status with the World Bank, which provides credit on preferential terms to developing countries, might be considered an unwise policy even by a government dominated by the far left. Another technique is to make special efforts to include (in the syndicate) banks from countries with presumed political leverage over the borrowing country. A third is to finance specific projects within the country which presumably will have visible economic benefits to the country instead of making loans to be repaid from a general balance of payments generation of foreign exchange. It is conjectured that a successor government might be more inclined to meet external debt service on such a project than on nonspecific debts incurred by the previous regime.[8]

A second dimension of country risk relates to the ability of a country to generate sufficient foreign exchange to meet obligations denominated in foreign currencies. This problem is economic rather than political in character, and its analysis is primarily concerned with an appraisal of the external economic outlook of a country. Respondent banks mentioned the following factors as significant:

1. The relative rate of inflation as shown by the trends of the wholesale and retail price indexes
2. Trends in the balance of payments statistics

7. S. M. Yassukovich, "The Growing Political Threat to International Lending," *Euromoney*, Apr. 1976, p. 12.

8. A critic holds this assumption to be an unrealistic assumption on the grounds that debt incurred to finance projects originated by a discarded regime are likely to be repudiated by the successor government even though the projects have clear benefits to the country. (*Euromoney*, Apr. 1976, p. 15.)

3. Trends in official foreign exchange reserves and exchange control policies
4. The performance of the currency in foreign exchange markets and the past record of currency devaluations
5. The amount of external debt and annual servicing requirements related to the status of the balance of payments
6. The availability to the country of standby credits from international agencies

However, since some of these data may be unavailable or their reliability subject to considerable doubt, skilled inferences are often essential to an evaluation of the risk potential.[9]

The obvious policy to control country risk exposure is to set specific loan limits for every country based on an assessment of its economic strength and political stability, and all respondents had such a policy. In policy implementation, however, significant differences were apparent. Some indicated that they had established zero limits for a number of vulnerable countries.[10] Others would permit a moderate general authority for any country, say a few million dollars, but beyond that amount country guidelines controlled credit exposure, and here too zero limits beyond the general authority were not uncommon. Finally, it was the position of a few that, except for situations clearly involved in serious political turmoil, reasonable levels of country risk could be assumed with minimums of at least ten to twenty millions of dollars. The apparent reason for the latter position was that recognition as a full-fledged international bank in the world-wide financial community required a willingness to participate on a reasonable basis in Eurocurrency loan syndicates for the developing countries which dominate many areas of the world, particularly Africa and, to a lesser extent, Asia. Also those banks with

9. Based on these factors and one other, the literacy percentage of the population, an economic formula to rank countries has been recommended. A geometric relationship between the formula rankings and country exposure limits would be established through reducing limits by a specified percentage as the ranking declines. (H. H. Hartleben, "Country Exposure Guidelines," *Journal of Commercial Bank Lending,* Aug. 1972, pp. 10–12.)

10. Exceptions to the zero limit policy were sometimes made to finance exports of U.S. customers to these countries. In this case the debt was short-term in character and related to specific shipments of goods wherein the total amounts presumably would be relatively moderate.

extensive networks of branches, representative offices, and subsidiaries (affiliates) in most areas of the world cannot realistically be highly negative on country risk and still justify the extensive overseas facilities.

As of late 1976 there was considerable controversy concerning the prudence of some U.S. banks, presumably those with extensive facilities overseas, with respect to their control of country risk exposure. The extreme negative view was expressed as follows:

> Eighteen major non–oil producing, lesser developed countries are in hock to big U.S. banks to the tune of $21 billion—that's about 10% of these banks' loans. . . . These relatively poor nations are to international banking what real estate investment trusts are to domestic banking. In plain language, a potential disaster. . . . Banks tapped oceans of petrodollars at relatively low interest costs, and reloaned them at high interest rates and high placement fees. But standards were lax. . . . The bankers got into this position because they were a bit greedy. But through their greed, they did serve an important international need. Don't be surprised, therefore, when the banks ask to be bailed out.[11]

The problem of Zaire in Africa is illustrative. According to one source, as of late 1976 that country owed $162 million to the 12 largest U.S. banks and had been in default on principal and interest for a year; negotiations to "restructure" the debt had yet to begin and litigation against alleged preferential treatment of some official institutions in the United States and elsewhere had been instituted.[12] The decline in the price of copper, the major export commodity of Zaire, coupled with the escalation in the prices of oil imports, had apparently triggered the default, and other countries may well face similar problems.

On the other side, there was the view that the situation had been exaggerated. The following comment of a banker involved in international banking reflects this position:

> To be sure, there are a dozen or so nations with heavy debt

11. "Money and Investments," *Forbes,* June 15, 1976, p. 87. In a subsequent article, an anonymous banker was quoted as holding that "the greatest threat hanging over banking today [is] those tens of billions of dollars of shaky loans to poorer countries of the world. There were $19 billion in such loans last year; there will be perhaps $12 billion this year." (*Forbes,* July 1, 1976, p. 76.)

12. *Wall Street Journal,* Aug. 11, 1976, p. 6.

> burdens which have sizeable term and non-trade obligations to U.S. banks. In practically every case, however, the countries have rich natural resources or enjoy long-standing ties to the United States. . . . In the case of such countries as South Korea, the Philippines, Taiwan, or Israel, it is reasonable to expect that the day of default would be forestalled indefinitely as long as the stake of the U.S. Government in their economic and political stability remains high.[13]

Because hard data and information on exposures are not available, it is difficult to determine which view is the more reasonable. However, there is some evidence that a more defensive posture on country risk emerged in 1975–76, which may be a tentative indication that previous policies were excessively liberal. According to one source, in the first half of 1974, bank Eurocredits of $1.6 billions were extended to middle and lower income developing countries, but in the last half of 1975, only .6 billion was extended to the middle income category and practically none to the lower income group.[14] Therefore, greater sensitivity to country risk may have become established policy in a number of banks, but of course prior excesses may remain a problem for some years.

## Currency risk

Since U.S. banks prepare their position and income statements in terms of dollars, currency risk can be defined as the exposure to loss because of existing holdings of or future claims to foreign currencies that may decline in value relative to the American dollar. With the advent of floating exchange rates, foreign exchange rates have become more volatile, and significant movements in one direction or another have persisted for periods of several months or more. Therefore, the risk dimension of uncovered foreign currency loans greatly increased as a consequence of the move to floating rates, and there is no evidence that a return to relatively fixed rates is under serious consideration. The following statement of one respondent is, therefore, indicative

13. C. S. Ganoe, "U.S. Banks' International Loans under Scrutiny," *Euromoney*, Mar. 1976, p. 13. Mr. Ganoe is a senior officer of a large bank in Philadelphia.

14. D. L. Babson and Co., "Uncertain Outlook for International Financial Markets," *Weekly Staff Letter*, Mar. 18, 1976, p. 3.

of the preferred policy position with respect to currency risk and the alternative options to eliminating it:

> No foreign exchange risks are to be carried in the international loan portfolio. If loans denominated in foreign currencies are not funded in the same currency, the Loan Department will obtain a forward exchange contract from our foreign exchange dealers at the main office. If a contract which covers the entire term of the loan cannot be written at the inception of such loan, the loan agreement must provide for conversion at our option to U.S. dollar obligation should forward cover be unavailable at the next rollover or funding date.

However, two respondents indicated that they sometimes accepted currency risks for two reasons. One would be in cases of currencies where the outlook for strength against the dollar appeared highly probable. Second, moderate-size exposures might be considered if there were compelling reasons to provide service to the customer and a hedge position were not available. As the assumption of any significant currency risk necessarily is a speculative operation inconsistent with prudent banking policies, there may be reason to question policies which tolerate such risk, even though the profit opportunities may appear attractive at certain times.

### "Rate-gap" risk

Offshore sources of funds to U.S. banks are almost entirely limited to purchased deposits (borrowings), either in the Eurocurrency markets or in the domestic markets of the country in which loans are denominated. The reason is that U.S. banks generally are not prepared to offer full banking services in the domestic markets abroad in competition with large indigenous banks, which often branch on a nationwide basis. The term of the purchased funds may range from an overnight basis to possibly several years, but, as Table 15–2 shows, the great proportion of Eurocurrency deposits held by U.S. banks (70 percent as of November 1975) usually have a term of three months or less.

As a consequence, international loans are almost always priced on a spread basis, wherein the loan rates are specified as a given Eurocurrency rate plus a premium. For example, if a loan for a

TABLE 15–2
MATURITIES OF PURCHASED EUROCURRENCIES
(U.S. Banks in England as of 11/19/75)

| MATURITY | AMOUNT (In $ Billions) | PERCENTAGE OF TOTAL |
|---|---|---|
| Less than 8 days | 15.89 | 23.7 |
| 8 days–1 month | 11.52 | 17.2 |
| 1–3 months | 19.49 | 29.1 |
| 3–6 months | 13.07 | 19.5 |
| 6 months–year | 3.51 | 5.2 |
| 1–3 years | 2.03 | 3.0 |
| Over 3 years | 1.52 | 2.3 |
| Total | 67.03 | 100.0 |

Source: Bank of England, *Quarterly Bulletin* 16, No. 1 (Mar. 1976), Table 22.

six-month period were funded and priced on the basis of a purchase of a six-month deposit, then we would have a matched maturity on that transaction. However, it might seem desirable to offer a price based on the six-month deposit rate and fund the loan with a sequence of one-week deposits. If that decision was made, a rate-gap risk would be assumed. The risk exposure may be defined as the degree of probability that short-term rates on the weekly deposit rollovers could increase to levels which would result in a negative yield spread on the loan.

Some risk in this connection may be difficult to avoid as the term of some loans may not exactly correspond to the term of available deposits. But it also may be consciously assumed as a matter of policy because the yield curve is typically upsloping in

TABLE 15–3
RATE-GAP POLICIES
(Respondent Banks)

| FREQUENCY OF EXPOSURE | TERM OF RATE-GAP | | |
|---|---|---|---|
| | FEW DAYS | WEEK | OVER A WEEK |
| Frequently | 2 | 3 | 3 |
| Sometimes | 3 | 1 | 1 |
| Rarely | 1 | 2 | . . . |
| Never | 1 | 1 | 3 |

the Eurocurrency market. Therefore, if interest rates remain stable, rate spreads are almost always improved if loans are funded with short-term deposit rollovers rather than matched maturities. Table 15–3 shows that there were significant differences between the respondent banks with respect to their policies on rate-gap exposures. Several followed a discretionary policy based on their evaluation of the interest rate outlook, and these banks indicated that in general average returns had been improved thereby. However, one admitted that the rapid escalation in Eurocurrency rates in 1974 had caused negative spreads for several months. At the other extreme, one respondent had the policy of avoiding rate gaps entirely while the remainder would accept gaps of a week or less but avoided those over a week.

The risk exposure in this connection is appropriately monitored on a portfolio basis, and computer programs have been designed for this purpose. Each day the maturities of fund sources are compared with the interest-rate period of the assets (the maturity of many loans may be several years but rates are reset every three to six months.) The cumulative long or short position by total amount and number of days will be shown, and gaps can be eliminated or widened through purchases of long deposits or short deposits as appears appropriate on the basis of the indicated market outlook. In one bank, for example, the policy was to reduce a cumulative short position (rate gap) to a point where a 1 percent increase in rates would not decrease profits on the portfolio by 10 percent or more.

## International Loan Policies

### International credit universe

For purposes of policy criteria, assets generated from the international operation might be classified as follows:

1. Interbank deposits and loans
2. Loans to finance international operations of domestic customers, either through parent company or overseas subsidiaries
3. Local currency or Eurocurrency loans to foreign domiciled customers, including private sector companies, governments and agencies

4. Participations in syndicated Eurocurrency term credits to multinational firms, governments, and government agencies

With the exception of category 2, it might be generalized that international credit relationships lack the close and personal contacts on a recurring basis that typify a large proportion of domestic credits. As one bank put it:

> . . . except for a few situations in which we are supporting the operations of domestic customers, it cannot be said that the bank has a civic responsiblity to undertake anything but the most prudent international risks.

In short, to a considerable extent, the intermediation process on the international scene more closely resembles the impersonal management of domestic money market operations and security investments than the management of a commercial loan portfolio. As a result, policies and policy implementation may be based to a greater degree on specific quantitative criteria and reactions thereto (such as the computer program outlined above for monitoring and adjusting the rate-gap exposure) than is characteristic of domestic lending policies, which are typically highly flexible and subject to ad hoc exceptions based on subjective judgments.[15]

*Interbank credit policies.* All respondent banks reported that their policy was to establish a list of eligible banks and to set specific credit limits for each. The list is reviewed and eligibility and limits are revised periodically. Deposit placements, direct lines and loans, and total guarantees of credits made to others were included in the total exposure subject to limits. In general, policies in this area may have become more conservative in recent years, since several banks participating in the international markets failed in the 1974–75 period. Some losses in fact were incurred even on settlement of foreign exchange transactions with those banks on which the exposure was a day or less.

15. Those individuals who prefer to reach decisions through the application of specific quantitative guidelines and computer-based financial models and analyses may well be more comfortable in the international area than in the domestic area, where subjective and intuitive judgments make the decision-making process appear somewhat vague and less subject to so-called scientific solutions.

Respondents regarded the eligible lists and limits thereunder for deposit placements as highly confidential in order to avoid invidious comparisons and consequent public relations problems. However, the lists seem to vary with the extent of participation in the international markets; banks with a single or a few overseas offices limit deposit placements to the major visible banks active in the Eurocurrency markets, mainly large U.S., Canadian, Continental European, British, and Japanese institutions. Respondents with multiple branches and offices overseas may include banks in the less developed countries. The only specific standard for limits mentioned was that an exposure beyond 10 percent of the eligible bank's total capital was unusual and limited to large, strong banks in stable countries.

*International credits for domestic customers.* The major service that U.S. banks can perform for domestic customers overseas in the lending area, as distinct from export-import transactions and contacts overseas, is to provide local currency loans or in some cases to arrange a syndicate for a large Eurocurrency term credit. In general, if the request is supported by a parent guaranty or "comfort letter," the credit analysis and decision is usually made in the home office groups responsible for the parent, and the international function is limited to funding through purchased currencies in the local market or Eurocurrency market. If there is no parent support, then up to certain limits the decision could be made either overseas or in the international department of the head office. While lending activities in this area remain important, their relative significance has declined in recent years. For example, one respondent London branch indicated that such loans a decade ago represented 70 percent or so of the total loan portfolio but as of 1976 the proportion had declined to less than 40 percent. Moreover, there are no special policy issues on these credits. However, only in exceptional cases is collateral taken on loans to acquire assets overseas, because legal and technical problems make security interests cumbersome. In addition it might be noted that pricing is often based strictly on a yield spread basis without supporting balances required.

*Foreign customer loans.* Table 14–3 indicated that some banks with formal international departments and at least one branch overseas do not attempt to solicit foreign customers actively on a direct basis. Some dollar lines may be extended to foreign banks from the home office, but except for irregular calls abroad the posture is rather passive. Business will be accepted if requested but penetration of indigenous banking markets abroad is considered outside the scope of the operation. However, a few of the large regional banks consider local currency loans to foreign-domiciled customers a significant part of their activities. As the branch networks have expanded, multicurrency credit facilities to foreign companies have become a significant part of the product line. For example, a branch in Britain might offer a British company sterling accommodation plus credits denominated in other currencies as required to finance the company's operations in other areas of the world.[16]

But it is unusual for a foreign company to regard a U.S. facility as its major banking relationship. Therefore, direct local currency loans are usually sporadic or of a type not within the policy framework of local banks. Term loans extending for seven years or more with covenants similar to domestic term loans represent an example of a product that U.S. banks have successfully marketed abroad to foreign companies. The policy problem is to attract sufficient business in competition with the indigenous banks and yet maintain a tolerable risk exposure. Some U.S. banks consider they have been reasonably successful in this respect, but others, as indicated above, are hesitant to engage in an active direct lending program to foreign companies outside of participations in syndicated credits.

*Syndicated Eurocurrency term credits.* Syndicated credits have become a very important factor in the international loan markets. Governments, government agencies, and private sector companies often have credit needs beyond the prudent capacity of indigeneous financial institutions or of any single bank wherever located. On the other hand, the large supply of Eurocurrency deposits available on a world-wide basis represents a funding

16. Purchased local currency deposits from banks, corporations, governments, or, occasionally, wealthy individuals represent the usual funding source. If such deposits are not readily available (Greece and Austria were examples) reciprocal lines with local banks were used as the funding source.

source that can meet these demands. The logical solution to accommodate these demands in the Eurocurrency markets is the syndicated loan where one or more lead banks form a syndicate and offer participations to perhaps ten or more other international banks with active Eurocurrency operations.

In essence these credits resemble private placements of new bond issues except that their maturities are usually serial and for less extended periods of time. The lead banks receive the equivalent of an underwriting fee and participations are purchased strictly on an impersonal investment basis. The decision to participate or not will probably include the following factors: (1) credit status of borrower or guarantor, if private sector; (2) country and sovereign risk appraisal; (3) adequacy of rate spread; and (4) portfolio goals of international account (capital adequacy, etc.). In most instances, the policies and decisions with respect to participations will be made in the home office, although some banks allow branches or subsidiary units discretion on participations up to certain limits.

As these credits are more or less widely syndicated, the general nature of the borrowings and terms are usually publicized. Table 15–4 shows selected placements in this market during the first

TABLE 15–4
SELECTED PUBLICIZED TERM EUROCURRENCY CREDITS
(March through July 1976)

| ISSUER | GUARANTOR | AMOUNT* (In Millions) | TERM |
|---|---|---|---|
| Bluebird Navigation, Ltd. | Fuji Bank Ltd. | 26 | medium |
| Kingdom of Denmark | ...... | 500 DM | medium and long |
| Kingdom of Thailand | ...... | 100 | 5 years |
| Olivetti International S.A. | Ing. C. Olivetti & Co. | 20 | medium |
| Banca Nacional de Cuba | ...... | 200 DM | ...... |
| Imperial Chemical Industries | ...... | 100 S | ...... |
| Caixa Economica Federal | Republic of Brazil | 100 DM | medium |

Source: *Euromoney,* May–July issues, 1976.
* Dollars if not specified DM (German marks), S (British sterling).

half of 1976, and the data were selected to show the spectrum of borrowers, amounts, and currencies that typify the syndicated market. A review of the placements as published in several issues of *Euromoney* magazine suggests that governments and their agencies dominate but the private sector is also important, often with guarantics of large parent companies or large international banks. In general, therefore, credit risk tends to be a lesser factor than the other risk factors in the decision to participate in a syndicated loan. Country and sovereign risk were the principal base for criticism of exposures in this market in 1976. The following observation is indicative of such criticism:

> . . . considerable press comment has been given to the banks' exposure in the non–OPEC developing world. There is little evidence that the distribution of geographical credits is shifting; the non-oil LDCs have raised a further $725 million, the oil producing LDCs $263 million, and the industrial world accounts for the remaining $970 million. . . . Thus the non-oil LDC borrowers (the category that has aroused much of the recent concern) continue to account for over 40% of the syndicated credits and throughout 1976 they might expect to raise a total of $9 to $11 billion.[17]

Therefore, there is evidence that some large international banks remain aggressive in tolerating country risk exposure on syndicated credits despite revelations of existing problems and predictions of more to come in the non–oil-producing, less developed countries. The alleged reasons for the tolerant policies are the need for portfolio volumes to support the investment in the international program and the attractive spreads offered on the deals. Very large lead banks might be in a position to tolerate considerable country exposure on syndicated credits, but as there is no customer relationship involved for smaller participating banks, strict policy limits on country risk exposure on such credits would seem prudent, despite the attractive nominal yields.

### Pricing policies: Yield spreads

A few dollar lines and transaction loans to foreign customers—Japanese banks, for example—may be structured and priced simi-

17. Amex Bank, London, "Market Commentary," *Euromoney*, May 1976, p. 114.

larly to domestic credits—the prime rate with adequate supporting balances. However, the great majority are structured strictly on a yield spread basis, with loan rates specified in relation to the cost of the purchased deposits (borrowings) used to fund the credits. On term loans rates are usually reset every three or six months in relation to the cost of purchased deposits in the currencies in which the loans are denominated, plus fixed yield spreads which are negotiated at the origin on an ad hoc basis.

In the 1964–73 decade, many U.S. banks entered the international market on an active basis for the first time, and competition to obtain adequate volume through rate concessions resulted in the view that some were accepting yield spreads of a less-than-optimal nature. The following statement is indicative of the problem at that time:

> At home, many direct and indirect costs of a new department might be overlooked or even lost in the total head office operation, but as a separate operation in an overseas office, operating costs are laid bare and measured quite easily. These pressures have caused many banks to accept offerings of easy business at rates substantially below fair compensation. The initial goal of most of the new operations seemed to be to do business at any price to get launched and to cover some of the overhead.[18]

"Fair compensation" may be construed in several different ways. However, using the capital budgeting concept, it would represent average yield spreads that provide returns on the capital necessary to support the international portfolio approximately equivalent to the opportunity cost returns available on such capital in the domestic operation. D. R. Mandich in a separate analysis essentially used this approach, based on the following assumptions:

1. A deposit-to-capital ratio of 15 to 1, or a loan portfolio of $16 for every dollar of capital
2. Operating expenses that would absorb ¼ percent to ¾ percent of the portfolio, depending on the size of the operation

18. D. R. Mandich, "Pricing International Loans," *Bankers Magazine,* Spring 1971, p. 72. In the same article Mandich indicated that in 1970–71, loan spreads (excluding interbank deposits) of 1% were "common"; ½% to ¾% spreads were "regularly available," and some had been structured on ¼% spreads.

3. An opportunity cost goal of 13 percent to 15 percent return on capital after taxes at a 50 percent estimated rate
4. Cost of funds varying between 5 percent and 8½ percent

On the basis of these assumptions, the arithmetical results show that average spreads of 1½ to 2¼ are required in order to achieve the rate-of-return goals, with the proviso that this might be shaded a bit if Eurocurrency interbank trading operations provided modest returns and were considered riskless.[19]

There is considerable evidence, therefore, that many banks' rate-spread policies on international loans were indeed of the "loss leader" type in the expansionist years. However, as noted above, less aggressive postures in both domestic and international operations seemed evident in many banks in 1975–76, consequent to the problems encountered in certain major loan areas (REIT and tanker credits were conspicuous examples) and to increased regulatory concern with adequate capital support for the risk asset position. The feedback to rate spread policies, as might be expected, was a general shift upward in the targets for such spreads.

Table 15–5 shows the policies of the respondent banks as of 1976 with respect to rate spreads on various categories of international credits. The distribution of the responses suggests the following tentative conclusions as to prevailing policies: First, on lines and short-term transaction credits, most expected normative spreads of between 1 and 2 points. However, a significant proportion would still accept somewhat lower spreads in this category, presumably on loans to major customers for competitive reasons. On the other hand, spreads in excess of 2 points were generally infrequently achieved here, possibly because loans requiring large spreads usually have a risk dimension that is unacceptable.

19. D. R. Mandich, "International Loans: Profit Center or Loss Leader," *Journal of Commercial Bank Lending* 51 (Sept. 1972): 40–42. In the light of this analysis the following comment of an international banker during the highly competitive era of 1971–73 is interesting: "I doubt seriously whether many branches in London are measuring their success in terms of return on capital. They're engaging in types of business and pricing practices that their head offices would never engage in at home." (F. D. Pettit, Vice President, Citibank of New York, as quoted in the *Wall Street Journal,* Nov. 24, 1972, p. 1.)

TABLE 15–5

RATE SPREADS ON INTERNATIONAL CREDITS OF RESPONDENT BANKS

(As of 1976)

| TYPE OF CREDIT | RATE SPREADS (in Points) | | | | |
|---|---|---|---|---|---|
| | LESS THAN 1 | 1 TO 1½ | 1½ TO 2 | 2–3 | OVER 3 |
| *Eurocurrency Credits* | | | | | |
| Lines and transactions | | | | | |
| Frequently | 2 | 6 | 1 | . . . | . . . |
| Sometimes | 3 | 1 | 5 | 2 | . . . |
| Rarely | 2 | . . . | . . . | 3 | 2 |
| Never | . . . | . . . | 1 | 2 | 5 |
| Term loans | | | | | |
| Frequently | . . . | 3 | 4 | . . . | . . . |
| Sometimes | . . . | 2 | 3 | 5 | . . . |
| Rarely | 2 | 2 | . . . | 1 | 2 |
| Never | 5 | . . . | . . . | 1 | 5 |
| *Other foreign currency credits** | | | | | |
| Lines and transactions | | | | | |
| Frequently | 1 | 3 | 2 | 1 | . . . |
| Sometimes | 3 | 3 | 2 | . . . | 1 |
| Rarely | 2 | . . . | 1 | 3 | 1 |
| Never | . . . | . . . | 1 | 2 | 4 |
| Term loans | | | | | |
| Frequently | . . . | 2 | 3 | 1 | . . . |
| Sometimes | . . . | 1 | 1 | 2 | 1 |
| Rarely | 1 | 3 | 2 | 1 | 2 |
| Never | 5 | . . . | . . . | 2 | 3 |

* One respondent essentially made only Eurocurrency credits and did not respond to this section.

Second, as in domestic pricing policies, rate spreads in the term loan category were moderately above those on lines and transaction loans. In this area, spreads of 1½ to 2 clearly dominated the universe. The surprising fact was that spreads above 2 points were not much more frequent on term credits than on lines and transaction loans. The only logical explanation for this result is that large credits, often syndicated in nature, to governments and large multi-national corporations are more dominant here than in the short-term category. Because large borrowers are in a position to shop the loans on a competitive rate basis, competitive pressures on rates in the term loan category are more intense. However, it appears that the modal rate spread on the international universe as a whole was about 1½ points as of 1976, which was distinctly above that indicated in the early seventies. The average spread, therefore, was still at the low side of the "adequacy" computation suggested by Mandich, but apparently rate spread policies were no longer dominated by the "loss leader" approach evident in earlier years.[20] Although conjectures about the future are always uncertain, the expansionist phase of U.S. banks overseas seems to be mostly completed. The result—because of a reduction in competitive pressures from new entrants seeking to develop a significant international presence—may be a reduction in the tendency of rate spreads to be nonoptimal.

## International Credits: Decision-Making Structure

### Domestic customers: Overseas requirements

In the home office, both the loan group handling the parent company's domestic business and the international department typically participate in the decision-making process. The domestic loan group participates because it is intimately familiar with the credit position and the overall financial requirements of the corporation, both domestically and internationally, as well as with the history and status of the major deposit and loan relationships with the customer. In short, this group ordinarily makes the fundamental decisions as to appropriate size and terms of the total credit accommodations to the entire corporate complex, on the basis of (1) the existing and prospective profitability of the deposit and other business obtained from the client and (2) an appraisal of the risk exposure.

The international department provides advice concerning the

20. Two respondents indicated their policy was to accept a minimum spread of 1½ points on large syndicated Eurocurrency credits and indicated that their refusal to participate in the $1 billion syndicated five-year term credit to the government of Spain priced at a spread of 1⅜ in June of 1976 was evidence of the firmness of this policy. (Terms of this loan described in *Wall Street Journal*, June 21, 1976, p. 6.)

specific options available to implement credits in the area concerned. Availability of local currencies, forward cover, and possible participations from international subsidiaries, affiliates, or correspondents would be among the factors on which the international department provides advice. In addition, foreign affiliates often have underwriting departments to handle long-term borrowings, either in the form of straight bonds or convertible issues. Therefore, the international department may be in a position to appraise the possibility of obtaining financing in the long-term capital markets overseas, particularly the Eurobond market.

To illustrate, the decision-making structure for overseas financing of a customer may be as follows: First, the head office group handling the parent company is the primary negotiating and decision point on the overall credit relationship with the customer. Presumably the loan committee, and possibly the executive committee, approve the size and structure of all proposed credit arrangements. Second, assuming the decision to assist the customer in his foreign financing needs is affirmative, representatives of the international department would be introduced into the negotiations with the customer, and the required credit package would then be structured.

*Implementation options.* As an example, assume that the credit needs include a combination of both foreign currency short-term loans and term financing for capital asset requirements. Exploration of the options available to provide these credits would then proceed. On the short-term foreign currency needs, the options might include: (1) direct loans funded with purchased local currency time deposits, (2) Eurocurrency loans with funds acquired by a foreign branch in the required currency, (3) foreign currency loans funded with dollars converted into the required currency on the spot market accompanied by forward-exchange cover, and (4) an accommodation loan from a foreign correspondent or affiliate. The first option might be the most expedient, because it is direct and uncomplicated. Also, it should be noted that Eurocurrency deposits and forward cover are available for only about a half-dozen of the leading currencies. As to the fourth option, the availability and cost of the required funds would probably dictate whether it should be considered.

On the term needs, the options might include: (1) Eurocurrency loans funded through a foreign branch, (2) Eurocurrency loans on a participation basis with other banks with which the domestic customer is affiliated, (3) a foreign currency loan through purchased time deposits in that currency, (4) a Eurobond issue underwritten or directly placed by an affiliated overseas commercial or merchant bank. In addition, an Edge Act subsidiary may make a direct investment in a Eurobond issue, but respondents indicated that this is rarely done, because Edge Act corporate resources are primarily reserved for investment in foreign financial institutions.

The home office international department would presumably have the major responsibility for the decision as to which of the above options are most desirable for a given credit package. Foreign branch personnel might be invited to make recommendations, particularly if the request originated in a subsidiary overseas. Moreover, the options' relative cost and feasibility, unlike those of most domestic credit arrangements, can change over short periods of time, depending on such factors as variations in the cost of forward-exchange cover in various currencies, changes in Eurocurrency rates as compared to rates on locally generated funds, and the availability of purchased foreign currency time deposits.

Therefore, many international credits may require more active monitoring than do similiar types of domestic credits; the syndicated term loans to U.S. multinationals represent an exception, as these generally require little attention after the original package has been structured.

### Foreign customers: Branch authorities

The loan authorities of branch management abroad varied widely. Generally as the international operation expands in scope and size, the tendency is to decentralize the decision-making process. For example, in the case of most respondents, decisions on participations in syndicated term credits were made entirely in the home office. However, where the international operation had expanded into an extensive network of overseas facilities and offered extensive services to foreign customers overseas, the regional executive officers were granted authority to reach decisions on syndicated loans originated in their areas, their funding mechanisms, and consequent rate-gap exposure.

In the branches per se, loan authorities varied from zero to $5,000,000. In those cases where the branch was strictly a booking office for Eurocurrency deposits, all decisions are made in the home office. In others, the branch officers were encouraged to solicit business from foreign customers, both corporate and governmental, and, in order to give them stature with such customers, they were granted authorities of $1,000,000 to $5,000,000. For example, in one London office which also had regional European supervisory responsibility, it was estimated that 60 percent to 70 percent of the total number of credits generated in the region were made under local loan authorities. But when large syndicated credits approved in the head office were included, the dollar percentage decreased to about 20 percent. Moreover, senior officers from the home office frequently visit overseas facilities and are in constant telex or phone communication with management abroad. As a consequence, monitoring of loans to foreign customers extended in the overseas branches may be almost as close as loan committee reviews of domestic credit decisions.

## APPENDIX

The questionnaires reproduced here were used to obtain the views of eight large banks in the Midwest on lending policies and practices. The same banks provided the information on international policies, and this information in turn provided much of the essential material for enumerating the elements of policy and analyzing the reasoning behind policy formulation. The order of the questions corresponds to the order in which the subjects are discussed in the text.

### Organization of Commercial Lending Functions

1. What loan authorities are given to the following?
   - Assistant Cashiers (Loan Officers)
   - Assistant V. P.
   - V.P.
   - Loan Group
   - Other (please indicate)
2. Please list loan committees and their loan authority if less than legal limit.
3. Does the bank have specialized industry groups or loan officers specializing in loans to certain types of borrowers? Please indicate specialties.
4. Does the bank have written loan policies to guide lending officers?
5. Does the bank have a loan "controller" or "loan review" officer?
6. What review, if any, is made of loan requests rejected by a loan officer?

### Personnel and Training Policies

1. In recent years, have the majority, some, or few of the loan officer trainees had the following educational backgrounds?
   a. MBA from a business school
   b. BBA from a business school
   c. AB from a Lit. School
   d. Other (please indicate)

2. What proportion of your lending officers have been trained within your organization as contrasted to being brought in as a lending officer from another institution?

3. How long are trainees typically assigned to the following functions?
   a. Spreading statements
   b. Answering credit inquiries (correspondence)
   c. Preparing written credit reports for loan divisions
   d. Serving as assistants to loan officers
   e. Other (please specify)

4. Are trainees rotated among the loan divisions on a regular basis either by their choice or because of bank policy?

5. Are trainees assigned to any other area of bank for six months or more as a general policy? If so, please indicate areas.

6. What has been the turnover rate for loan officer trainees?

7. What steps have been taken, if any, to bring representatives of minority groups (blacks) into the loan officer training program? Do you have any such trainees now?

8. What is the length of training before a trainee becomes a lending officer?
   a. Minimum
   b. Average
   c. Maximum

9. Does the bank regularly review the progress of trainees and are the results of the review communicated to the trainees?

10. What estimated percentage of the officers in the consumer and mortgage loan areas have come to their positions as follows?
    a. Recruited and trained within these departments of bank
    b. Transferred from another department of bank at officer or near officer level
    c. Hired from outside bank at officer level

11. If transfers from other departments of bank are a source of mortgage and consumer credit officers, which departments are the principal sources?

### Lines of Credit, Transaction Loans, and Working Capital Loans

Information policies

1. If collateral is clearly adequate (marketable securities), do you

regularly, sometimes, rarely, or never require the following information on a business loan?

a. Financial statements
b. Purpose of loan (except Regulations G and U waiver)

2. In the case of a new customer of moderate size, how many years' financial statements are usually requested on:
   a. Short-term loans (lines of credit)?
   b. Term loans?

3. Audit requirements: unsecured credits

| | (Thousands of $) | | | |
|---|---|---|---|---|
| | Under 250 | 250–500 | 500–1,000 | Over 1,000 |
| a. Term loans and revolvers: | | | | |
| Always | | | | |
| Frequently | | | | |
| Sometimes | | | | |
| Rarely | | | | |
| b. Lines and transitions | | | | |
| Always | | | | |
| Frequently | | | | |
| Sometimes | | | | |
| Rarely | | | | |

4. Do you regularly, sometimes, rarely, or never require that commercial lines or loans be supported by the following information?
   a. Visit to customer's place of business and report thereon
   b. Checking with suppliers to borrower
   c. Checking with customers of borrower

Open lines of credit (unsecured)

1. On open lines, what is expected period of complete payout during year?
   a. Finance companies
   b. Industrial companies
2. If a company is growing rapidly, will unsecured lines be renewed despite absence of a payout for two years or so? If not, what are typical actions taken when payouts do not take place?
3. Do you grant "courtesy lines" to good customers who do not request them?

4. Do you grant open lines regularly, sometimes, or rarely to any industries (utilities) where payout is to come from long-term financing at an indefinite future date? Please indicate industries, if any.

Other

1. Do you have any clear policy on "side venture" requests (quasi-permanent loans to provide financing for new ventures, including real estate deals, entered into personally by executives of companies that are good customers)? Please indicate nature of policy, if any.
2. If a modest-sized company is making satisfactory earnings progress and the commitment seems adequately secured, will you more or less ignore a closely inadequate equity position and deposit balances in relation to bank debt?
3. It is typical for lending officer handling accounts of this nature to be more tolerant of strained position than loan committee?

### Correspondent Accommodation

1. Does the bank accommodate correspondent banks regularly, sometimes, rarely, or never on the following types of loans?
   a. Lines of credit (overlines)
   b. Transaction loans (over legal limit)
   c. Consumer loans (blocks of paper)
   d. Term loans
   e. Other (please specify)
2. Are the following factors on such loans included regularly, sometimes, rarely, or never as a matter of policy?

   *Terms:*

   a. LIFO (on your share)
   b. Financial statements of borrower
   c. Correspondent balances related to accommodations accepted
3. During the "tight money" period of 1973–74 did the bank sell any loans to:
   a. Correspondents (domestic or foreign)?
   b. Foreign branches?
   c. Parent holding company or a subsidiary thereof?
   d. Others (please specify)
   e. Types of loans sold

4. During this period, were loans sold under repurchase agreements? If so, please indicate nature of buyers as in (3).

### Rate and Supporting Balance Policies

1. Estimated rate premiums on loans
(Frequent, Sometimes, Rarely, Never)

| | Prime | ½–1 Over (110%) | 1–2 (110–120%) | 2–3 (120–130%) | Over 3 (Over 130%) |
|---|---|---|---|---|---|
| a. Lines of credit | | | | | |
| b. Transaction loans 90–180 days) | | | | | |
| c. Working capital commitments (Secured by receivables) | | | | | |
| d. Revolving credit | | | | | |
| Floating | | | | | |
| Cap. | | | | | |
| Fixed | | | | | |
| e. Term loans | | | | | |
| Floating | | | | | |
| Cap. | | | | | |
| Fixed | | | | | |

2. Supporting balances: estimated universe

| | Frequent | Sometimes | Rarely | Never |
|---|---|---|---|---|
| a. Finance Companies | | | | |
| None (price adjusted) | | | | |
| Specified percentages | | | | |
| b. Other commercial loans: | | | | |
| None | | | | |
| 10% | | | | |
| 15% | | | | |
| 20% | | | | |

c. Commitment
(facility fees)
Lines of credit
¼ to ½
½ to 1
Revolving credits
¼ to ½
½ to 1
Term loans
(until takedown)
¼ to ½
½ to 1

d. To obtain prime rate, balance average % expected: ______

e. Balance computation:

| | Yes | No |
|---|---|---|
| Collected balances used? | | |
| Account servicing deducted? | | |
| Reserve requirements deducted? | | |

### Term Loan and Leasing Policies

1. Does your bank make business loans for following maturities? (Please indicate one of the following opposite each indicated maturity: regularly, sometimes, rarely, or never.)

| | Secured | Unsecured |
|---|---|---|
| a. 5 years ______ | | |
| b. 7 years ______ | | |
| c. 10 years ______ | | |
| d. 12 years ______ | | |
| e. 15 years ______ | | |

2. What is estimated average maturity of term loans?

3. Term loans: amortization policies

| | Frequent | Sometimes | Rarely | Never |
|---|---|---|---|---|
| a. Straight-line annual amortization | | | | |
| b. Balloon maturity | | | | |
| Half of loan or more | | | | |
| Less than half of loan | | | | |

c. Delayed amortization
   2 years or less
   Over 2 years
d. No amortization
   (bullet maturity)

4. Are term loans made on a participating basis with long-term lenders such as life insurance companies (frequently, sometimes, rarely, or never)?

5. Are most rates set at time of a term loan or do they (frequently, sometimes, rarely, or never) vary during life of loan in accord with variations in:

   a. Prime rate?
   b. Eurodollar rate?

6. Would the bank make term loans for the following purposes under normal conditions—regularly, rarely, or never?

   a. Purchase of control of other companies
   b. Purchase of minority interest in other companies
   c. Acquisition of assets not required in business (airplane, land purchase)
   d. Retire portion of equity (buy-out of an owner)

7. Are the following provisions used always, frequently, sometimes, rarely, or never in your term loan agreements?

   a. Working capital floors
   b. Commitment fees (if take-down deferred)
   c. Fixed asset expenditure limits
   d. Limitations on lease obligations
   e. Dividend restrictions
   f. Salary restrictions
   g. Negative pledge clauses
   h. Restricting sale of assets
   i. Earnings acceleration clause
   j. Audits and interim financial reports
   k. Restriction on borrowings from other banks
   l. Controls on inventories and receivables
   m. Restriction on total borrowings
   n. Establishing minimum net worth requirement
   o. Restricting acquisitions of other companies
   p. Restriction on sale of stock of principals
   q. Restricting mergers with other companies
   r. Maintain existing management

8. What action is usually taken in case of violations of covenants where there is no default on interest and principal payments?
9. What proportion of term loans (by number and $ amount) would you estimate are secured?
10. On secured term loans are the following types of collateral taken frequently, sometimes, rarely, or never?
    a. Mortgage on land and buildings
    b. Chattel mortgage on equipment
    c. Assignment of inventories and receivables
    d. Hypothecation of marketable securities
    e. Assignment of stock interests in subsidiaries or affiliates
    f. Personal guaranties of principals
    g. Assignment of lease rentals
    h. Assignment of proceeds of life insurance
11. Are the following adjustments made frequently, sometimes, rarely, or never during the time a termloan is outstanding, assuming no default on interest or principal payments?
    a. Amount of loan
    b. Amortization schedule (maturity)
    c. Change to less restrictive covenants
12. On "revolving" credits what are the bank's policies in the following areas:
    a. Maximum and average maturities of commitments?
    b. Commitment fee (range)?
    c. Is commitment frequently or infrequently subject to reduction in successive years of commitment period and so specified in the loan agreement?
13. Does your bank engage in direct leasing? If so, please indicate kinds of equipment.

14. Leasing policies

| | Frequent | Sometimes | Rarely | Never |
|---|---|---|---|---|
| a. Origination | | | | |
| Referred by brokers | | | | |
| Generated internally | | | | |
| b. Types of leasing arrangements | | | | |
| Operating leases | | | | |
| Full payment | | | | |
| Residual value in estimated full payment | | | | |
| Residual *not* in full payment estimate | | | | |
| Purchase options | | | | |
| Stated at outset | | | | |
| Fair market value at termination | | | | |
| Length of term | | | | |
| Up to five years | | | | |
| 5 to 10 years | | | | |
| Over 10 years | | | | |
| Leveraged leases | | | | |
| Percent equity | | | | |
| 20% | | | | |
| 21–30% | | | | |
| Over 30% | | | | |
| Length of term | | | | |
| 5 years | | | | |
| 5 to 10 years | | | | |
| Over 10 years | | | | |

## Collateral Policies

1. On receivable loans please indicate policies in the following respects:
   a. Percentages of loans to receivables of industrial and commercial companies (average and range of percentages)
   b. Percentages of loans to contractor receivables (both on non-bonded and bonded jobs)

c. Outstanding loan-receivable audits
d. Continuous borrowing under receivable assignment (two or more years)
e. What estimated percentage of receivable loans are made under a dominion of funds arrangement?

2. Are the following types of inventory loans made and, if so, are they made frequently or infrequently?
    a. Commodity loans against bills of lading or bonded warehouse receipts.
    b. Field warehousing loans.
    c. Floating liens on all inventories. (If so, how is collateral valued?)
3. What is the policy, if any, on rate spread over prime rate on loans secured by receivables and inventories (average and range of spread)?
4. Does the bank make loans secured by receivables and/or inventories in participation with nonbank financing sources?
5. On loans secured by equipment please indicate the policies in the following respects:
    a. Percentage of loan to appraised and/or purchase price of equipment (average and range of percentages)
    b. Maximum term on equipment loans (new and used equipment)
6. Does the bank have any specific policies as to the collateral values of the following types of securities (loan as percentage of value)?

| | Individuals and Others Except Security Brokers | Security Brokers |
|---|---|---|
| a. Goverment bonds | | |
| b. Other bonds (municipal or corporate) | | |
| c. Listed stocks (outside Regulation U limits) | | |
| d. Unlisted stocks, but publicly traded | | |
| e. Large blocks of either (c) or (d) | | |

   f. Closely held shares
   g. Drafts directed to other with securities attached
   h. Securities owned under investment letter

7. Does the bank keep any records as to the amount of loans supported by securities of given companies, e.g., total loans secured by G.M. common stock?

8. Does the bank have any specific policies regarding total percentage of outstanding shares of any one company that it would lend against to any group of individuals?

9. What is the bank's policy regarding loans against common stock of correspondent banks?

10. In the case of loans to closely held corporations is it typical practice to require personal signatures of principals and/or spouses?

11. If loans are adequately secured, why does the bank care if there is a repayment program?

12. Does the policy on (11) vary with "tightness" or "ease" of monetary policy?

13. If balance sheet indicates a liability to principals, is the practice to subordinate regularly, sometimes, or rarely such debt during the period of borrowing from the bank on the following?
   a. Term loans
   b. Revolving credit
   c. Transaction loans
   d. Working capital loans
   e. Operating lines of credit

14. What is the bank's policy with loans to the mortgage bankers regarding collateral (loan percentage) against the following?

| | Completed | Construction |
|---|---|---|
| a. FHA & VA insured loans: | | |
| 1) Single family | | |
| 2) Multi-family | | |

b. Conventional loans:
   1) Single family
   2) Multi-family
   3) Commercial

15. What is the bank's policy regarding unsecured loans to mortgage bankers?

16. Do the bank's borrowing customers (mortgage bankers) pledge residential collateral at more than one bank?

**Retail Credit Policies**

1. Credit card policies
   a. What is range of "floor limits" and total credit limits on cards?
   b. What is range of merchant discounts?
   c. What is monthly charge to customers on unpaid balances after 30 days?
   d. Does bank give cash advances on cards as substitute for small consumer loans?

2. Does your bank grant personal lines of credit (check-credit)?
   a. What is range of amounts of such lines?

| 3. Terms on auto loans (new cars)? | Direct | Indirect |
|---|---|---|
| a. Average maturity (estimated) | | |
| b. Maximum maturity | | |
| c. Processing time | | |
| d. Rates | | |
| 1976 | | |
| 1974 | | |
| 1972 | | |

   e. Dealer rebates on indirect? (Yes or No ________)

4. Does bank make the following type instalment loans?

| | Frequently | Sometimes | Rarely | Never |
|---|---|---|---|---|
| a. FHA Title 1 Home Repair | | | | |
| b. Home Repair (non–FHA) | | | | |
| c. Appliances and Furniture | | | | |
| d. Unsecured | | | | |
| e. Boats | | | | |

5. Frequency of financing auto dealers' other needs?

| | Frequent | Sometimes | Rarely | Never |
|---|---|---|---|---|
| a. Car leasing programs of dealers* | | | | |
| b. Floor plans | | | | |
| New cars | | | | |
| Used cars | | | | |
| c. Mortgage financing of dealer facilities | | | | |

* Assignment of lease, chattel on car, and cross guaranty of dealer assumed.

6. Estimated percentage of outstandings by types of financing program

| | 1971 | 1975 |
|---|---|---|
| Credit card (Mastercharge or Bank Americard) | | |
| Auto loans | | |
| Other instalment loans | | |
| Single payment loans | | |
| Personal lines of credit | | |
| Total | 100% | 100% |

**Mortgage Loans**

1. Does the bank restrict mortgage loans to less than the maximum legal percentages of capital and/or savings deposits? If so, what are policy guidelines in this area?
2. Does the policy include any indication as to the desirable mix between conventionals and insured mortgages?
3. Does the mortgage department regularly make mortgages, sell them, and retain the servicing on them?
4. Please indicate the following practices on conventional residential mortgage loans:
    a. Range of rates
    b. % of appraised value
    c. Maximum maturity allowed
    d. Maximum amount of a mortgage loan
    e. Customer relationship requirement, if any
5. Does the bank make FHA or GI loans to non-depositors? Has policy ever changed in this connection?
6. Does the bank take end mortgages on new apartment construction, hotels, and motels?

7. Does the bank take end mortgages on other types of real property (stores, office buildings, etc.)?

8. Has the bank taken, or is it considering taking, equity type rates on commercial mortgages? If so, what are the alternative bases of such rates (gross rentals, sales, etc.)?

9. Has the bank bought mortgage loans made by other institutions in the 1967–76 period for its portfolio?
   a. From what institutions
   b. Nature of properties involved
   c. New or seasoned mortgages
   d. Location (in bank's area or outside?)

10. Does the bank engage in the following types of interim financing on residential tract construction?
    a. Mortgage warehousing for mortgage bankers against pledge of completed loans for which there is firm commitment on part of long-term lender.
       Percentage of such loans to collateral?
    b. Mortgage warehousing where there is no firm commitment from long-term investor. If so, percentage of loan to collateral?
    c. Loans to mortgage bankers to finance contractors. If so please indicate requirements.

### Loan Review and Administration

1. Please check the appropriate column for the limitations applied to the indicated category of loans during the tight money period of 1973–74.

| Category | Degree of Limitations | | | |
|---|---|---|---|---|
| | Great | Some | Minor | None |
| a. New customers (local)* | | | | |
| b. New customers (national)* | | | | |
| c. Term loans (existing customers) | | | | |
| Reduce maturity limits | | | | |
| Acquisition of other companies | | | | |
| Equity buyouts | | | | |
| Raise credit standards | | | | |
| Increase balance requirements | | | | |
| d. Lines (finance companies) | | | | |

* Assume supporting balances would be adequate.

e. Lines (nonfinance companies)
    Impose commitment fees
    Limit increases

f. Mortgages
    Residential
    Commercial
    Construction loans

g. Consumer instalment loans
    Indirect
    Direct

h. Other (if any)
    Please indicate nature

2. Do you require bank lending officers to fill out an annual "conflict of interest" questionnaire?

3. Do you restrict in any way the acquisition by loan officers of stock in borrowing customers? If so, how?

4. If a loan officer owns securities of a borrowing customer, is he allowed to participate in loan decisions to that customer?

5. Does the bank use a formal "profit center" approach in the following areas to appraise the results of lending activities?
    a. Commercial loans (breakdown?)
    b. Consumer loans
    c. Mortgage loans

6. If a "profit center" approach is not used, what means, if any, are used to evaluate the profitability of various loan activities?

7. Has the bank established a special program for making commercial loans to minority groups in the inner-city areas?
    a. What has been the approximate number and dollar amount of such loans?
    b. Do you obtain special guaranties on such loans regularly, sometimes, or rarely? What guaranties are used?
    c. Do you provide financial management or other assistance (please specify) to such customers?

## International Loan Policies

1. Loan frequency by types of loan (*not* deposit placement)

(F = frequent, S = sometimes, R = rarely, N = never.)

| | Lines | Term |
|---|---|---|
| | FSRN | FSRN |
| a. Direct to foreign governments | | |
| b. To foreign companies (nonfinancial) | | |
| 1) with their govt. guarantee | | |
| 2) without govt. guarantee | | |
| c. To foreign financial institutions | | |
| 1) banks | | |
| 2) finance & ins. co's. | | |
| d. International subsidiaries of U.S. companies | | |
| 1) with parent guarantee | | |
| 2) with "comfort" letter | | |
| 3) without either (1) or (2) | | |
| e. Other (please indicate only if frequent) | | |

2. Rate and risk policies

| | Rate Spread (Frequent Sometimes Rarely Never) | | | | |
|---|---|---|---|---|---|
| | Less than 1 | 1½ | 1½–2 | 2–3 | Over 3 |
| a. Eurocurrency loans | | | | | |
| 1) lines and short-term loans | | | | | |
| 2) term loans | | | | | |
| b. Other foreign-currency loans | | | | | |
| 1) lines and short-term loans | | | | | |
| 2) term loans | | | | | |

c. Do you accept rate "gaps" in funding of Eurocurrency loans of

| | A Few Days? | A Week? | Over a Week? |
|---|---|---|---|
| Frequently | | | |
| Sometimes | | | |
| Rarely | | | |
| Never | | | |

d. Do you limit "country risk" by setting maximum loan exposure in countries or regions?

Any exceptions? (Please indicate countries excepted.)

e. Do you accept "currency risks"?
(Frequently, Sometimes, Rarely, Never)

f. Deposit placements of Eurocurrencies with banks

| | Yes | No |
|---|---|---|
| 1) Restricted to eligible list of banks? | | |
| 2) Limit set for each bank? | | |

3. Branch office policies

a. Personnel policies

| | Yes | No |
|---|---|---|
| Managers rotated from U.S.? | | |
| Managers from host country? | | |
| Language competence required? | | |

b. Functions of branches (Frequently, Sometimes, Rarely, Never)

| | London or Nassau | Other |
|---|---|---|
| Book Eurocurrency transaction originated in U.S. | | |
| Purchase time deposits of local currencies as needed for loans | | |
| Make local currency loans to foreign customers | | |
| Make local currency loans to U.S. company foreign subsidiaries | | |
| Other *major* functions (Please list in summary form.) | | |

c. Do branch managers have discretionary loan authority?

If so:

| Limits (in $ equivalent) | |
|---|---|
| Secured | Unsecured |

## INDEX